JUVENI

THE CHILL

Dr W. E. Cavenagh originally trained as an economist at London University and spent some years in business management before her marriage to a chartered accountant. After the war years, spent in the Factory and Welfare Department of the Ministry of Labour in Birmingham, she became a lecturer in Social Study at Birmingham University. She has been a member of Birmingham Education Committee since 1946, a magistrate in the adult and juvenile courts since 1949 and is a past chairman of the Association of Social Workers.

Dr Cavenagh now lectures in Criminology and was called to the Bar in 1964. She has published articles in a wide variety of journals dealing with social and legal matters and with the administration of justice.

JUVENILE COURTS,
THE CHILD AND THE LAW

W. E. CAVENAGH

PENGUIN BOOKS

Penguin Books Ltd, Harmondsworth, Middlesex, England
Penguin Books Inc., 3300 Clipper Mill Road, Baltimore 11, Md, U.S.A.
Penguin Books Australia Ltd, Ringwood, Victoria, Australia

First published as *The Child and the Court* by Victor Gollancz 1959
This revised edition first published in Pelican Books 1967

Made and printed in Great Britain
by Richard Clay (The Chaucer Press) Ltd,
Bungay, Suffolk
Set in Monotype Baskerville

CONTENTS

ACKNOWLEDGEMENTS

My thanks are due to the many magistrates, clerks, social workers, police officers, psychiatrists, psychologists, and others who have readily and helpfully discussed with me over the years a number of the points raised in this book, and to Master I. H. Jacob for helpful comment and advice.

The editors of *The British Journal of Criminology* (formerly *The British Journal of Delinquency*) have kindly allowed me to include material from my articles published in their issues of January 1957 (special number on juvenile courts), July 1961, and April 1966 (special number on the white paper *The Child, the Family and the Young Offender*). I have also been permitted by the editor of *The Lawyer* to include material from my article published in the issue of Hilary 1962 and, by the editor of *The Magistrate*, to include material from my article of June 1966.

INTRODUCTION TO THE
PELICAN EDITION

THERE are at present about 820 juvenile courts in England and Wales. Out of an approximate total of sixteen thousand active lay magistrates in the country as a whole about 5,060 men and 3,450 women are members of juvenile courts.

The juvenile court is one of the special courts which have developed within the general system of summary courts. These have both a criminal and a civil jurisdiction and, with very few exceptions indeed, are presided over by lay magistrates. At the present time such summary courts finally determine about ninety-eight per cent of all criminal charges heard.

Juvenile courts are distinct from ordinary summary courts in their composition, in their jurisdiction, and to some extent in their procedure. But most of the law they administer is the ordinary law of the land, which on the sentencing side now contains many special provisions relating to the younger offender. Most of these special provisions extend to cover offenders of up to twenty-one years of age but the law relating to the liability, treatment, or welfare of offenders is administered up to their seventeenth birthday in the juvenile court. There are also provisions for dealing with young people in the juvenile court not as offenders but as young people in need of care, protection, or control.

The juvenile court and the law it administers has evolved from the old common law and must be seen against that background. Although the special juvenile court was not established in the law until the passing of the Children Act, 1908, sometimes called the 'children's charter', its development was only a part of a much wider movement towards reform of the penal system and the criminal law and its administration which gathered force throughout the nineteenth century and is still continuing today.

The first step which made possible the eventual setting up of a special court for the separate trial of juveniles was the passing of an Act in 1847 enabling the lay justices to deal summarily with thieves under fourteen years of age instead of committing them for trial before a judge and jury at a higher court. After the Summary Jurisdiction Act, 1879, virtually all cases against children were dealt with summarily in magistrates' courts. The practice of keeping children separate from adults was developed by the magistrates in various places, for example in Liverpool and Manchester, before this became obligatory under the Children Act.

The next stage in the evolution of the juvenile court was the special selection of magistrates to serve in it. In London under the Juvenile Courts (Metropolis) Act, 1920, stipendiary magistrates were nominated as chairmen by the Secretary of State and sat with two lay magistrates. Since 1936, however, London chairmen have usually been lay magistrates and the system of Home Office nomination of juvenile court magistrates has never spread to the rest of the country where about eighty per cent of juvenile offenders are dealt with. Yet the procedures and practices of the London juvenile courts under chairmen such as Sir William Clarke Hall (1866–1932), one of the Secretary of State's first nominees, have done much to shape attitudes in the juvenile court as a whole.

In the rest of the country, under the provisions of the consolidating Children and Young Persons Act, 1933, magistrates to serve in the juvenile court are elected from among their own number by the magistrates of each petty sessional division and are appointed for periods of three years at a time. Each juvenile court appoints its own chairman.

Specially constituted juvenile courts have not developed in Scotland (where the administration of justice is based on a different legal system) to the same extent as in England. The law relating to the trial of juveniles in separate courts from those in which adults are tried is enforced, but only about sixteen per cent of juvenile cases are heard in courts which have been specially constituted – that is, presided over by specially selected magistrates or judges.

Almost all the juvenile court magistrates in England and Wales serve also in the adult courts. Thus the juvenile courts are closely integrated in the general system of administration of justice, and there is to some extent a two-way flow of ideas and attitudes between the juvenile courts and the adult courts, and between the courts and the general public. An opinion seems to be growing among younger or more recently appointed justices that the sort of personal qualities, attitudes, and capacities desirable for service in the juvenile court are probably equally to be desired in the adult court. Some would go further and doubt whether a person who could not conceivably be regarded (apart from his age) as suitable after training for service in the juvenile court is likely to make a good magistrate at all.

Lay magistrates have administered legal justice in England for more than 600 years and in Wales for more than 400 years. The work on the criminal side has grown very considerably during this century and there has been a tendency to increase the power of the lay magistrates' courts to deal with more serious forms of crime. It is estimated that, of those magistrates appointed since 1945, probably at least half have voluntarily and in their own free time attended educational and training courses in fields of study relating to the practice and procedure of the magistrates' courts and to the children and adults who appear before those courts. Since the beginning of 1966, training has been made obligatory and includes additional special instruction for those magistrates who are appointed to the juvenile courts.

Recent official proposals relating to the treatment of juvenile offenders seemed likely, if adopted, to lead to a considerable change in the part played by the juvenile court by greatly diminishing the number of cases which it would be necessary to bring before the court at all. But none of the proposals appeared to involve fundamental changes in the actual procedure of dealing with a juvenile who was so brought. There is talk in other quarters of proposals for strengthening the legal element in the summary courts (as has been done in the quarter-sessions) – for example, by altering the position of the legally qualified clerk in relation to the Bench, or by the appointment of more stipendiary magistrates. Any such changes would have repercussions in the juvenile court. But whatever proposals are made it may be thought that a more widespread understanding of the present place and functions of the juvenile court may itself make a positive contribution towards more realistic discussion of possible changes.

CHAPTER I

THE MAGISTRATES' COURT: I

It is now half a century since the establishment of juvenile courts. The history of these courts over the last fifty years is the story of an attempt to modify the procedure for the administration of justice step by step in the light of growing experience in the juvenile courts and of increased knowledge about children. There are many provisions for the diagnosis and treatment, both educational and social, of children's needs which did not exist in 1908 and which fall quite outside the penal system. Since the Second World War the social services generally have expanded almost beyond recognition. We now have an all-embracing system of secondary school education up to fifteen years of age, and of provision for special educational treatment up to the age of sixteen. The health services have greatly increased and include the provision of what may well eventually become a network of child and parent guidance services. Since 1948 we have had an integrated service for the care of children deprived of normal home life. These are not provisions designed specifically to meet the needs of the delinquent child, but clearly their existence has considerable bearing upon the work of the juvenile courts, since they greatly increase the range of services available to delinquent children over and above those provided specifically for the use of the courts, such as approved schools and borstals, detention centres and attendance centres, classifying schools and remand homes, supervision and probation. When we add to these features the advances which have been made in the understanding of child development and of the social and emotional factors in child delinquency, it is clear that the juvenile court today is at work in a world which is very different in highly relevant respects from that in which it was originally designed.

What is, or should be, the effect of these changes upon the place of the juvenile court in our society? Do they mean that the whole system by which children are brought before a court of law under a judicial system based upon the procedure for dealing with adult offenders is no longer appropriate and ought to be swept away? Do they merely imply the necessity for further modifications both in the procedure and, still more, in the methods open to the courts in dealing with juveniles against whom charges are found proved? Or are changes in the law required, to enable the juvenile courts to deal more directly and freely with the roots of criminality rather than its fruits?

A searching question, often not explicitly formulated yet certainly lying behind much of the doubt about the place of the juvenile courts today, is one as to the age at which it is appropriate to apply the concept of legal justice in society's dealings with individuals. Is legal justice suitable for children at all, or, if it is, are the old bottles capable of containing the new wine? How far does the present system enable the juvenile courts to work along lines which are different from those of the ordinary courts?

The courts which deal with children are a matter of interest to every person concerned in any way in children's welfare or the administration of justice in summary courts, i.e. teachers and social workers, the staffs of social agencies and of statutory departments, magistrates' clerks, lawyers, and, of course, magistrates themselves. Each tends to approach the matter from that aspect with which he is most familiar – the child, the family, the social services, the law, the administration of justice. Some are more aware of treatment requirements, others of the need to preserve civil liberties. The discussion is sometimes further confused by the introduction of examples from the practice of countries whose legal systems differ in various important respects from our own.

In this book it is hoped to show the English juvenile court of today against the background of the ordinary summary court, of which it is a development, and to discuss its practice and procedure in terms related to practice and procedure in summary courts generally. In order to do this an account of the adult court is given first. This is not comprehensive in every detail, but includes particularly those features which are important to an understanding of any summary court and therefore of how and why the juvenile court works in the way in which it does. The treatment of courts throughout this book is, so to speak, defendant-centred with a view to focusing attention finally on the situation, as it appears to a magistrate, of the child who stands before the court.

THE COURTS OF SUMMARY JURISDICTION

The present juvenile courts are courts of summary jurisdiction hearing applications relating to juveniles and charges against them. There are still other summary courts which hear particular classes of cases, such as the domestic court for the hearing of summonses for desertion or neglect to maintain. By far the greater part of the work of the juvenile court is concerned with criminal charges, mainly larceny, and the usual procedure is therefore best understood in the light of the procedure for trying criminal charges in the adult court which will now be described.

The rough outlines of this procedure are known to most people at second hand. The defendant hears a short statement of the accusation against him read out by the clerk and is then asked whether he pleads 'guilty' to the charge or 'not guilty'. If he pleads 'guilty' it is likely that only an abbreviated and formal account of the case against him will be offered by the prosecution, after which the Bench will proceed to announce the sentence. If, however, the defendant pleads 'not guilty', matters will be dealt with at greater length. The prosecution call their witnesses, who give their evidence. The defendant is then invited to question the witnesses. There may, at this point, appear to the Bench to be no case to answer, and if so they will dismiss the charge. But if, as is much more common, there does appear to be a case to answer, the defendant is now invited to give his answer. He can do this according to his preference, either going into the witness-box and taking the oath, or simply telling his tale (i.e. making a Statement) from where he is standing. If he chooses to give evidence upon oath he may be questioned about what he has said, or about anything else which is relevant, even though he himself has not mentioned it. If, however, he chooses not to go into the witness-box, he cannot be questioned beyond, for example, being asked to clarify some part of what he has just said, of which the meaning is not clear to the Bench. Whichever way he answers the charge he may next call in support any witnesses that he has. After hearing the two sides, prosecution and defence, the Bench decide whether to convict or acquit, and publicly announce their decision. If they decide to convict they pass sentence after hearing the defendant's record, and whatever information is known, or may be obtained for this purpose, about him.

The procedure thus outlined is simple and economical in its character. There is an absence of unnecessary stages or ceremonial. The business of the court does indeed often go forward very briskly. On Monday mornings, between 10.0 a.m. and lunchtime, a busy court in a large urban area may well dispose of a mixed bag of seventy or more pleas of 'guilty' to charges of 'drunk', 'drunk and disorderly', or other minor offences.

In itself the procedure does not appear to need the imposing buildings in which in fact it is often carried out. But what are the requirements which the court premises must meet in order to function efficiently? Besides the actual courtroom there need to be places where parties can consult their legal representatives, where witnesses can wait till called, where prisoners can be held until their case is heard, where magistrates can foregather beforehand and retire during cases to consider their verdict. There needs to be office accommodation for the magistrates' clerk and his assistants dealing with the endless paper-work attached to the courts. There may well be cloakroom and toilet facilities for all concerned.

The courtroom itself needs to be large enough to accommodate the Bench and their clerk, the court officers, the parties and their representatives and witnesses, representatives of the Press, and, in addition, a reasonable number of the public, since in this country, with exceptions in a very few classes of cases, the courts are public. Children are not admitted. They are prohibited, under the Children and Young Persons Act, 1933, Section 36, from being present in court, except as witnesses, during the trial of other persons. These numbers already imply quite a large room. But, in addition to accommodating these people, if the proceedings are to be orderly and comprehensible certain arrangements have to be made in regard to the siting of participants.

The members of the Bench need to be near enough to each other to discuss the case, but not feel or look crowded. It is a help if there is sufficient distance separating the Bench and their clerk from everyone else in court to make discussion and consultation possible without every word being audible to the parties. The clerk must be sufficiently near to the Bench for consultation if necessary, but not so near that he appears in effect to participate as a matter of course in all the deliberations of the magistrates. Witnesses giving evidence need to be visible and easily audible both to the Bench and to the parties and their representatives if any. The door to the retiring room should be easily accessible to the Bench and not also be used by other persons, e.g. prisoners *en route* to the cells. Most of these requirements need to be met in any premises proposed for use as a court. They have to be borne in mind even in connexion with the special needs of the juvenile court to be considered later (see Chapters 5, 6, and 7), and many juvenile courts are held in a room used for an ordinary court at other times.

The procedure for hearing cases in summary courts, though simple, is formal, particularly, for example, in such matters as the giving of evidence. It is designed to secure that justice is done, and therefore it is important that the court be conducted in an orderly manner so that this procedure can be carried out. Most courts have a formal atmosphere in themselves, due to the fact that they are arranged in a way which indicates a certain order, formality, and authority about the proceedings and the offices, independently of the personal qualities and abilities of the particular individuals filling these offices. In many courts the magistrates sit several feet above the floor of the courtroom, while the clerk is suspended like Mahomet's coffin midway between heaven and earth, and the defendant – not to put too fine a point on it – is found still lower down. In some large urban areas a busy court bears a strong resemblance to a crowded public meeting at which trouble is expected. There may be a hundred or more members of the public present, plus an impressive contingent of uniformed police.

The only legal status the police – as police – have in these courts is that of litigants. The frequency of their appearance in the role of prosecuting party, coupled with the fact that in many courts they act as ushers and court officers generally, has given rise to an unfortunate confusion in the minds of a large section of the public who refer to the magistrates' courts as 'the police courts', under the impression that this is the correct title and description, with all that it implies. It must be admitted that a member of the public, being shown round a busy court building today – noticing members of the Force acting as doormen, call boys, office messengers, citizens' advice bureaux, and charge officers; seeing in the magistrates' own room the pictures of former stipendiaries labelled 'Police Magistrate'; and recollecting perhaps that when he dialled the telephone number of the courts he was greeted with the words 'Police here' – may well be excused if he is confused as to the role of the police in relation to the administration of justice.

THE BUSINESS OF THE SUMMARY COURTS

The business of the summary courts is concerned,[1] to the extent of nearly sixty-five per cent of the total number of cases, with traffic offences. Far behind come the larceny cases (about nine per cent), followed by the drunk and disorderlies (around six per cent). The remainder consist of railway offences, assault, indecency, nuisance, etc., and cases committed to assizes and quarter-sessions (e.g. murder, manslaughter, robbery, burglary and house-breaking, rape, carnal knowledge, etc.). There are special courts dealing with domestic cases, desertion, neglect to maintain, bastardy, etc.

The incidence of delinquency, in the sense of persons having been proved guilty of an offence against the law in any one year, is under two per cent of the population. If indictable offences only are considered it is less than half of one per cent. (For other aspects of the statistics relating to the proportion of criminals in the population, see *Out of Step* by J. Trenaman.)[2] As, however, only about thirty-nine per cent of the offences known to the police to have been committed are ever cleared up (as no evidence is found which enables a charge to be brought and proved against anybody), the percentage of people actually committing offences in any one year may be assumed to be somewhat higher. It would be unwise to pretend to further exactitude, since it is not known how many of the people who did commit offences which have not been cleared up committed more than one of them. It must also be remembered that among the people, particularly householders, who report that an object is missing, e.g. a watch, ring, or money, some probably forget to inform the police when the missing object turns up later in some unexpected corner.

There is a marked relationship between the commission of offences and age and sex, and between age and sex and type of offence. In particular, the incidence of indictable offences among those young persons aged thirteen to fifteen is much higher than among the rest of the population, but crime in general decreases steadily after the age of twenty-one is reached and is very small among the over-forties. Norval Morris in *The Habitual Criminal*[3] thought there might well be a sort of criminal maturation going on, showing itself in the type of offence typically committed at each stage in the life span of offenders, since begging, sleeping out and 'vagrancy types of crime, larcenies, and receiving tend to occur early both in the criminal's life span and in his criminal career', while 'forgery, robbery, and extortion occur late in both these respects'. There would need to be considerable study of the years in between before anything like a complete picture could be offered, but such suggestions are important to remember in forming a mental picture of the work of the courts against the background of criminality in general.

The incidence of convictions among men and boys is far greater than that among women and girls at all ages, the general proportion being about eight men to every woman convicted. Women shoplift more, they forge and 'utter' to about the same extent, but they are left far behind in traffic offences, other larcenies, and drink charges – largely due without doubt to their much more limited opportunities in these fields.

Statistics of crime are divided into indictable and non-indictable offences. Indictable offences are generally thought of as the more serious ones. This was true in the early days of our law and it is still roughly true today. The history of indictment takes us back to a time when our law and our courts were concerned mainly with keeping the peace by regulating the exaction of vengeance and retribution between private parties. But later some offences were recognized as more dangerous to peace and good government and the common good than others, and so the state took upon itself the right of action and punishment in such cases. But, before the time of the king's judges was taken up in hearing the case, it had to be shown that there was a prima facie case, and particulars of this were drawn up in a bill of indictment. The most important thing about a trial on indictment, from the layman's point of view, is that the accused person's guilt or innocence is decided in a higher court, and by a jury, not by a judge. The judge decides on the sentence if, and only if, the jury make a finding of guilt.

Until comparatively recent times it was thought that the test as to whether an offence was indictable or not (i.e. as to whether it should go before a jury) was the extent to which it was an act to the prejudice of the public – a public mischief. But nowadays the statute which creates an offence also says whether there is a right of jury trial or not. The result of these historical developments is that robbery, murder, and shoplifting are indictable offences, but so also are throwing things at railway carriages to endanger the passengers, cheating at play, and injuring a letter-box – whereas cruelty to animals, assaulting a police constable, taking and driving away a motor-car, driving while un-insured, etc., are not.

There are a number of offences which, though indict-able, can be tried summarily if the accused person agrees, e.g. larceny from shops and stalls. In determining whether to try a case of this nature summarily, the court will hear representations by the prosecutor or the accused person and will consider the nature of the case, the adequacy of the punishment the summary court can impose, and the absence or presence of circumstances making the offence a serious one. If the court does decide on summary trial, the accused person must be told of his rights.

If a magistrates' court tries summarily an offence which is also triable at quarter-sessions on indictment, then, in the event of his conviction, an accused person may be com-mitted to quarter-sessions for sentence if his character and antecedents require, in the opinion of the Bench, the in-fliction of greater punishment than they can impose. This power of the court must also be explained to an accused person before he makes his choice as to the manner in which he wishes to be tried.

This power to commit to quarter-sessions for sentence

after conviction in the summary court can be very important because it is not until a person has been convicted that the court is told of his previous record. It is also not until after conviction that an accused person can ask the court to take into consideration other offences which he admits. Thus, a person who is convicted of stealing may, if he has a history of previous convictions for crime, deserve a more severe prison sentence than the six months which is the most the summary court can impose. These convictions would be unknown to the court when deciding to try the case summarily, and the proper course to take after his conviction would be to commit the offender to quarter-sessions for sentence, since that court is not limited in its power to impose a sentence except by the act of parliament creating the offence.

A fairly common example of the kind of case referred to above is where a person who has falsely pretended he is collecting for a genuine charity, though in truth he is only obtaining money for himself, has visited scores of houses and collected small sums from a great number of them. In practice, he may be tried on only two or three – in themselves minor – charges, but, on conviction, will ask for all the others to be taken into consideration. This will undoubtedly increase the gravity of the offences and would give the summary court convicting him power to commit for sentence since, in the court's view, a heavier sentence is now merited than lies within its power to impose.

A form of words by which a person may be asked whether he wishes to be tried by a jury or summarily, and by which he may be warned of the possibility of being committed to quarter-sessions for sentencing, is provided in the Magistrates' Courts Act, 1952. In practice, the court will probably explain matters to the accused in whatever words it thinks are most likely to be understood, and what its clerk says will probably run somewhat as follows:

'The prosecution has said that this is a proper case to be tried summarily and the court are prepared to do that, but whether they can or not depends on your choice. You have the last word. You can be tried here if you agree. If you don't agree and the prosecution can show to the magistrates that, on the face of it, you have committed this offence, then you will go for trial to quarter-sessions at Warwick on the [date] of [month] and there you will be tried by a jury. If, however, you do agree, you can be tried by the magistrates here today. But if you agree to be tried by this court, and the magistrates find you guilty of this offence, they can send you to the quarter-sessions to be sentenced if they feel that their powers of punishing you are not great enough when they hear your character and antecedents if you have any, and of course they don't know yet whether you have any antecedents or not. That simply means other offences that you may have been found guilty of on previous occasions or other offences you might want to have taken into consideration today.'

When the charge against a defendant has been proved, the next stage will normally be for the court to pass sentence. The severity of the sentence which the court can pass in any given case is limited to the maximum laid down by parliament in respect of that offence. The maximum term of imprisonment to which an English summary court could sentence anyone on one offence is six months and the highest fine is £100. Its power as to the sentence it may impose is therefore somewhat limited. However, the aggregate fine for a number of offences is unlimited, e.g. nine offences of larceny could lead to a maximum total fine of £900, although the maximum total length of imprisonment for more than one indictable offence tried summarily is twelve months.

THE METHODS OF DISPOSAL

There are a variety of courses open to the summary court according to the case. It may be that the court does not wish to punish the convicted person at all. If so, it may choose one of the following: It may give the defendant an absolute discharge, in which case the matter is finished with, although, of course, the conviction remains on the record. A variant of this is the conditional discharge for a period not exceeding twelve months – a discharge subject to the condition that no further offence is committed during that time. If an offence is committed, the offender may be sentenced not only for that offence but also for the original one as well (Criminal Justice Act, 1948, Section 7). At first glance very similar to the conditional discharge, but with one all-important difference, is the probation order (Criminal Justice Act, 1948, Section 3). The offender is placed on probation under the supervision of a probation officer for a period of not less than one year nor more than three years. Requirements about behaviour may be embodied in the order. If the probationer fulfils these requirements, and also commits no further offence during the stated period, the matter ends there. If not, however, he may be brought back to court and sentenced for the original offence as well as for the new one. Probation differs from the conditional discharge in that the consent of the defendant must be obtained, and the form of the order is more flexible, allowing the court to include requirements which it thinks will help the defendant. The most important aspect, however, is that the defendant has the help, advice, and friendship of a trained and experienced person in his effort to keep out of further trouble.

However, it is usually felt that when a person has been convicted of an offence he ought to be punished. By far the most frequent punishment awarded by the summary courts is the order to pay a fine. A first offender must be given time to pay if he asks for it, but the court may fix an alternative punishment to be awarded in the event of non-payment of the fine. The court may commit the convicted person to prison, either as an alternative to payment of a fine 'forthwith', or with the option of paying a fine.

A person between the ages of fifteen and twenty-one, convicted by the magistrates' court of an offence punishable on summary conviction with imprisonment, may, if the court is satisfied on various relevant points (Magistrates' Courts Act, 1952, Section 28) that he ought to be sent for borstal training, be so sent, but *not* by the magistrates' court direct. All it can do is to commit the youth or girl in custody to the quarter-sessions with a view to sentence. The magistrates' court can, however, itself commit to borstal where a defendant is a persistent absconder from an approved school or has been guilty of serious misconduct there.

There are two further penal provisions especially for people under twenty-one which may be used in cases where the court has power to pass a sentence of imprisonment and in view of the previous record. Such a person may be ordered to attend an attendance centre for periods adding up to not more than twelve (or, in exceptional circum-stances, twenty-four) hours, or be sent away to a detention centre (usually for three months), according to the circum-stances. These provisions were made for the first time under the Criminal Justice Act, 1948, and, as far as people between the ages of sixteen and twenty-one are concerned, the pro-visions as to detention centres have only recently been put into force, and the first attendance centre for this age group was opened in December 1958.

The use of imprisonment for offenders under twenty-one was restricted under the Criminal Justice Act, 1948, Section 17 (2). Imprisonment was not to be imposed on these offenders except when the court was satisfied that no other method at its disposal was suitable. There was an effective check on the misuse of this exception in that the court must state in writing its reasons for being satisfied. Under the First Offenders Act, 1958, this restriction now covers all adult offenders except in respect of imprisonment in default of payment of fines, costs, damages, or com-pensation.

The courts' power to imprison an offender under twenty-one has been restricted still more narrowly by the Criminal Justice Act, 1961, which is intended completely to eliminate prison sentences of intermediate or short length on offenders in this age group. This Act prohibits any court from passing a sentence of imprisonment on a person who is 'within the limits of age which qualify for a sentence of Borstal training' (Section 3), except where the sentence is either under six months or over three years in length.

There are two sentences designed for a particular sort of offender which cannot be used by the summary courts at all but only by the higher courts. These are corrective training and preventive detention (Criminal Justice Act, 1948, Section 21), and they are used for persistent offenders. There the similarity ends. Corrective training is intended for younger, still reclaimable people and may be used for anyone who has reached the age of twenty-one. The sentence may be for not less than two or more than four years. The sentence of preventive detention is simply to prevent the commission of further offences by an apparently incorrigible and persistent offender aged thirty or more and may be for not less than five or more than fourteen years. However, arising out of a practice direction of the Court of Criminal Appeal it now appears that it is not, hereafter, the intention to confirm sentences of corrective training passed on persons who have already served a borstal sentence or are over thirty years of age, or sentences of preventive detention passed on persons aged under forty years. ([1962] 2 All E.R. 905)

It will be apparent from a consideration of the penal provisions outlined above that the law allows, and even at times enjoins, a very considerable differentiation of treatment between different sorts of offenders who are tried in the summary courts, and that age, character, and record as well as the offence are considered to be of importance in selecting the appropriate course of action in dealing with offenders.

The selection of the appropriate course of action is described as 'a particularly important part of the work of justices' in the *Report* of the Royal Commission referred to below (page 29). As new methods of dealing with persons found guilty come into operation, justices are expected to study them. Newly appointed justices are now, of course, expected to go much farther than this and to take advantage of courses of study provided by their own magistrates' courts committee and by the Magistrates' Association or otherwise. They are urged and expected not to sit to adjudicate but merely to observe until they have at least begun to fit themselves for the duties which they are required to perform. Since the beginning of 1966 training has been obligatory. The object of training is not to give the lay magistrate a thorough knowledge of the law but an understanding of his own duties in administering it, and especially an understanding of what is meant by 'acting judicially' and by 'a judicial mind'. Whatever else may be included in training this is indispensable for every magistrate serving in any court, whether the court is one dealing with adults or with juveniles.

THE SELECTION AND APPOINTMENT OF LAY JUSTICES

An understanding of the method by which lay justices are selected and appointed is essential to a realistic appreciation of the working of the juvenile court, since outside London it is from the general panel of justices in each area that those to serve in the juvenile court must be chosen. The appointment of lay justices to sit in the summary courts is made for most areas by the Lord Chancellor on the advice of advisory committees of which the membership is secret but the secretaryships are known. Their job is to find the men and women who are best qualified to be justices and to recommend them for appointment. All other considerations are to be subordinate to personal suitability. The difficulty is, of course, for the committee, especially in a large area, to know who is suitable. The Royal Commission on Justices of the Peace, reporting in 1948, thought that 'the dominance of political representation on advisory committees' was one reason why the system tended 'to look too much to certain sections of the community for candidates for appointment as justices'.[4] How far this situation has been remedied it is difficult to say. Appointment as a lay magistrate is regarded as an honour, so that in order to avoid the suspicion of bias in the award of this honour one would expect the advisory committee to include representatives of the more powerful bodies participating in the life of the area. In the large town one has the impression that the justices selected by the advisory committee include people of all classes and of most of the more obvious religious and political persuasions. It seems easier in the case of men to get an idea of their suitability or otherwise since they are often known through their work with political, religious, trade union, industrial, commercial, professional, or other groups, including sometimes voluntary social service. Women, even today, have fewer avenues through which to become known. In some areas certain bodies such as the Girl Guides appear to be regarded as a source of suitable recruits, while being the wife of a man who is himself a prominent member of one of the groups listed has sometimes seemed to outsiders to be almost the only identifiable qualification of some persons appointed. While, however, the number of men about whom the advisory committee could be expected easily to obtain reliable information is probably far greater than that of women, this may to some extent be offset by the fact that it is often very difficult for men, already involved in these various extra activities, to offer the further time required to serve on the Bench, whereas middle-aged women are available in much larger numbers. Although the present scheme can easily be criticized, the problem of how to select justices is extremely complex. The scheme ought obviously to be open to as few objections and pitfalls as possible, but, within the limits of any given scheme, the quality of the appointments made and eventually the quality of the advisory committee itself will depend on the general appreciation of what is required and what are the essentials of English justice as it ought to be administered in the summary courts.

THE DEFENDANT IN COURT

One important way by which the general public gains a realistic picture of what goes on in the magistrates' courts, and what the roles and duties of the various participants are, is by first-hand information spread by those who have been there in any capacity whatever. This includes not only the representatives of the Press but also the general public, the witnesses, and the parties, perhaps particularly the defendant.

It soon becomes clear to anyone watching and listening in court that a number of the people participating are performing roles with which they are quite familiar. But many of the defendants have never been in that position before nor even perhaps watched court proceedings, and the ordinary citizen may well feel himself at a disadvantage in this unaccustomed role. The court situation, its size, formality, and publicity, the conspicuousness and isolation of his position, and the feeling of being required to perform according to rules, the details of which are unknown to him but appear familiar to the other side, all tend to handicap him.

In English law there is a presumption of innocence. A person cannot be assumed to be guilty of an offence until the offence is proved against him in court according to the proper rules of evidence. The charge will therefore be read over to the defendant and he will be asked whether he pleads 'guilty' or 'not guilty', even if he was caught in the act. It is important to realize that the court's duty is confined to examining the charges, hearing what is said on both sides and reaching a verdict, and then pronouncing sentence. It is not part of the function of the court to undertake any part of the punishment itself. The appearance in court and the court proceedings are not part of the punishment. They could not reasonably be so, since by no means everyone who appears in court is guilty, and in law no one is until a verdict of guilty is reached. Even where the defendant is guilty, the penalty is in the sentence, plus any social punishment such as loss of job or respectability which may be consequent upon the court case, and should not include an attack by the clerk or the Bench during the case. In practice, it is not difficult for a certain punitive atmosphere to gather about the proceedings; for example, a person who was addressed as 'Jones' when the charge was read over, suddenly becomes 'Mr Jones' on pleading not guilty, only to revert to plain 'Jones' on the charge being found proved. The manner in which the clerk addresses the defendant is possibly the most important single factor in enabling the latter to do his best to defend himself, or disabling him by making him feel – whatever is said – that his case has been prejudged in one person's mind at any rate, and that the finding there was not in his favour. There is all the difference in the world between the clerk who says, 'Now, Mr Smith, I will just explain the procedure in these courts. First of all we . . .', and the one who starts in tones of exasperation, 'Now come on, Smith, wake up and take your hands out of your pockets.'

In most cases a defendant who has a right of trial by jury nevertheless chooses summary trial, but whether on any basis other than the wish to get the matter finished is not known. Often he seems, after gazing vaguely round, to reach a sudden decision on hearing the words '. . . tried by the magistrates here today'.

The prosecution then open their case and call their witnesses. Very often in the magistrates' courts the police are the prosecuting party. Police witnesses often give their evidence out of a little notebook from notes alleged to have been made independently of each other and at the time of the incident, and are followed in the witness-box by a second officer who corroborates the first. The wording used is often startlingly similar because most of the cases and the evidence in support are of a type which recurs frequently and they have no special features other than place, date, and time. The defendant is entitled to question the witnesses at this point, and this is a serious hurdle for the novice. He may have just heard what he believes to be a tissue of inaccuracies or at least a highly tendentious and unjustified interpretation of his behaviour. He is only anxious to get his denial in as quickly as possible and does so. The clerk may pull him up sharply, 'I said ask questions, not tell your story . . .', or he may say, 'Mr Brown, you will, as I explained, have an opportunity to tell the court your side of the story later but at the moment you have an opportunity of putting questions to the witness. Did you want to ask him . . . ?', and the clerk may reformulate as questions the gist of what the defendant had started to say. A sharp remonstrance may well have the effect of silencing a defendant entirely: although it is of vital importance to his case that he should question the prosecution witness on the points with which he disagrees, he seems to feel that he has made a bad impression on his judges and had better take no further risk of appearing a fool.

When the prosecution have finished their case and there seems, on what they have said, to be a case to answer, it is the defendant's turn. In giving him the choice between going into the witness-box and giving his evidence on oath, or telling his story from where he stands, the court has somehow to get it across to the defendant that in the first case he can be questioned and in the second case not, without making it seem that they are advising him to do one thing rather than the other, or that they will not believe his story if he is not speaking on oath. In the case of a woman defendant in a large and crowded court, she may very well choose not to give evidence on oath because she would rather stay where she is with her back to the public than walk across to the witness-box and face them.

It is a curious feature of many courts that the seating of the persons taking part in the trial is so arranged that the defendant has, in effect, to choose between facing the magistrates, who after all are the people trying the case and on whose opinion of his evidence his whole reputation and future may depend, or turning to face whichever of the parties is putting questions to him. The angle through which he and other witnesses turn may be anything from about forty-five degrees to nearly a hundred and eighty, and he cannot face in both directions simultaneously. Nor is it usually at all necessary that he should, but the result of this situation in some courts is that an already nervous witness may be asked repeatedly by the clerk to 'speak to the magistrates, please', or to 'turn and face the magistrates', while at the same time his questioner is, so to speak, pulling at his other sleeve. Anyone who has played the parlour game in which the player is required to stroke the middle part of his anatomy in one direction while simultaneously patting the top of his head with the other hand, will have some idea of the kind of ability required in the witness in these circumstances.

Sometimes a defendant appears to have no idea which are the material points in the prosecution's evidence against him, or not to realize that the Bench know nothing about him excepting what has been put by the prosecution. In these cases a Statement can be very inadequate as a defence and the situation is difficult to help.

When it comes to calling his witnesses, a defendant who is not legally represented often appears to be at a total loss. He either had no witnesses or he never thought of bringing them with him or he didn't feel he could ask them to miss time at their work. Offers to adjourn the case to enable him to bring his witnesses are often not accepted and the case proceeds without them, the defendant's evidence remaining without their corroboration, which might or might not have been forthcoming.

Members of the public listening to the replies of some of the witnesses in a criminal case may sometimes be excused if they misunderstand the implications of the terms 'witness for the defence' and 'witness for the prosecution'. The witnesses are not themselves fighting the case; they are being called before the court by the parties who are. Their function is to answer as truthfully as they can the questions which are put to them. It is the job of the defence and the prosecution, respectively, each to try to put the truth as revealed by the witnesses in the light most favourable to his client, and a witness who quite obviously supposes he is there as an advocate has not only mistaken his function but is also likely to make a bad impression and to injure his 'client's' case. The most convincing witnesses are often quite simple people who apparently easily appreciate this fact, or at any rate take the questions at their face value and have no trouble in answering straightforwardly.

The evidence of an accomplice should be corroborated. It is not contrary to law to convict on the uncorroborated evidence of an accomplice, but it is considered unsafe to do so. For example, in a recent case two defendants, A and B, alleged to have acted together, each made statements to the police. At the trial A withdrew his statement completely and pleaded not guilty. The withdrawal was accepted by the court, with the result that the whole of the evidence remaining against A consisted in the statement made by his alleged accomplice, and in view of this situation it was decided to dismiss the case against A. Some weeks later X, who was not known to be connected with either A or B, and who was on probation at the time after being convicted of another offence, confessed to having committed this one.

The evidence given by a witness must consist of facts and not opinions unless the witness has been called as an expert on the points in question. Belief as to either the guilt or the innocence of the defendant on the part of a witness who is not in a position to know any of the facts is not evidence. The function of deciding upon the guilt or innocence in any case belongs to the Bench. The expert witness's opinion is evidence as to fact in so far as the matters on which he is giving his opinion really do lie within his professional competence.

Hearsay evidence is not generally admissible. It is not enough to have arrived on the scene after the assault, and to have been told by a bystander who it was that struck the bus conductor, if the accused denies that it was he, and the said bystander is not produced in court to give evidence.

THE JUDGES' RULES

Statements made voluntarily by the accused to the police and later offered by them in court in evidence in the presence of the accused, for example, 'I asked her why she did not stop at the Halt sign and she replied, "I never do stop at that one" ', are admissible. A difficulty arises, however, when a statement alleged to have been made to the police and signed by the accused is produced in court as evidence and the defendant, while admitting that he made the statement and that the signature is his, asserts that it was not made voluntarily and that the contents are not true. In general, in the case of an adult of normal intelligence born and brought up in this country it is difficult to imagine how this could happen. The questioning of suspected persons by the police is regulated by the Judges' Rules, a copy of which is displayed at the police station. Furthermore, there is always the risk that any irregularities would be reported to the court by the accused person. However, if the defendant does say, for instance, that he was kept at the station and questioned right through the night, and that, finally, in order to get home or on the promise that no action would be taken against him he signed a confession, the Bench has to consider whether in the light of these remarks the statement is or is not admissible as evidence. If it was in any sense not a voluntary statement it is not admissible. In view of the police denials, it is a question of whose view of the matter is to be accepted. It does not follow that the police version must be accepted because not to do so would suggest doubts about their truthfulness, since the same would apply, where there is a conflict of evidence, to any other witness whose credibility has not hitherto been put in question. The defendant can usually produce no witnesses in support of his statement, but if the circumstances described, in such a case, were true, this might not be at all surprising.

This difficult problem is one with which most Benches are probably not very often faced. When it does arise, however, it is of great importance, since an unjudicial or biased attitude on the part of the Bench could cause people to lose confidence in the administration of the law and to feel that the police as prosecutors are in some special position in relation to the Bench. Each case has to be reviewed on its merits and in the light of whatever has been said on both sides. If it does appear to the Bench that an element of compulsion, whether intentional or otherwise, may well have been present on the part of the police, the statement will probably be regarded as inadmissible.

The Judges' Rules refer to statements by persons suspected of crime, or by prisoners in police custody. They are not laws but are administrative rules, the result of deliberations by a committee of judges, and are circulated for the information and guidance of the police. Among other things it is laid down that, while there is no objection to a police officer questioning people about a crime when he is still trying to discover who did it, yet, as soon as he has reasonable grounds for suspecting that a person has committed an offence, then he must caution the suspect before questioning him further. When a person is actually charged with, or informed that he may be prosecuted for, an offence, a rather more strongly worded caution must be administered and, after this caution, questioning of the accused should normally cease. A person making a voluntary statement must not be cross-examined.

A police officer taking a statement is to 'take down the exact words spoken . . . without putting any questions other than such as may be needed to make the statement coherent, intelligible and relevant . . .' (Rule IV (*d*)). When two or more people are charged with the same offence and statements are taken separately, a police officer who wishes to bring to the notice of one accused any written statement made by another is to do this, not by reading the statement aloud but by handing the person a true copy of the said statement without saying or doing anything to invite any reply or comment. If the recipient starts to say something he is to be cautioned immediately (Rule V).

Thus however short and informal in character a statement may be, the taking of it is a formal matter. The editor of *The Magistrate* notes [5] a case in which a statement 'consisted of seventeen lines of introductory cautions, signatures, counter-signatures, etc., although followed only by a laconic "I done it, mate!"'

In announcing the new rules (1964), the Lord Chief Justice referred to an 'overriding principle', namely, that a fundamental condition of the admissibility of a statement in evidence against a person is that it should have been voluntary. If the court is satisfied that a statement was made voluntarily, it may well admit it even though the Rules were not complied with, since the whole object of the Rules is only to ensure that statements admitted are voluntary statements.

In the preamble to the Rules the point is made that, at any stage of an investigation, a person should normally be able to communicate and consult privately with a solicitor. It is also pointed out that police officers, otherwise than by arrest, cannot compel any person against his will to come to or remain in any police station. The Rules do not only apply to police officers but (Rule VI) say that other persons charged with the duty of investigating offences or charging offenders shall, so far as may be practicable, comply with these Rules.

It will be agreed that the Judges' Rules, if carried out, do offer fairly comprehensive protection against improper treatment by the police. Although it is probable that few first offenders actually know of them as such, certainly many adults are aware that regulations of some kind exist, and in some instances even refuse to say anything at all except in the presence of their solicitor.

CHILDREN IN COURTS

It sometimes happens that children are called as witnesses to give evidence in cases being heard in the adult courts. There are general provisions under the Children and Young

Persons Act, 1933, Section 37, regarding children who may have to appear as witnesses in courts. These provisions are intended to protect the welfare of the children, at the same time avoiding interference with the ordinary requirements of the administration of justice. This is a somewhat difficult tightrope to walk, as will be seen more clearly in connexion with the discussion of juvenile court procedure.

The general provisions include powers to clear a court while anyone who, in the opinion of the court, is a child or young person is giving evidence in cases relating to conduct contrary to decency or morality. There is also power to prohibit publication in newspapers of any particulars calculated to lead to the identification of a child or young person concerned in proceedings of this kind in any court.

There is a further provision in the Act of 1933 that where 'a child of tender years' (Section 38) is called as a witness and the court thinks that he does not understand the nature of an oath but is sufficiently intelligent to understand the duty of speaking the truth, his evidence may be received in spite of not being given on oath, but, if it is for the prosecution, it must be corroborated in material particulars by some other evidence in support which implicates the accused.

The welfare of children as witnesses has recently received further consideration. It is provided under the Children and Young Persons Act, 1963, Section 27, that, in committal proceedings for a sexual offence, the evidence of a person under fourteen must, as a general rule, be given in the form of a statement made in writing by, or taken in writing from, the child so far as it is admissible, the child not being called as a witness. All these are very important provisions which seem to have a proper regard on the one hand for protecting children from injury through the effects of undesirable publicity, and on the other for protecting accused persons against the natural inadequacies of children as witnesses.

While it is often true that children 'of tender years' giving evidence in court show signs of very great strain, yet, in some suggestions for protecting them (e.g. that they should not be cross-examined), there is a risk of destroying their value as witnesses in a court of trial, for example, by putting them in a privileged position as witnesses which could not be justified from the point of view of an attempt to get at the truth. In a recent case of alleged indecent assault, a young man was charged with having indecently handled a little girl in the course of delivering goods to the door of her mother's house. The Bench consisted of one man and one woman with the woman magistrate as chairman. The mother of the child, a very excitable foreigner, who had not seen the alleged offence, had given evidence of a disturbing character as to what she said was the state of the child on returning to the sitting-room after talking to the young man at the door. The child also gave evidence which was of a rather confused nature and delivered in a whisper. The legal representative of the accused then turned towards the Bench and said to the chairman, 'I don't want to upset the little girl in any way. Perhaps it would be better if I didn't ask her any questions, what do you think?' From the child's point of view it would certainly have been much better, but the Bench, although thanking him for his consideration, felt obliged to reply that the question whether to cross-examine any of the prosecution witnesses was one which he, as defending solicitor, must decide for himself – presumably in the light of the needs of the defence. With this the solicitor proceeded to put questions to the child, who answered clearly and quietly and with such unexpected effect that the defendant was pronounced not to be guilty. It is very unfortunate when young children are required to appear in such cases or indeed in any cases in a criminal court. If, however, they do appear, then justice must not be prejudiced in an attempt to protect them. No one with experience of such cases would deny that there are instances where an innocent person runs a risk of being put in serious peril through the intellectual and emotional immaturity of a child witness, and through the otherwise justifiable anxiety of those present to protect the child from strain. The situation is aggravated when, not only is the charge one which by its nature implies that the victim has been subject to a serious emotional shock, but the case is not finally brought until an interval of two or even three months has elapsed after the alleged event. Meantime the child has been taken over the circumstances many times by friends, neighbours, and police, none of them being in a position to know the facts at first hand, but some of them expressing very strong emotional reactions about the incident on the assumption that a great deal will be alleged and that even more happened. In these cases the strain on some children of giving evidence in court and the possibility of damage to them is probably greatly increased, in addition to whatever harm was done by the alleged incident itself. It could be argued that it is even more difficult to prove the charge sometimes in such a situation, since the child is not fully aware of the inconsistencies and contradictions in the picture he or she has formed *since* the event and which, in reply to questions, he or she presents to the court.

CHAPTER 2

THE MAGISTRATES' COURT: II

AFTER both the prosecution and the defence have finished putting their case the Bench must make up their minds whether to acquit or convict. Very often something has come out in the evidence which convinces all members of the Bench as to what is the proper verdict. The Bench in the adult court may consist of two magistrates or any other number up to and including seven. In the Lord Chancellor's view three is the most suitable number and five should be the maximum. In busy courts which sit daily and where the magistrates are able to have plenty of experience it is usual to see only two or three on the Bench. An uneven number is much the more convenient, since it enables a decision to be reached even in the event of a disagreement. If they are in disagreement, the Bench are likely to retire, compare notes, talk things over, and very likely send for the clerk so that he can remind them of the position in law in regard to the particular charge, i.e. as to who has to prove what, and as to what evidence has been given.

THE MAGISTRATES' CLERK

The relation between the magistrates and their clerk is a keypoint in the administration of justice in the summary courts. In the *Notes for New Magistrates* (1966) published by the Magistrates' Association, this relationship is summed up very well in the sentence 'In each magistrates' court the magistrates' right-hand man is the clerk.' The good running of the court depends on the extent to which the chairman and his colleagues are able to make the maximum correct use of their 'right-hand man'. In as far as it appears that the Bench are using their clerk correctly, the public will have confidence that both Bench and clerk are doing their own work and that the judges in the court are, in fact as well as in form, the magistrates and not the clerk.

Under the provisions of the Justices of the Peace Act, 1949, ultimately all clerks must have a professional qualification, but at present the clerks are qualified either professionally or by experience. How is the professional expertise of the clerk used in his position as right-hand man to the Bench in the magistrates' court?

In a magistrates' court the justices are judges of both fact and law. They decide whether the case is proved or not and impose any penalty. It is therefore not proper to consult the clerk as to the fact of the guilt or innocence of the accused. The clerk is, however, the person to turn to on points of law. It often happens that the justices wish to be informed as to what the law is on certain points or whether, for example, the facts found by them do constitute an offence in law (and this is a question of mixed law and fact). As the clerk takes a note of all the evidence he can also refresh the memory of the Bench as to what was actually said.

However, the decision when actually reached, whether on law or on fact, is the responsibility of the magistrates. The decision of the court must be the decision of the justices and not that of the justices and their clerk. When it comes to deciding on the sentence, the same principles apply, and the magistrates would not be in order in asking the clerk for his opinion as to the sentence which they *ought* to impose. As a matter of common sense, however, in making their decision, they might, and very often do, ask him what sentences are usual for the offence in question. This is a practice which makes, or should make, for uniformity of sentence for the same offence where at least a degree of uniformity of circumstances exists. It allows deviations from the usual sentences in such cases to be made with conscious intention, thus enabling a considered and rational opinion to be formed as to the just and consistent penalty in the particular instance. This should avoid the passing of a sentence which appears simply to reflect the personal prejudice or idiosyncratic views of the strongest personality on the Bench on any particular day.

Having said this, it must be remembered, however, that if the Bench are seen to be conferring with their clerk, but not with each other at all, before announcing either the verdict or sentence, members of the public watching from the well of the court may draw certain conclusions as to what the conference is about. It was once pointed out that everything that the Bench might properly say to their clerk could safely be, and indeed should be, audible to every person in the courtroom. There is a great deal to be said for this proposition, though unfortunately it is only the experienced and competent chairman who has sufficient confidence to put it into practice. If the clerk always and as a matter of course goes into the retiring room with the justices when the verdict and sentence are to be considered, and returns with them as they all file back into court again to announce their decisions, the presumption that he has been there in order to join in their discussions is excusable.

While, in a particular case, there may be aspects of the matters on which the justices have to make up their minds with which the clerk can help, there are always in every case matters on which it is not within his competence as clerk to the court to help the justices and in which his opinions have no status. The proper use of the clerk's professional contribution can be made, and will be assumed to be being made, if he is sent for at the appropriate moment and returns to the court again on his own while the magistrates remain behind to discuss the further matters which concern them alone.

An intelligent, interested, and tactful clerk, with a good professional attitude to his work and an understanding of all that his duties include, in the widest sense, can decisively affect the quality of the court's work. Whatever formal theoretical training is arranged for the magistrates, the most important and valuable training that they receive will be on the practical side in the day-to-day work with the clerks. Many clerks seem to feel this and to accept the responsibility, developing an attitude towards the Bench rather like that of a father who may reproach his offspring in private but will allow no criticism from outsiders. Such an attitude was engagingly displayed in the reply made to a solicitor who suggested that the Bench were probably unaware of the provisions of section so-and-so of the Magistrates' Courts Act, 1952: 'I would have you know, Mr X, that *my magistrates* are fully conversant with the Magistrates' Courts Act, of 1952, and with every other Act that deals with procedure in these courts!'

REACHING A VERDICT

Generally, before a finding of guilt the magistrates must have been able to satisfy themselves, not only that the offence was actually committed and by the person charged but also that he intended to commit it. This is the principle of '*mens rea*' or criminal intent, and does not apply to all offences by any means, e.g. speeding. Where it does apply, however, and in the case of normal adults it is usually fairly obvious that the defendant was capable of forming a criminal intent and is clear from his actions immediately after the offence that he had in fact done so. A woman may take a pair of stockings to the shop door without paying for them first in order to verify the colour. But, if she then puts them in her pocket, goes out into the street, and walks rapidly away from the shop in the direction of the bus stop, with every step she takes it becomes more difficult for her to give a convincing answer to the allegation that she was intending to avoid payment. The facts are against her.

A correct verdict must be one which is supported by the evidence. This sounds like a simple and obvious proposition. That it is not always so in practice is shown by the reports of appeal cases in the High Court given in the various Law Reports from time to time (though most appeals from magistrates' courts go to quarter-sessions).

In considering their verdict the Bench have to decide not whether the defendant has done the thing with which he is charged but whether his guilt is shown in the evidence. It is quite possible for a member of the Bench to feel a strong personal conviction that the accused has indeed committed the act, and yet agree that in law he must be found 'not guilty'. A new magistrate may well have an occasion in the first few months of service when he feels tempted to suggest that the verdict of 'not guilty' should be announced by the Bench in the following form: 'We find you not guilty of the offence with which you are charged and warn you in the strongest possible terms *not to do it again.*'

A case recently heard before a magistrates' court may serve to illustrate a number of the points which have been made above. A man was charged with having committed an indecent assault upon a young female by indecently exposing himself to a little girl of six who was in the company of her brother in a half-finished house on a building site. The court was cleared for the hearing of the case and, as the accused's solicitor had announced that the plea would be one of not guilty, the witnesses were also out of court. As the charge was read the accused man looked as sorry a picture of wretchedness and guilt as could be imagined, with something quite extraordinarily furtive and unprepossessing about his manner.

It appeared that a complaint had reached the police on a Sunday afternoon, nearly two months previously, that such an offence had occurred. On the following day two uniformed policemen had called for the children and had taken them in a police car to the site. There were a number of unfinished houses, but the car was driven without hesitation to a particular one and the two policemen got out. They disappeared into the house and almost immediately reappeared accompanied by a builder's labourer. With this man between them they came up to the car and said to the little girl something to the effect of 'Is this the man?' The child thought it was and as a result a charge was preferred. The defence, however, was one of mistaken identity.

The little girl was called at an early stage. She was too young to take the oath, but the court, having satisfied itself that she understood the importance of speaking the truth, received her evidence. This was a very painful proceeding, as she was in tears and so unnerved and frightened that she actually shook. She at first stood against her mother's knee in the witness-box, but, as the mother found it impossible to refrain from prompting her replies to each question, it was necessary, in fairness to the accused man, to ask the mother to stand down. This, strangely enough, produced no further deterioration in the witness's condition and she managed to tell the court, among other things, that the offence took place on the ground floor between the back door and the kitchen. She agreed to the prosecution's suggestion that if he was in court she would be able to identify the man concerned, and on being asked to look round and see if he was there she was able to point a wavering finger, not at the accused but at the clerk to the solicitor for the defence!

The young brother, aged fourteen, was then called and proved to be an excellent witness, straightforward and clear. As it was necessary for the younger child's evidence to be corroborated in a material particular he too was asked, among other questions, to tell the court exactly where the offence took place. In his answer he named a quite different place and, on being asked if he was quite sure, said that he remembered the place clearly and had no shadow of doubt.

When the Bench came to consider the verdict they were obliged to set aside any instinctive feelings they might have had as to the guilt of the accused and to consider only the evidence which had been given. The original identification was in a form which was worthless, while the one in court was in favour of the defence. The boy's evidence did not corroborate that of his sister as to the important and elementary fact of where the offence took place. In the event, the justices on coming back into court delivered their verdict as not guilty. Two points remained as memorable in the mind of at least one member of the Bench. One was the look of amazement on the face of the boy witness, as he took in what the chairman was saying. The other was the remark of the clerk after the parties had left the court, 'Your worships will be interested to hear that this is the twelfth time that X has appeared on a charge of this kind. He has eleven previous convictions and has served several prison sentences!'

It is difficult not to feel in such cases that a guilty man has got off scot-free and that justice has rather obviously not been done. Would the verdict have been the same if the Bench had known the facts about the defendant's previous history? This story was told by the writer to an elderly continental judge, who at this point said with great satisfaction, 'Ach! so after all he was guilty! By our system it is better because we have the record!' In English law, however, evidence that the defendant has committed previous offences is not usually admissible, and this is one of the most striking differences in practice between our courts and those of some other countries. Having a record probably makes the chance of being suspected considerably greater, and this in itself may increase the risk of detection. But suspicion is not proof. The police were so sure of their man that they carelessly omitted to obtain a most important piece of evidence as to identity. They staged an identity parade which was worthless for the purpose. The little girl identified the only person she was offered when he was shown to her in a highly suggestive situation, namely, standing between two uniformed policemen. Would she have picked the same man out from among fifteen other builders' labourers if the identity parade had been properly done at the time? Nobody knows, and only the offender himself knows who in fact committed the offence. Whether that man was the one who stood in court is now a matter for speculation only, since a person cannot be tried a second time for the same offence, when once he has been acquitted.

CONSIDERATIONS IN SENTENCING

After the verdict, if it is one of guilty, comes the sentence. Before passing sentence the Bench will inquire whether there is any record of previous offences having been committed by the convicted person and, if there is, these will be recounted. If the offender is aged twenty-one or more his criminal record as given to the court will not include any offences of which he was found guilty before he was fourteen (i.e. as a child), and any such offences are disregarded (Children and Young Persons Act, 1963, Section 16). The man in the dock will have an opportunity of challenging and correcting any statement which may have been made. If there is no record, or even if there is, the Chairman may ask the police if they have any information about the prisoner and, if they have, this too will be given in his hearing. It usually takes some such form as 'Y is a married man with a wife and three children in Ireland. He came to this country two years ago and has been here ever since, except for short holidays at home. He is in lodgings here on his own. He is a quiet-living man and he hasn't been in any trouble till now.'

Sentencing has not reached the stage of being an exact science, but in some summary courts a sort of conventional tariff evolves in regard to the lower ranges of offence and penalty. In this way the penalty is fitted to the crime, and the guilty defendant may have, if he knows the tariff, whatever satisfaction attaches to getting what he expected. There is, however, no certainty of uniformity as between one Bench and another, and farther up the scale the lack of uniformity can be quite startling, e.g. fines of £15 and £50 respectively for the offence of being drunk in charge. Sentences may also vary greatly as between one court and another even when judges are sitting, e.g. binding over compared with a sentence of two years' imprisonment for cases of bigamy tried within a few days of each other by different judges.

With rare exceptions we do not in this country have

prescribed minimum sentences, and the range of variation is therefore limited only by the maximum. But such differences as those quoted above are felt by many people to be a mistake. They are on the whole unpopular with the clerks, and other legally-minded persons. They may arise from different views as to the heinousness of the particular offence, but they may also be due to the effort to fit the sentence either to the particular circumstances of the offence (whether extenuating or otherwise) or to the offender.

While many magistrates agree that there is not a sufficient degree of consistency between the sentences passed by different courts for common minor offences, there is, on the other hand, some resistance on grounds of principle to the idea that the courts themselves might adopt a generally agreed policy and so come into line with each other. In some areas these ambivalent feelings have been resolved by discussions between neighbouring courts without any binding resolutions being passed. Each Bench is as free to operate as previously, yet each is better informed on local practice and has been encouraged to examine its own policy in sentencing. Justices who profess themselves quite unable to accept 'guidance' as to what sentences they *ought* to pass nevertheless often fall into line on discovering, in general discussion, that they are quite out of step with their colleagues sitting on other days or in neighbouring courts.

On the question of variations between sentences passed on different offenders for the same offence even when charged in concert, Mr Justice Hilbery, delivering judgment in the Court of Criminal Appeal in the case of *R.* v. *Ball*,[1] made an interesting statement. He is reported, in *The Times* of 20 November 1951, as speaking in reference to 'the principles which must guide a court in deciding what was the right sentence to pass on any prisoner', as follows:

When two persons were convicted together it was often right to discriminate between the two and to be lenient towards the one and not towards the other; for the character and bearing of the one might indicate that there was a chance of his reform if a lenient course were taken. The argument of one prisoner that his heavy sentence must be reduced because a fellow convict received a light sentence had of itself no validity or force.

The view that it is often right to discriminate in sentencing so as to recognize and allow for 'the chance to reform' is considered to be of particular importance in relation to young offenders. It may happen that a child is dealt with by the adult court, for example, after he has been charged jointly with an adult, or he may be before the court not as an offender at all, but to be dealt with after charges of wilful neglect have been proved against his parents. The 'Principles to be observed *by all courts* [author's italics] in dealing with Children and Young Persons' are set forth in the Children and Young Persons Act, 1933, Section 44. A duty is laid on the court to 'have regard to the welfare of the child or young person and . . . in a proper case take steps for removing him from undesirable surroundings, and for securing that proper provision is made for his education and training'.

If the purpose of the court is to protect the public from crime this must evidently be done mainly by means of sentencing such as is likely to diminish it. The objects of sentencing were considered by the (Streatfeild) Inter-departmental Committee on the Business of the Criminal Courts which reported in February 1961.[2] The Committee refer to sentencing as an effort to control future events: (1) by stopping the offender from offending again, (2) by deterring individual offenders, and (3) by protecting society from the persistent offender, and the Report contains a review of the information which might be relevant as far as these three objectives are concerned.

But it is not known if, or what, sentences deter potential offenders, though we proceed on the assumption that all do and some more than others. The deterrent effect of punishment, at least upon the offender who suffers it, is commonly assumed. Yet Norval Morris in the investigations reported in his book *The Habitual Criminal*[3] found that forty per cent of one of his groups of recidivists had already suffered imprisonment before the age of twenty-one. In regard to both of his groups, the evidence was that the length of prison sentence a man served had no relation to the amount of time between his release and his committal for his next offence. A longer sentence did not bring him nearer to rehabilitation. Punishment did not deter. Margery Fry in *Arms of the Law*[4] examines the proposition that fear is an adequate sanction against law-breaking and argues forcefully that the psychological assumptions behind such a proposition appear to be mistaken. Our naïve trust in penalties 'needs to be revised in the light of careful statistical information . . . and guidance . . . from social psychology'.

The relation between crime and punishment is a matter which arouses heated controversy as was shown in discussions on flogging and on capital punishment. The only point of certainty which seems to emerge is the not very helpful one that, in the case of the individual offender, capital punishment appears to punish, to be an effective deterrent, and finally to reform in the sense of removing all wish to commit further offences! But what the effect upon potential offenders may be no one was able to say with any certainty. The situation is that, whatever future researches may reveal, there is at present no recognized body of penological knowledge to which the Bench can turn for guidance in finding a sentence which will be effective.

In court the guilty defendant seems usually to expect to be punished, but in practice the elements of punishment, deterrence, and even of reformation in sentencing are not easy to disentangle, and it is difficult, for example, to see what purpose would be served by a sentence which contrived to be punitive without deterring the offender himself or others, or tending to reform. If there was a strong risk that the punishment might actually increase criminality in general, then clearly it could not fulfil the purpose of the courts in sentencing. From the point of view of the individual offender also, a rational sentencing policy would mean that, in choosing between the different available methods of dealing with him, the court should consider the type of personality they have before them in the offender.

A great deal more could be said about the matters which ought to be considered before sentence, but perhaps the most important point to note is that none of them would arise for consideration at all if the appropriate penalty for each offence were fixed by law, and had to be applied whenever guilt was established. As it is, there is a very great degree of latitude allowed, especially in the direction of leniency, and such freedom to choose implies a duty to choose responsibly. This duty is understood and accepted by many, probably by most, magistrates, and, although statements may sometimes be made during conferences and discussions to the effect that certain kinds of offence ought invariably to be punished in a particular way, such remarks always raise suitable protests.

REMANDS FOR INQUIRY AND REPORT

The difficulty, then, which may face a conscientious Bench, in deciding how to deal with a convicted offender, is not only that of knowing what matters ought to be considered but also that of the dearth of properly established knowledge in some of these fields. But, when it comes to knowing what sort of a person they have before them and what methods are or might be available for use, a great deal of information can be obtained by a court which chooses to ask for it. Under Section 26 of the Magistrates' Courts Act, 1952, if a person has committed an offence which could be punished with imprisonment and if the court 'is of the opinion that an inquiry ought to be made into his physical or mental condition before the method of dealing with him is determined the court shall adjourn the case to enable a medical examination and report to be made'. Under the provisions of the Magistrates' Courts Act, 1952, Section 105, the court may remand the prisoner either on bail or in custody. An accused person on bail during a remand for medical examination can be required, for the purpose of the examination, to reside in a specified hospital (Section 26). Under Section 14 of the same Act a court may, after conviction, adjourn a case 'for the purpose of enabling inquiries to be made or of determining the most suitable method of dealing with the case'.

These powers enable the court to adjourn a case so that they may have an opinion, for example, from the prison medical officer, a psychiatrist, a probation officer or other social worker, a remand home warden, a psychologist, or indeed, presumably, from any expert upon any relevant matter within his professional competence.

The fact that many courts make only infrequent use of their power to inform themselves before deciding upon a sentence is probably due to a number of reasons. It is often difficult or even impossible to make sure that facilities for adequate examination by one or more experts will be available, and that the offender will cooperate by placing himself at their disposal in the time allowed, unless he is remanded in custody. An additional reason for a remand in custody arises if the offender has no fixed address. But whatever the reasons the remand in custody is a deprivation of liberty. By law it must not be used as a punishment, and many courts hesitate to use it, even for a proper purpose, unless the offence or the record is a serious one or the court is contemplating the possibility of a prison sentence. There are fewer difficulties in the way of obtaining a report from the court's own social worker – the probation officer – than from other experts, since he is available on the spot either to interview the offender or to make arrangements for interviews. Probation officers, although not used nearly as often as they might be, are probably used in the ordinary courts much more often than other experts. The use made varies in extent from that in which a case is put back for half an hour so that the probation officer can see the convicted offender in the cells, to that in which a case is adjourned for three weeks so that the probation officer may actually work with the offender on the solution of his problems and explore as far as possible his total social situation for the information of the court.

Section 43 of the Criminal Justice Act, 1948 deals with the making of reports by probation officers to the courts (other than a juvenile court) and states that 'a copy of the report shall be given by the court to the offender or his counsel or solicitor'. There is a provision that, where the offender is under seventeen and is not legally represented, a copy of the report need not be given to him but 'shall be given to his parent or guardian if present in court'.

THE COMPETENCE AND CONTRIBUTION OF THE EXPERT

This power to obtain reports can only be used effectively if the court is itself clear as to what is the professional competence of the particular expert and what kind of information it is hoping he will furnish. In addition, the court should make clear to the expert why the report is being asked for and what sort of information it is hoped to obtain. For instance, a court which invites a medical officer untrained and inexperienced in psychiatry to tell them whether an offender is suffering from any mental disease and, if so, whether he could successfully be treated, is asking the doctor to report on matters outside his professional competence.

In this connexion two general points have to be kept firmly in mind by the court. In the first place none of the reporting experts is, as such, an expert in penology nor is his professional responsibility in any event the protection of the public against crime. These are reasons why it ought not to be considered to be within the function or competence of any of the reporting experts to give advice to the Bench as to how a delinquent *ought* to be dealt with by the court. This is a matter which lies within the competence of the court alone to decide, and in deciding it the court will have to take into consideration other factors in addition to the welfare of the offender.

It must be frankly admitted that opinion on the function of the reporting expert is far from unanimous even among those who work in the courts. Reports by probation officers were the subject of discussion, following remarks alleged to have been made by the Chairman of Bedfordshire Quarter-Sessions Appeals Committee on 11 September 1956:[5]

He [the chairman] said that a passage in a report by a Leeds Probation Officer states 'Unless the accused can be compelled to accept rehabilitation at some centre I am of the opinion that a term of imprisonment is the only alternative to bring him to his senses.' 'What justification in law is there for such an observation from a probation officer?' asked the chairman.

These remarks were referred to the following month by no less an authority than the Lord Chief Justice in addressing the Magistrates' Association at their annual general meeting. He took care to point out that he was not giving a judicial decision but he felt bound to say it seemed to him the learned Chairman's remark was wrong. Lord Goddard based his view on the power given to the magistrates, by Section 43 of the Criminal Justice Act, 1948, to ask a probation officer for a report. Magistrates ought not to be under the impression that if the report recommends a particular course the probation officer 'is going outside his functions . . . because that is the very thing you have asked him to do and unless you get a full and frank opinion from him, the opinion is worthless'.[6]

These views were widely commented upon. In June 1957 the case for the Chairman of the Appeals Committee, so to speak, was summed up neatly by the Clerk to the Dartford justices writing in *Probation*. He pointed out that Section 43 neither prohibits a probation officer from giving his views nor authorizes him to do so, but that the statutory provisions relating to the duties of probation officers in giving reports would appear to exclude anything other than factual information as to the circumstances or home surroundings of the subject.

Up to the time of writing, the last word on this controversial topic would seem to be that contributed by the Streatfeild Committee. Here the probation officer is seen as one who may well be able to give a reliable opinion, founded on actual and substantial experience, on the likely effect of different forms of sentence – especially as compared with the effect of a period of probation. Since such opinions 'relate only to one of the considerations in the court's mind: how to stop the offender offending again' they do not constitute a recommendation as to the sentence the court ought to pass. But 'they represent material which will not usually be available to the court from any other source and may therefore be essential if the sentence is to be based on adequate material'.[7]

The Committee give six examples of the kinds of opinion a probation officer might properly express. Only two actually mention alternatives to probation and these are in each case borstal or detention, which are of course available only for offenders under twenty-one. But detention is a punitive sanction and is the prison equivalent for offenders under twenty-one, so that, unless the Committee intended the probation officer to offer his opinion only in relation to young offenders (and there is no such indication in their Report), there would seem to be no objection in principle to the court receiving a probation officer's opinion that imprisonment would improve the behaviour of an offender over twenty-one. The Committee's views do not[8] 'mean that a probation report should ever go so far as to suggest, for example, that imprisonment for a certain number of months seems to be the best way of diverting the offender from his criminal ways', but this is because 'For one thing, the present state of knowledge is not such that anyone can confidently make such a precise forecast'. The fact is, of course, that in the present state of knowledge forecasts as to the effect of treatment or punishment cannot be precise whatever form of these they relate to, but under present arrangements for official after-care, the probation officer is likely to have as much or more experience with ex-prisoners as with ex-borstal or detention-centre inmates.

Some courts actually ask the reporting experts to give their opinion as to the suitability of the offender for a particular sentence. Others do not directly ask but nevertheless expect to receive advice and they do receive it. Yet others take an opposite line and are careful to reprove what they perceive as an infringement of their own prerogative. It appears, in short, to be a matter which is left to local option.

There needs to be some rethinking upon this whole subject, and the Streatfeild Committee has taken a long step towards this in its insistence that the probation officer's opinion 'about the kind of sentence most likely to benefit the offender' is an opinion about only one of the matters which the court has to consider before deciding upon sentence. 'The probation officer should never give his opinion in a form which suggests that it relates to all the considerations in the court's mind.'[9] The admonition applies at least as strongly to the opinions of other reporting experts. The expert – unless he is actually to sit with the judge in court and hear the whole case, which is not his function – can in any event only make recommendations based upon the offender's supposed needs in some direction or other. On the other hand, as long as the court is a court of justice and the making of the order or passing of sentence is performed by justices, there ought to be some obvious relation between the order and the offence and record. There is no reason to suppose that an order or a sentence made on such principles will necessarily bear any relation to the needs of the offender, though in practice it may well do so, since there is a wide margin of what is adequate as a sanction for the offence, and within this margin there is ample room for individual considerations. But the court is there to deal with offenders in their capacity as offenders, and care should be taken not to lose sight of the fact that its functions are related to the punishment of offenders and the protection of the public against crime. The offence is the only reason why the court has any powers over the offender at all.

These are very difficult matters to reach a conclusion upon at a time when, on the one hand, so much emphasis is rightly being placed upon the need to rehabilitate the offender as well as punish him, and, on the other hand, questions of the rights and liberties of the subject have never been so relevant.

Penal measures ought not to be applied to an offender because of some incidental benefit which a social worker or a doctor thinks they would bring to him, but only if the court is of the opinion that the offence justified such a sentence. Nor ought social measures to be forced on an offender for medical, social, psychiatric, or educational reasons simply because a doctor or a social worker, a psychiatrist or a teacher tells the court that such measures would be good for him.

This appears to have been the conclusion reached by the (Wolfenden) Departmental Committee on Homosexual Offences and Prostitution, reporting in 1957: '. . . duration of the sentence should not be fixed by reference to any estimate of the time which treatment is likely to take. . . . If . . . the seriousness of the offence is such that a prison sentence is necessary, this should be awarded, as it were, on its own merits. . . .'[10]

These various experts, who have so comparatively recently joined the company of persons who play a role in the administration of English justice, would do well to study the rules of good professional practice observed by the bar today after centuries of experience in these matters. Sir Alfred Denning, in his admirable essay *The Road to Justice*,[11] writes of the duty of counsel in these words:

In England today every counsel who is instructed for the prosecution knows how essential it is to be fair. The country expects it. The judges require it . . . he must state the facts quite dispassionately whether they tell in favour of a severe sentence or otherwise . . . no counsel is allowed to suggest to the judge what the sentence should be. That is for the judge alone. No counsel must attempt by advocacy to influence the court towards a more severe sentence. . . . If counsel for the accused should ask the judge not to inflict a prison sentence but to bind him over to be of good behaviour, counsel for the prosecution must not get up and say that he opposes it.... Tradition demands that he should act, not as an advocate to condemn the accused, but as a minister of justice to see that he is fairly treated.

It is the practice in many other countries, including many of the states of America, for the prosecution to call for particular sentences. It is not the custom here, and it is probable that the experts and welfare advisers in those countries are also used in a rather different way, in relation to the work of the courts, from the way in which one would hope they would be used in English courts, where the procedure and the ideas of justice upon which that procedure is based are different in important essentials. It must be remembered that the question here at issue is not that of the nature of medical, social, psychiatric, or educational competence *per se* but rather of the administration of justice.

APPEALS

A person who, having pleaded not guilty, is nevertheless convicted in a magistrates' court has a right of appeal to quarter-sessions against either the conviction or the sentence or both. But if his plea was one of guilty he can only appeal against sentence. Although probation is not, strictly speaking, a sentence, a convicted person may appeal against the making of a probation order. There is a further right of appeal in some cases to the High Court. As a quite distinct procedure there is a right of appeal direct from the magistrates' court to the High Court by way of case stated on a point of law only. In no case can an appeal from the decision of a magistrates' court go higher than the High Court.

Appeals to quarter-sessions are heard by the recorder sitting alone in boroughs which have their own quarter-sessions. In other places they are heard by an appeals committee of the county quarter-sessions consisting of not more than nine magistrates, including a legally qualified chairman and deputy chairman.

Although appeals from the magistrates' court go to quarter-sessions and are not recorded for the guidance of the court below, yet the guidance of the higher courts which lay down certain principles in sentencing, such as the relevance of a position of trust in the commission of an offence (cf. *R.* v. *Fell*,[12] reported in *The Times* of 22 January 1963), is felt in the general traditions and practice of the courts, and more immediately through the advice of the justices' legally qualified clerk as to the current state of the law.

The matters that we have been considering up to the present have been related mainly to the adult court. They have been dealt with in detail as a necessary background for a discussion of the juvenile court. They include among other things the selection and appointment of members of the Bench and the parts played respectively by the Bench, clerk, parties, and witnesses. They include the court premises, the nature of the business which comes before the court, the procedure of trial, remand, and expert reports, the alternative sentences available, the issues that have to be taken into account in coming to a decision, and the provisions for appeal. In looking at the development and present situation of the juvenile court against this background, we have to consider what is, or ought to be, the relevance to the features we have described of the fact that the defendant or subject of an application is a child.

CHAPTER 3

JUVENILE COURT PROCEDURE

SUMMARY courts to deal exclusively with juveniles were first established by law under the Children Act, 1908, Section 111, which defined a juvenile court as a summary court when hearing charges against children or young persons not jointly charged with adults, or applications relating to children or young persons at which their attendance is required, and when sitting in a different building or a different room from that in which the ordinary sittings of the court are held, or on different days or at different times. Today the juvenile court is still a court of summary jurisdiction, though modified in certain respects as to constitution and procedure and also as to the place where the court is held. These modifications are intended to protect the juvenile from contamination through contact with criminal courts and especially with adult offenders. Their object is to prevent his being handicapped by youth and immaturity whether he is a defendant, or the subject of an application, or otherwise, and to assist towards his reclamation where necessary.

THE JURISDICTION OF THE JUVENILE COURT

Since 1908 a number of further enactments, and rules made under enactments, have dealt with the constitution, jurisdiction, and procedure of these courts. Several departmental committees and royal commissions have reported upon matters which to a greater or lesser degree concern the juvenile court. Of particular importance were the Departmental Committee on the Treatment of Young Offenders, which reported in 1927 and resulted in the Children and

Young Persons Acts of 1933 and 1938 with their amending Act of 1952; the Curtis Committee on the Care of Children, which reported in 1946 and was followed by the Children Act, 1948; and the Ingleby Committee on Children and Young Persons, which reported in 1960 and was followed among other enactments by the Children and Young Persons Act, 1963. Each of these marks some more or less important stage in the effort to adapt the use of the summary courts to the needs and capacities of children.

A court of summary jurisdiction has both criminal and civil jurisdiction. The trial of offences constitutes by far the greater part of the business of the juvenile court, and in these cases it administers the ordinary law of the land, which is as applicable to juveniles as it is to adults. Although there are minor modifications in procedure, the mode of trial also remains essentially the same for juveniles as it is for adults. It is in the less formal atmosphere of the juvenile court, the selection of magistrates with special qualifications, and the use made of methods available for dealing with young offenders that most scope has been given for differentiating between adults and juveniles.

Whether a trial procedure designed for dealing with adult criminals is suitable for juveniles at all has now, in the light of modern views about children's needs and capacities, become a highly controversial question. But the question itself is not new. In 1836 a Royal Commission of Inquiry was set up to consider whether there ought to be 'any distinction in the method of trial between adult and juvenile offenders'. The result of these deliberations was a report to the effect that such a distinction would not be desirable unless it was brought about by way of increasing the summary jurisdiction of the magistrates, and in 1847 an Act was passed giving the justices power to try children under fourteen summarily for simple larceny. The Summary Jurisdiction Act of 1879 widened the jurisdiction of magistrates' courts still further so that after that date most child offenders were brought before the justices and not tried at the assizes or quarter-sessions. In this way and to that extent it may be said that the ordinary procedure of criminal trials had already been modified before 1908 in respect of child defendants, although these were still being dealt with alongside of adults, some of whom were hardened criminals.

Some twenty years after the setting up of the juvenile courts the legal principles underlying the trial of juveniles were again considered during the deliberations of the Committee on Young Offenders.[1] Several witnesses thought that the trial of young persons for offences should be entirely separated from criminal jurisdiction, as had been done more or less completely in some other countries. The Committee noted the example of New Zealand,

where in the Child Welfare Act, 1925, it is expressly provided that when a child is brought before a children's court charged with an offence it shall not be necessary for the court to hear and determine the charge, but it may act after taking into consideration the parentage of the child, its environment, history, education, mentality and any other relevant matter.

But the Committee's final conclusion was that there was a danger in ignoring the offence 'on which the action of the court in dealing with delinquents must be based'. The juvenile court should not cease to be a court of justice. Development should proceed on existing lines without any fundamental change of legal principle and the juvenile court was the best tribunal for dealing with all the offences by young people which cannot be met by warning. This conclusion was reached after an examination of possible alternatives in the shape of police or school tribunals.

Almost thirty years later (in 1956), under the chairmanship of Lord Ingleby, the Committee on Children and Young Persons was set up to inquire into, and make recommendations on, the working of the law in England and Wales in relation to juvenile court matters and also on the question as to whether local authorities should be given further responsibilities for preventing or forestalling the suffering of children through neglect in their own homes.

This Committee reported in 1960. It saw as a problem

fundamental to the juvenile court system the difficulty of trying to meet the social and welfare needs of the young offender from a seriously disturbed home through the criminal jurisdiction of the juvenile court. In attempting to do so, they said, the court often appeared to be trying a case on one ground and then dealing with the offender on some quite different ground. Thus, for example, the petty theft might bring 'a disproportionate sentence', embodied in an order based not on the seriousness of the offence or record but on the unsatisfactoriness, as it appeared to the Bench, of the boy's home. The Committee thought such a difficulty was inherent in combining the requirement for proof of a specified event or condition with a general direction to have regard for the child's welfare. They rightly saw as a characteristic of criminal jurisdiction in this country the maintenance of some recognizable balance between the weight of the order or sentence and the gravity of the offence. The practical difficulty in submitting child offenders to the criminal jurisdiction was, as they saw it, that the extent of a child's social need and the gravity of his offence were not necessarily in proportion to each other.

The Committee considered various alternative solutions which were suggested to it including non-judicial or quasi-judicial tribunals to deal on a compulsory or voluntary basis with children up to various ages. It examined, but rejected, proposals to sweep away the juvenile court altogether in favour of Scandinavian-type administrative boards having compulsory powers divorced from any system of trial and outside the courts. Its final conclusion was that state intervention should continue to be dependent upon proof of certain specifically defined allegations since 'the maintenance of this basis is essential if State intervention is to be fitted into our general system of government and be acceptable to the community.'[2] It was a short step from this to the recommendation that a court provides the most effective machinery for doing this and that the juvenile court should be retained, though 'in its dealings with younger children and with children whose primary

need is for care and protection it should move further away
from the conception of criminal jurisdiction', and that the
age of criminal responsibility should be raised to twelve,
with the possibility of being raised to thirteen or fourteen
at some later date, child offenders under that age being
dealt with under civil procedure.

It is against the background of this general line of thought
and policy – which yet contains the seeds of further possible
change – that the proceedings of the juvenile court today
must be considered if the system is to be understood and
appreciated, and its value assessed.

PROCEDURAL MODIFICATIONS

From 1908 onwards there has been a series of statutory
provisions designed to prevent the contamination of
juveniles by hardened offenders during even the preliminary
stages of bringing a juvenile before the court. He has now,
under the main Act (Children and Young Persons Act,
1933), to be separated from adult defendants while detained
at a police station, going to or from court, or when remanded in custody. A girl must be in the care of a woman. A
juvenile awaiting trial must normally be released on bail,
but if that is not done because the charge is very grave (e.g.
homicide) or for certain other specified reasons, provision
is made for him to be detained in a remand home. At
present, if a young person is fifteen years of age or more and
is too unruly to be kept in custody in a remand home, he
may in certain circumstances be remanded to prison, but
under the Criminal Justice Act, 1948, Section 27, there is
provision for remand centres to be provided for the reception of such juveniles and for the custody during remand of
young people aged seventeen to twenty-one. It was more
than ten years before this provision even began to take
effect, but at the time of writing nine centres have been
opened including four which have accommodation for
women and girls as well as boys. The Act provides that

where a centre is available prison must not be used in the remand of juveniles.

There are at present the two general provisions already mentioned (Sections 36 and 37 of the main Act) which help to safeguard the interests of juveniles in contact with any courts. These respectively give power to clear any court (except for the press representatives) while a child or young person is giving evidence in certain cases, and place a prohibition on children being present in a court during the trial of other persons. There is also a prohibition on the publication by the press (or, since 1963, by sound or television broadcast) of any identifying particulars relating to a child concerned in such proceedings.

A related point of importance is the attempt to safeguard the privacy of the juvenile who is himself the subject of court proceedings. The juvenile court, though public, has never been an open court. The only people who may be present (Sections 47 to 49) are the parties and their legal representatives, members and officers of the court, persons directly concerned in the case, and 'such other persons as the court may specially authorize to be present'. These provisions, however, do not exclude the press (though they are again prohibited from publishing identifying particulars) and in this way the character of the court as a public court is preserved. The court or the Secretary of State may dispense with this prohibition, but only if satisfied that to do so would be in the interests of justice. If it is not so dispensed with, any person who contravenes this prohibition renders himself liable on summary conviction to a fine not exceeding £50 in respect of each offence. A contravention of the provisions of this Section was reported in the *Manchester Guardian* in April 1955. This report was headed 'Newspapers Fined: Breach of Juvenile Court Rules', and stated that in one case the name of a school attended by a girl witness, and in others the name of the witness, had been published. The fine inflicted was £10 in each case. The nature of the identifying particulars may vary according to circumstances; for instance, the statement that a 'grammar-school boy living in the village of X admitted to stealing a number of articles' may well serve to identify the defendant if X is a small village and there is only one child who attends a grammar school, whereas a similar statement in another context, e.g. 'a London grammar-school boy', is quite vague.

Police officers usually attend at the juvenile court, being concerned in the proceedings. As in the adult court, it is preferable for the case to be conducted by a professional advocate, the police officers concerned being called as witnesses, and appearing in uniform or not according to whether they are on or off duty at the time. As in the adult court, it is inadvisable to use police officers as court ushers, since the child will draw the obvious inference that as litigants they stand in some special relationship to the court. Where police are in the court in the way of duty they should normally wear uniform.

The most elastic of the categories of those persons who may be present in the juvenile court during a trial is that of persons 'specially authorized'. This wording was used in the Children and Young Persons Act, 1933, and it is rather stronger than that of a similar clause in the original provisions under the Children Act, 1908. In between the passage of these two Acts, the Committee on Young Offenders in their Report[3] had complained in no uncertain terms that the number of persons actually present was often 'unduly high'. They noted that it sometimes amounted to 'twenty, thirty, forty, or even fifty persons'. In some courts it had been the practice to admit 'students who are taking a course of social service', but while students might well find it useful to know about the conditions of work in a juvenile court the Committee thought that the practice of admitting them was prejudicial to the interest of the young people concerned. Having a large number of people present changes the whole character of the court and seriously affects its usefulness. They thought that any new statute ought to make it plain that the court should be as private as possible and that only people immediately concerned with the case being tried should be allowed to be present. Other persons should only be admitted '*in exceptional circumstances*' [author's italics] by special leave of the court. In spite of the Committee's recommendations, however, nothing was said in the new Act (of 1933) about authorization of attendance by outside persons at the juvenile court having to be given only in exceptional circumstances, while the Ingleby Committee contented itself with pious repetition of the phrase 'as private as possible'. That position remains unchanged today, and in some areas is so abused as to run counter to the whole spirit of the Act.

The premises in which juvenile courts sit today vary greatly in suitability for their purpose, and there is in any case an evident diversity of view as between one Bench and another as to what constitutes suitability. Some courts, such as Liverpool and Birmingham, are held in separate specially built premises. Others sit in the same building as the ordinary courts or even in the actual courtroom used on other occasions by those courts. Others again sit in premises which were not built to serve as any kind of court but as offices or committee rooms.

The Committee on Young Offenders commented unfavourably on a similar situation in 1927.[4] They thought it much more important to have the juvenile court in premises which were quite separate from those in which the ordinary courts functioned than to get even the best accommodation in the latter. Such a separation, they thought, 'is one of the best ways of emphasizing the difference of treatment between the juvenile and the adult; and it is the only effective method of keeping the juvenile from the undesirable associations of the adult court'. The Committee went so far as to recommend a general requirement that juvenile courts should be held in their own separate premises.

This recommendation was not adopted in the Children and Young Persons Act, 1933, and might probably have proved impracticable in the circumstances of the time, but the Committee made out a good case for it. They wished to make it possible to furnish and arrange the courtrooms more

suitably for their special purpose. Such things as furnishing
and arrangement have an effect on a young offender's
mind and may thus have a marked effect on his demeanour.
It is natural for a child to try to interpret the meaning of his
surroundings and the aim should be to justify an estimate
of the importance of the occasion which is neither too high
nor too low, and to suggest an inquiry rather than a trial,
'no dock, witness-box, or lofty bench'. Evidence had been
received that the strangeness and formality of their surroundings were often a cause of misunderstanding to the
juveniles appearing in court. Tables and chairs should be
arranged so that the juvenile can stand conveniently near
the presiding magistrate and is enabled to understand who
are the persons adjudicating on his case. These are points
which are all just as valid today, though not all members of
juvenile courts would agree on the details as suggested and
though by Section 17 of the Children and Young Persons
Act, 1963, a juvenile court may now be held in the ordinary
courtroom provided that at least one hour elapses between
its sitting and that of any other court.

'SPECIALLY QUALIFIED' MAGISTRATES

The Bench in a juvenile court today is constituted according
to the Lord Chancellor's Rules made under the Children
and Young Persons Act, 1933, containing decisions as to
arrangements which were only arrived at after many years
of experience. It seems surprising to us now that no special
provisions were made in the Children Act, 1908, as to the
constitution of a court of summary jurisdiction when sitting
as a juvenile court. The Committee on Young Offenders
was much more in line with today's views in saying, as it
did,[5] that the constitution of the juvenile court was probably
'the most important question which we have to consider in
this part of our inquiry'. They rejected the idea that any
age limit, or selection by professional qualifications, educational or otherwise, would secure inevitably the right

choice of magistrates for this work, but thought that experience of social work among youth would be a valuable
asset. The qualities which are 'needed in every Magistrate
who sits in a juvenile court are a love of young people,
sympathy with their interests, and an imaginative insight
into their difficulties. The rest is largely common sense.'

Members of provincial juvenile court panels today often
discuss the London system of appointment – juvenile courts
set up directly by the Secretary of State – and compare it
with their own, weighing up the pros and cons. The Committee on Young Offenders did the same. They saw that
outside London the selection of magistrates for the juvenile
court was largely haphazard and sometimes very unsuitable, and they wondered whether it would be wise to extend
the London system, in spite of certain disadvantages, to
the rest of the country.[6] Although tempted by the fact that
such a step would give considerable emphasis to the separation of the juvenile court from the ordinary courts, the Committee finally rejected the idea, because it would have
involved duplication of the present system for the local
administration of justice. They felt sure that some satisfactory
method of appointment could be developed from the local
system and they attached 'great importance to local interest
and local initiative in this as well as in other matters connected with the administration of justice'.

They recommended that advisory committees should
have their attention specially called to the needs of the
juvenile courts for people with special qualifications for
dealing with children and young persons and the choice
'should not be narrowed by consideration of the political
party to which a person may belong'. The number of
justices sitting in the juvenile court ought ordinarily to be
limited to three and never exceed five (in 1927 the number
sitting at any time varied widely from place to place, being
not unusually five or six and sometimes reaching as many
as ten!). Justices should be elected annually to the juvenile
court panel. They should only be re-elected as long as they
remain suitable in mind and body for such work. The

statute ought to contain general directions on these points and the constitution of the juvenile courts should be governed by Rules made by the Lord Chancellor.

As a result of these recommendations, provision was made under the Second Schedule of the Children and Young Persons Act, 1933, for the constitution of the juvenile court to be regulated along the lines suggested. There must now be at least two justices, if they are lay justices (the stipendiary can sit alone as he can in his other courts), but not more than three. One of the justices should, if possible, be a woman, and in an emergency two women may sit alone.

The justices to serve on the juvenile court panel are now chosen by the whole body of justices for the petty sessional division from among themselves. In 1949 the Home Office in a circular letter [7] on the selection of new juvenile court panels reminded justices' clerks that the Lord Chancellor's Rules required the appointment of people 'who are specially qualified for dealing with juvenile cases'. The letter quoted from the Report of the Royal Commission on Justices of the Peace (1948) to the effect that the need in the juvenile courts was for 'men and women who have not merely a love for children, but real appreciation for the surroundings and way of life of the type of child who most frequently finds his way into the juvenile courts'. In a later letter [8] the Secretary of State again used the phrase 'specially qualified', but omitted to quote from the Report and forbore to give any further guidance as to what these 'special qualifications' might be held to comprise.

By Rules made under the Justices of the Peace Act, 1949, Section 14, justices are required to retire from the juvenile court panel on attaining the age of sixty-five years. This requirement was recommended in the Report of the Royal Commission on Justices of the Peace, which also expressed the view [9] that the most suitable age for first appointment to the juvenile panel was between thirty and forty and that, save in exceptional circumstances, no one should be appointed for the first time when over the age of fifty.

Clerks have been asked to bring these recommendations to the notice of justices before the latter proceed to make new appointments to the juvenile panel. The recommendations clearly intend that juvenile panel justices should be in the normal age range of experienced parents or grandparents, but no older. The proposition seems almost too obvious to have needed stating, but, in fact, when the retirement rule came in it did result in the retirement of quite a number of juvenile court magistrates verging on the age range of great-grandparent. No further changes in these general arrangements were suggested by the Ingleby Committee in 1960.

THE ATTENDANCE OF PARENTS

When a juvenile is brought before a court, for any reason whatever, his parent or guardian may be required to attend (Children and Young Persons Act, 1963, Section 25), and shall be so required where the court thinks it desirable unless the court is satisfied that it would be unreasonable to require his attendance. Not all courts insist on the attendance of both parents in obviously trivial cases. In these cases it is often the mother who comes to court, since she either does not go out to work or, even if she does, she stands to lose less than the father in missing half a day. In some districts it is in any event the mother who holds the purse-strings and who comes, therefore, to pay the expected fine. Attendance of the parent or guardian can be required at all stages of a hearing, but it is often dispensed with where, for example, a juvenile makes a formal appearance in court for the purpose of a further remand while news is awaited as to the availability of some suggested opportunity for treatment. Another case where a parent is not required to attend is where he has already lost parental rights and the juvenile has been removed from his custody by order of the court. In general, however, a parent is required to attend and does so. This enables him to take part in the proceedings and it also enables orders to be made against him. Parents who do not attend may be brought in on a warrant if required, and a note to this effect is usually enough to secure their attendance unless – as too frequently happens, alas – there is some convincing reason for non-attendance such as hospitalization or death, imprisonment or 'whereabouts unknown'. No national records are kept, but discussion with magistrates in different parts of the country strongly suggests that juvenile courts usually take a firm line on this point and insist on the attendance of both parents at court, and that this is generally accepted so that it is very seldom necessary to issue a warrant.

The association of the parent with the child in the juvenile court is helpful in many ways. The child has the support of a familiar adult while the court can get a better picture of the family from which the child comes and the relationship between him and his parents. There is an opportunity of bringing the parents' responsibility home to them and of trying to obtain their cooperation in the course proposed. It is often helpful, too, in giving the court some idea as to how far pressure on the parent might be likely to contribute towards more effective handling of the child and so towards better behaviour. It should not be forgotten that the appearance in court is an experience for the parent as well as for the child, and the parent's attitude at the end of a case is often a much more hopeful feature in the child's situation than appeared likely at the beginning.

SOCIAL INQUIRIES AND REPORTS

Where a juvenile is to be brought before a summary court charged with an indictable offence or as being in need of care, protection, or control, the court probation officer and the local authority must be informed beforehand, and, unless the case appears to be of a trivial nature, investigations must be made as to the home surroundings, school record, health, and character of the juvenile, so that this information may be made available to the court if the allegations are found proved and before any order is made upon the finding. In some areas such investigations, especially those into the home background, are not actually made until after a finding; in others they are made before the court proceedings take place. There are advantages and disadvantages in each course, both from the point of view of strict legality and civil liberties and from that of the atmosphere in the home and the family attitude to the offence before the trial as compared with after the finding. In any event the reports cannot be produced to the court until after a finding has been made. The following are examples of school and home reports submitted to the court.

Extract from home background report on
Shirley Y. Aged 14. Before the court for larceny of clothing
from a shop

HOME CIRCUMSTANCES

Shirley, her father, a labourer earning a basic wage of £12 per week, and sister aged ten live in a three-roomed Estates-owned house in a congested area of the city. The property is in a poor state of repair and, although the house is reasonably well furnished, it is in a deplorable state of neglect and filth and is verminous and bug-ridden. Neighbours are continually complaining that vermin from the Ys' house is affecting their homes.

Mrs Y deserted her family in 1959 and has, more or less, lived a life of vagrancy since. She is known to the Mental Health Dept. as a confirmed alcoholic and has several convictions for soliciting, vagrancy, etc., the last being nine months ago when she was sent to prison for six months. From time to time she visits Blank St during her husband's absence, causing a disturbance and greatly embarrassing her two children, who have had strict orders from their father to keep her out of the house.

Mr Y is a very heavy drinker and spends most of his leisure time in the local public house. He is an extremely difficult man to get on with and when a Home Help was supplied he turned her out. He has also antagonized neighbours who are no longer willing to try to help Shirley with the cooking and cleaning. He resents what he terms interference and although I believe he has a strong affection for his daughters, and is good to them in his own way, his attitude prevents others from giving them the help and affection they need so badly. He has no idea of their real needs and seems unperturbed by the conditions under which they live.

PERSONAL PARTICULARS

HEALTH: Shirley is strong and well developed, and her health seems to be excellent. She recently complained of feeling ill as a reason for not attending school, but the doctor could find nothing wrong.

SCHOOL: She is keenly interested in school subjects, and until recently intended to stay on until the age of sixteen.

LEISURE: attends Mass and is a member of the League of Mary. Is a keen swimmer, enjoys reading, and is very good at sketching and painting.

COMMENTS: When her reserves are broken through Shirley is an interesting friendly child with an eager way of talking and a charming smile which changes her whole personality. She is fiercely loyal to her father and compassionate towards her mother who has recently visited the home.

She has no natural aptitude for housework, but until recently has always made some attempt to tidy up. Recently there has been a general deterioration in her attitude. Attempts to discuss the theft have met apathy and withdrawal. Under all the circumstances, may I respectfully suggest a remand for full reports.

(signed)

Probation Officer

Extract from school report on Shirley Y

Regularity of attendance	*Good, till recently*
Health and physical standard	*Good*
Estimated ability	*Above average*
Education attainments	*Good average. Maintains a good standard in the 'A' form*
Any special interests or abilities	*Fond of reading*
Attitude to school work	*Good*
Behaviour in school	*Good*
Relationship with adults in authority	*Good*
Relationship with other pupils	*Normal*
Honesty and Reliability	*Not very honest or reliable*
General disposition	*A quiet girl who often seems withdrawn and sometimes even melancholy*

Attitude of parents   *Unknown. Never visit school*
                                                (signed)
                                                    Head Teacher

The local authority responsible for producing these reports on school and home life to the court is, since the
Children Act, 1948, the children's department, though it
is usual in most areas for the home investigation actually to
be made by the probation officer.

Before 1948 the local authority responsible was the education authority. This provision had been made in 1933 after
criticism by the Committee on Young Offenders[10] as to the
lack of information at the disposal of the juvenile court
when they came to the stage of trying to prescribe appropriate treatment for the offender. They had reported that in
many courts no background information was available to
the court at all except a police report on the character of
the home. Yet the school medical and educational records
might throw light on what treatment would be appropriate
and the education authority had officers in constant touch
with children's homes; their reports could be supplemented
by special inquiries made by the probation officers and
furnished to the court. The police could cooperate by reporting on the juvenile's behaviour outside home and school
and by notifying the education authority and the probation
officer before a court appearance, so that thorough investigations could be made. As a result of the Committee's
criticisms, relevant provision was made in the 1933 Act.
Since that time it should not have been possible for a
juvenile court to be left in complete ignorance of the child's
background in any but the most trivial cases. It would be
difficult to overestimate the importance of these reports in
enabling the court to function effectively, since by the
nature of their content they can give great help to the Bench
in making the difficult choice between a remand for further
investigation or an immediate order of one kind or another.

The use of these reports in court is regulated by Statutory
Rule made under the Children and Young Persons Act,
1933. According to the rule, where a juvenile is found guilty

of an offence the court shall take any such reports into consideration. They need not be read aloud, but the child must be told the substance of anything bearing on his character or conduct which is considered to be material to the manner in which he should be dealt with. The parent, if present, must be told about anything material to the order which has to do with his own character or conduct or that of his offending offspring, or the health or home surroundings of the latter. The parent or the defendant may produce evidence with reference to the report; the proceedings can be adjourned to enable them to do so and the writer of the report can be required to attend. As long as the Rule is complied with, the court can ask the defendant or the parent to withdraw from the court at some stage if this appears necessary in the defendant's interests.

THE FINDING OF GUILT AND THE AGE
OF CRIMINAL RESPONSIBILITY

Whether a child or young person is tried in the ordinary court (being jointly charged with an adult) or in the juvenile court, no conviction or finding of guilt is to be regarded as a conviction of felony for the purposes of any disqualification attaching to felony. This provision of the Children Act, 1908, was re-enacted in 1933 (Section 51) and is still the law today. The practical handicaps of having had a conviction have proved less easy to deal with. The Committee on Young Offenders recorded that the witnesses who appeared before them went so far as to say that, in their view, no conviction should ever be recorded in the juvenile court, because, however trifling the offence, the fact of having had a conviction could be such a serious hindrance in after life in regard to employment. The Committee quoted no actual instance of such hindrances, but stated that, although they realized that a change of name would do little to conceal the existence of the technical fact, on general grounds the juvenile courts should use a simple form of words different from that used in the ordinary courts. As a result, under the provisions of the Children and Young Persons Act, 1933, Section 59, the words 'conviction' and 'sentence' have ceased to be used, and instead there is a 'finding of guilt' and 'an order made upon such a finding'. The charge is usually read out in what the court and its clerk believe to be simple language, and the young defendant is asked whether the charge is 'true or untrue', or whether it is 'right', or some such appropriately worded question.

A child under the age of ten years cannot legally be held guilty of any offence, though he may be found to be in need of care, protection, or control at any age up to seventeen. The age of criminal responsibility was raised to eight by the Children and Young Persons Act, 1933, Section 50, after the Committee on Young Offenders had pointed out [11] that it had stood at the age of seven for hundreds of years, going on to say 'and the whole attitude of society towards offences committed by children has since been revolutionized. We think the time has come for raising the age, and . . .' (somewhat of an anticlimax after this magnificent opening) . . . 'we think it could safely be placed at eight.' In the 1933 Act it was placed at eight and it remained there until raised to ten in 1963 (not twelve as recommended by Ingleby) under the Children and Young Persons Act, Section 16.

To obtain a conviction in the case of a defendant between the ages of ten and fourteen the prosecution must prove not only that the child committed the crime but also, on evidence which is clear and beyond all possibility of doubt, that he had guilty knowledge that he was doing wrong. Where evil intention is an essential ingredient of the offence, a child is protected by a legal presumption that he has not sufficient capacity to know that what he did was wrong. This presumption may, however, be rebutted by evidence concerning his behaviour in relation to the alleged offence, as for example that on seeing the police officer the child took to his heels and, when caught, denied having the stolen articles which were afterwards found on him. The

Committee on Young Offenders appears to have placed considerable reliance upon this presumption for the protection of children who might be less mature than the normal and had not yet fully grasped the difference between right and wrong.

AGE LIMITS IN THE JUVENILE COURT (OFFENDERS)

The Children Act, 1908, had defined a child as a person under fourteen (the age had formerly been twelve under the Summary Jurisdiction Act, 1879), and a young person as one who is fourteen years of age or over but under sixteen. The Committee on Young Offenders recommended in 1927 that the top age should be raised to seventeen, since the important thing was to keep boys and girls out of the police courts as long as possible and experience since 1908 showed that there was no risk in including people up to seventeen within the jurisdiction of the juvenile courts. To include the eighteen-year-olds, however, would be quite another story. The court would have to deal with a number of much more serious offences committed by young people in whom an appearance before the juvenile court would be unlikely to induce a proper sense of their responsibility, and this might tend to change the whole character of the court. This left unsolved the problem of those seventeen-year-olds who were actually less mature than some of the younger people, and for them it was suggested that it might be possible to have a system of overlapping jurisdiction. This could be based either on a statutory classification of offences or on the discretion of the court. The first alternative was rejected as too difficult, and the second as placing 'an unfair responsibility upon the magistrates', although this method is one which has been adopted under some legal systems abroad. The Committee pointed out that for the discretion to be exercised here a radical alteration of our legal procedure would be needed, namely, disclosure of the defend-

ant's record before trial, and the transfer from juvenile to
ordinary adult court might itself be regarded by the defendant as having already prejudiced his case. They decided, therefore, to proceed with caution and simply
recommend that the upper age limit for the juvenile court
should be the seventeenth birthday. This recommendation
was put into effect in the Children and Young Persons Act
1933, Section 107, and is still in force at the time of writing,
the Ingleby Committee having recommended that it remain
unaltered.

THE RIGHT TO TRIAL BY JURY

The distinction in the method of trial between adult and
juvenile offenders, which was brought about by increasing
the summary jurisdiction of the magistrates in 1847 so as
to empower them to try children under fourteen for simple
larceny, has since gone somewhat further along the same
lines. After the Children Act, 1908, a child or young person
could be dealt with summarily, even though the offence
he was charged with was indictable (unless the charge was
homicide), if the summary court thought it expedient to do
so and if the parents (in the case of a child) or the young
person had no objection. If there was an objection, then the
right to a trial by jury could be exercised and the case would
not be heard summarily. By 1927 the evidence placed
before the Committee on Young Offenders had shown that
this right was being exercised very rarely indeed in the
juvenile courts. Only about a dozen young persons a year
were being sent forward for trial by jury and, of these
instances, practically none was the result of an election by
the young person himself or by a parent on behalf of a child.
The question arose as to whether it was worth preserving a
right which was hardly ever exercised and was presumably
of no importance to people under sixteen. It was argued that
the procedure could well be simplified by doing away with
this right, which was very difficult to make clear to a child,

or even sometimes to his parent, and was almost never exercised. The law already discriminated in important respects between adults and juveniles, e.g. as to imprisonment and as to the protection and training aspects in sentencing juveniles, and it was hoped it would discriminate increasingly in the future. Was it so important therefore to retain the right of election to trial by jury simply on the ground that it was a right common to all offenders from time immemorial?

In coming to a conclusion on this matter the Committee attached great weight to the fact that if their other recommendations were followed the juvenile court would in future be dealing with sixteen-year-olds. As this new group of young persons might well include some who had committed serious offences, the Committee contented itself with recommending only that children under fourteen (except in cases of homicide) should always be dealt with by summary procedure in the juvenile court, and provision was made to this effect in the Children and Young Persons Act, 1933. The Ingleby Committee recommended retention of the right, remarking that, as it was so seldom used, abolition would have little practical effect. This is how the procedure stands today (unless the child is jointly charged with an adult), although the relevant enactment is now the Magistrates' Courts Act, 1952, Section 21.

JUVENILES CHARGED JOINTLY WITH ADULTS

Juveniles charged jointly with adults were explicitly excluded from the jurisdiction of the juvenile court, under the Children Act, 1908, but the Committee on Young Offenders criticized this exclusion [12] on the ground that it was wrong that those juveniles should be deprived of the jurisdiction of the juvenile court. To remedy the situation they proposed that the hearing of a joint charge should, if the adult was under twenty-one, start in the juvenile court, and should continue there unless the adult, on being asked, raised an objection, whereupon the hearing could be remitted to the adult court. This provision was not carried into law and was not repeated in the recommendations of the Ingleby Committee. In fact provision is still made for the opposite procedure, and, under the Children and Young Persons Act, 1933, Section 46, a charge made jointly against a child or young person and an adult must be heard in a court other than a juvenile court. After the verdict the juvenile may be remitted to the juvenile court to be dealt with (Section 56). The Ingleby Committee recommended that this latter part of the provision should be altered so as to *require* the adult court to remit the juvenile to the juvenile court at that stage 'unless there is a special reason to the contrary' (Recommendation 33). However, this advice appears to have been ignored in drafting the 1963 Act.

ADULTS OFFENDING AGAINST JUVENILES

Some of the witnesses before the Committee on Young Offenders thought that, where a child is the victim of an offence by an adult, the trial of the adult should take place in the juvenile court so that the child could be protected and could be dealt with appropriately by people used to dealing with children. The Committee, rightly in our view, rejected this suggestion on the ground that the best juvenile courts would not be the most suitable places to try difficult cases of serious offences such as cruelty and indecency, and also that to bring such cases into the juvenile courts would defeat one of its main objects, namely, the separation of the juvenile courts from the atmosphere of crime. A certain amount of protection had already been given under the Children Act, 1908, Sections 114 and 115, and the appropriateness of the juvenile court to deal with children could be made use of at a later stage under its civil jurisdiction in relation to the juvenile himself if necessary. The

Committee recommended instead that, when a court had convicted someone of having committed one or more of certain offences against a juvenile, that court might have power to direct the child to be brought before the juvenile court, which might make whatever order appeared to be proper in the circumstance. Alternatively the first court, if it thought that it had the necessary information before it to enable it to do the job properly, might itself be empowered to make any order which the juvenile court might make. These two recommendations were embodied in the 1933 Act and this remains the position – again in spite of Ingleby's recommendation that the adult court should be required to remit.

JUVENILES IN NEED OF CARE, PROTECTION, OR CONTROL

Although by far the greater part of a juvenile court's work has to do with the trial of offences, yet the remaining cases with which it has to deal are of greater significance than their mere number might suggest. These include cases of children who come before the court as in need of care, protection, or control, children involved in school attendance cases, and children already in care whom the local authority brings before the court on the ground that they should be in an approved school.

The categories of children who figure in these classes of cases overlap each other very considerably. They also overlap with the category of children charged with offences. As many social workers are aware, it is often very much a matter of chance by which procedure the juvenile eventually reaches the court. Neglect and truancy and refractoriness are thought to be the seed-beds of delinquency. Refractoriness and truancy particularly are often the signals of a home situation with which the child is simply not equipped to cope. Whatever the nature of the proceedings which have been brought, it is often only too clear from the probation officer's report that grounds exist for other proceedings also, either in respect of the juvenile himself or of his parents.

The actual and recent case of Michael X may serve to illustrate this situation. Michael was brought before the court by the local authority (children's officer) as in need of care, protection, or control, being beyond control. The immediate cause of the proceedings was the parents' request to the Children's Officer to bring Michael before the court as he was running away from home, staying away for several days at a time without food or money, sleeping in old garages, etc. He was aged eleven years and four months.

Reports show that Mr X left Michael and his mother at home in Eire when Michael was two years old and they were living with the maternal grandmother. A year later Mrs X joined her husband in England and they had three more children, all girls. When Michael was eight he was brought over by an aunt to join his family. The parents say he got on well with them at first, but soon began to misbehave by telling lies, pilfering small sums of money, bedwetting, and running away from home. It is also alleged that he has interfered sexually with one of his sisters. The home is exceptionally well kept, clean, and comfortable with material standards well above the average for the area.

Mr X feels that Michael runs off to escape his share of housework; Mrs X feels there must be 'something wrong' with the boy. She used to beat him, but doesn't any more. Both parents are very disappointed. Mr X wants Michael taken into care. Mrs X only wants him at home if he stops running away.

Evidence is given in court that

there is no bedroom for Michael though there is a folding bed, which he is not encouraged to use, in a cupboard. He wets his bed. Latterly he has been made to feel that he is too bad to be loved and has been locked out of the house if he came home late. At school (when he is there) he is a lonely boy who prefers his own company, and, owing to very irregular attendance here and previously in Eire, appears very backward. Bigger boys tease him.

He has no set pocket money at present as a punishment and he has not been allowed to join a club. He has already spent a month in the Children's Home where, although the Warden reports that he was not a popular boy, he settled very happily and says he had many friends. He was ambivalent, and partly hopeful, about returning home and the parents agreed to try again. Within three weeks Michael had left home again and was away four nights without eating until he turned up at school filthy, dirty, and exhausted. By evening when the probation officer called he was crying with the pain of swollen legs with both parents having thrown in their hands to the extent even of being too apathetic to call the doctor. While being removed to hospital he told the probation officer he wanted to go from the hospital to the Children's Home and not come back home. Both parents appear to be suffering from having to admit defeat, but though genuinely upset they insist that they cannot possibly have him back if this kind of thing is likely to happen again – as it certainly will. They are quite incapable of understanding the particular needs of this child.

At the end of the proceedings in court Michael was committed to the care of the local authority as the only way of giving him the help and security he so badly needs.

The procedure for dealing with non-criminal cases is in many ways similar to that for trial on a criminal charge, though no question of criminal responsibility is involved. Witnesses must be sworn, the court is public though not open, the same standard of proof is required, and certain specific facts must be proved. This is important and significant, since these cases are nearly always opposed by the parents or guardians. The method by which the decision is arrived at is all the more important since, if the decision goes against the parents, they may entirely lose their parental rights over the child and he may be taken away from his home under an order committing him to the care of the local authority or some other 'fit person' or to an approved school. The parents or guardians may later apply to have the order revoked on the ground that they have now become able to fulfil their parental duties. This matter also will be decided by the court in the light of evidence produced and considerations put forward.

The attempt to deal with children in generally unsatisfactory circumstances which might be held to justify the
interference with parental rights and responsibilities has a
long history. Provision for such cases was consolidated
under the Children Act, 1908, and they were brought
within the jurisdiction of the newly established juvenile
court. Under Section 58 of that Act are listed all those
circumstances in which children under fourteen could be
brought before the juvenile court by anyone, for the purpose of being sent to an industrial (now known as an
approved) school or committed to the care of a fit person
with or without the supervision of a probation officer.
Action could also be taken in regard to young persons in
those circumstances. The circumstances listed are those
which would now be recognized as suggesting that a child
is 'in need of care, protection, or control', but the phrase
is not used at this early date. The list included children
found begging, frequenting the company of a reputed thief
or common prostitute, or lodging in circumstances likely to
encourage prostitution; a child against whom her father has
committed certain offences; or a child having no parent or
guardian or one who exercises proper guardianship.

The provisions of the Children Act, which were an
advance on what had gone before, and which as far as they
went are a recognizable forerunner of the provisions in
force today, nevertheless left considerable gaps uncovered.
The Committee on Young Offenders complained that the
provisions were inadequate to protect children in many
cases where such protection was urgently required – where,
for example, parents were not exercising proper care and
guardianship over a child who was living 'in the worst
possible circumstances', and yet, unless that child could be
found wandering or having committed an offence, there
were no grounds under the law as it stood on which he
could be brought before a court. In a number of cases,
although the moral welfare of a child was in danger, it had
been found impossible to get the child before the court
under any part of Section 58.

The Committee drew up two general provisions by which they thought the provisions of the Children Act, 1908, should be extended. These were to ensure the protection and treatment of:

1. Children and young persons under seventeen who have no parents or guardians, or parents or guardians who are unfit to take care of them, or who do not exercise proper guardianship, where the court is satisfied that the children or young persons are falling into bad associations or are exposed to moral danger or are beyond control.

2. Children or young persons under seventeen in respect of whom specified offences (such as cruelty or sexual offences) have been committed or who are living in homes where such offences have been committed in respect of other children or young persons and the court is satisfied that they require special protection.

These two provisions were covered in two of the three definitions of a 'child or young person in need of care or protection', given in the Children and Young Persons Act, 1933, and the juvenile courts were given power to deal with such cases. Still another definition was added by the provisions of Section 1 of the Children and Young Persons (Amendment) Act, 1952, namely, that of:

A child or young person who, having no parent or guardian or a parent or guardian unfit to exercise care and guardianship or not exercising proper care and guardianship, is ill-treated or neglected in a manner likely to cause him unnecessary suffering or injury to health.

In 1963, however, all previous definitions were swept away by the repeal provisions of the new Children and Young Persons Act. Section 2 of this Act sets forth the present definition. A child or young person is in need of care, protection, or control if he is beyond the control of his parent or guardian. Alternatively he is in such need if he is not receiving such care, protection, and guidance as a good parent may reasonably be expected to give and, in addition, is suffering from any of certain specified conditions. The conditions are set out in Section 2 Sub-section 2 of the Act as follows:

(a) he is falling into bad associations or is exposed to moral danger; or

(b) the lack of care, protection, or guidance is likely to cause him unnecessary suffering or seriously to affect his health or proper development; or

(c) any of the offences mentioned in Schedule 1 to the principal Act has been committed in respect of him or in respect of a child or young person who is a member of the same household; or

(d) he is a member of the same household as a person who has been convicted of such an offence in respect of a child or young person; or

(e) the child or young person is a female member of a household a member of which has committed or attempted to commit an offence under Section 10 of the Sexual Offences Act, 1956.

A weak link in the provisions to protect and help neglected children has always been at the point of the initial responsibility for investigating and taking action. By the provisions of the Children Act, 1908, a duty had been laid upon the police authority to take action under Section 58, and they were only to be relieved of this duty if the education authority decided to take action, or someone else was already doing so, or it appeared undesirable to do so in the child's own interests. In 1927 the Committee on Young Offenders pointed out that since the duty laid upon the police authority was only in respect of proceedings which could be brought under Section 58, numbers of neglected children and young persons were never brought before the court because their cases did not fall within the provisions of Section 58 and 'there is no authority whose duty it is consistently to see that all suitable cases are considered and dealt with'. In their Report the Committee paid public tribute to the National Society for the Prevention of Cruelty to Children. A public debt of gratitude was owing to this Society, which had 'performed a remarkable public service in discovering cases of cruelty and neglect, and in bringing such cases before the courts when necessary'.

As a result of these comments, provision was made by the Children and Young Persons Act, 1933, Section 62, that any local authority, constable, or authorized person who has reasonable grounds for thinking that a juvenile is in need of care or protection may bring him before a juvenile court. Under this provision the 'local authority' was the local education authority; the person 'authorized' is the appropriate officer of the National Society for the Prevention of Cruelty to Children, which Society has been authorized by the Secretary of State to institute proceedings in suitable cases. The local authority, however, not only *may* bring a juvenile before the court in the circumstances defined in the Section, but they have a statutory duty to do so unless they are satisfied that this would be undesirable in his own interests or that some other person is about to take proceedings.

With the coming into force of the Children Act, 1948, the duties of the education authority in this matter passed to the children's department. In 1952 the Children and Young Persons (Amendment) Act, Section 2, considerably strengthened the duty of the local authority in the matter of investigation where the authority receives information suggesting that any child or young person may be in need of care or protection. In such instances the local authority now has, under this Section, a duty to cause inquiries to be made unless it is satisfied that such inquiries are unnecessary.

Under the Children and Young Persons Act, 1963, Section 1, the local authorities now have a still further duty, and this is 'to make available such advice, guidance and assistance as may promote the welfare of children by diminishing the need to . . . bring children before a juvenile court'.

A child out of the control of his parent or guardian could, under the provisions of the Children Act, 1908, be brought before the court by them. The Poor Law authority could similarly bring before the court a child who was maintained in a workhouse or a Poor Law school. The children's department is the successor to the Poor Law authority, since this provision still exists in the Children and Young Persons Act, 1933. The Committee on Young Offenders complained that, if the parents did not bring such children before the courts, there was no power to deal with them unless they came into the scope of Sub-section 1 of Section 58, already referred to. Furthermore, in the case of young persons over fourteen the parents had no power to bring them before the court as out of control at all. After the 1933 Act, not only were young persons brought within the scope of the proceedings but also in many cases where parents did not take the initiative in bringing their difficult offspring before the court the local education authority, and after 1948 the children's department, was able to bring proceedings on the ground that the child or young person was in need of care or protection, as defined in the 1933 Act. Now, however, for the first time, under the provisions of Section 3 of the 1963 Act, parents and guardians are actually prohibited from themselves bringing a child or young person before the court as out of their control. But they may instead request the local authority to do so. If the request meets with no response, then the parent or guardian may, after the lapse of twenty-eight days from the date on which the notice of request was given in writing, apply to the juvenile court for an order compelling the local authority to act. A juvenile who has already been committed to the care of the children's department may be brought before the court by that department itself as refractory and as needing to be sent to an approved school.

After 1908 a local education authority bringing a truanting child before the summary court, under the provisions of Section 12 of the Education Act, 1876, must bring the child before the juvenile court (Section 58 (6) of the Children Act, 1908). If he came within one of the circumstances listed in Section 58 (1), the local education authority could ask the court to proceed under that part of the Act.

At present the position is that the education authority may bring the parents before the summary court and that court (whether or not the parents are convicted), if satisfied that the child has not been regularly attending school, may direct that the child be brought before the juvenile court to be dealt with. It may happen that the ordinary court does not direct the child as above. The Education Act, 1944, Section 40, as amended by the Education (Miscellaneous Provisions) Act, 1948, Section 11, 1st Schedule, under which these proceedings are taken, does not say the court *must* do this but only that it may. The position was, until 1953, safeguarded by a further provision that if it appeared to the local education authority that punishing the parents would not get the child back to school, then they had a duty to apply to the court for such a direction and the court must give it unless they were satisfied that no such direction was necessary in order to get the child to go to school. However, since these provisions came into force a further step has been taken with the passage of the Education (Miscellaneous Provisions) Act, 1953. Under Section 11 of that Act the education authority may now bring a child directly before the juvenile court to be dealt with as a truant, regardless of whether they are or are not also instituting proceedings in the ordinary court against the parents.

CHAPTER 4

THE POWERS OF THE JUVENILE COURT

ALTHOUGH most of the business of the juvenile court is similar to that of the adult court in that it consists of the trial of offences, the class of offence is somewhat different. In the adult courts in 1965 only about fifteen per cent of the total offenders were people convicted of indictable offences; of the non-indictable cases about seventy-seven per cent were convicted of traffic offences and six per cent of drunkenness, etc. The numbers of motoring offences are rising and in future years may become a still higher proportion of the whole, particularly if the present crime wave takes a downward turn. In the juvenile court, on the other hand, fifty-two per cent of the total offenders were convicted of indictable offences – mainly larceny, with breaking and entering as the next highest category. Traffic and motoring offences figure much less in the total, though the actual numbers of the serious non-indictable offences of taking a motor without consent and driving while uninsured rise steeply from the age of fourteen. Stealing is at its peak among fourteen-year-olds and the incidence of convictions for indictable offences in the whole population was highest among boys aged fourteen, where it was about seventy-three per cent higher than among men in the age-group twenty-one to twenty-five.

HAVING REGARD TO THE WELFARE OF THE OFFENDER

In the juvenile court, then, the magistrates are in the majority of cases faced with a person whose offence is such that had he been an adult he could have been sentenced to imprisonment, and in deciding how to deal with him they are able to consider almost the whole range of methods available to the juvenile court. They may take no action at all, but instead give an absolute discharge or one conditional on good behaviour for twelve months. If they think action is called for, they may consider the alternatives of punishment, such as a fine, a period of detention, or – if the offender is over ten years of age – attendance at an attendance centre, in the hope of deterring him from further wrongdoing. And, finally, they may choose instead one of the more constructive measures – a probation order or committal to a 'fit person' or to an approved school. Where there is more than one charge the court may work out what it hopes will prove a fruitful combination of two measures, for example, a fine on one offence with probation on another, though some Benches would regard a combination of punishment with probation as infringing the main principles of probation. This view received some support from the case of *R. v. Evans* [1958].[1] In that case the Court of Criminal Appeal held that, while there did not appear to be anything in the Criminal Justice Act, 1948, which expressly prohibited a probation order being made at the same time as an order for detention in a detention centre, the making of a probation order in such circumstances was contrary to the spirit and intention of the Act, and that there was the further objection that the probation order could not be effective until the offender was released from the detention centre. It was also the view taken by the Committee on Young Offenders.[2]

Corporal punishment, which was a method of treatment available to both the adult courts and the juvenile courts, was finally abolished as a sentence of the courts in 1948 under the Criminal Justice Act. Females could not in any event be whipped, and the whipping of boys as a juvenile court sentence had very greatly decreased. In 1927 the Committee on Young Offenders, noting that in 1925 only 1·86 per cent of those found guilty had been ordered to be whipped, gave, with three reservations, carefully qualified approval to the continuance of the practice under safe-guards, but in 1938 the Committee on Corporal Punishment recommended abolition for offenders of all ages and this became the law in 1948.

Juveniles almost always admit the charge in court, since they have usually been caught in the act, or have admitted it to the police following betrayal with full circumstantial details by a friend, a co-partner in the enterprise. That part of a court's work which consists in deciding on the evidence whether a defendant is guilty or not is therefore at a minimum in the juvenile court. On the other hand, the decision as to what should be done with the offender is even more important in this court than in the adult court because of his youth, and because of the bearing of a wise decision upon what might otherwise develop into a criminal career. The emphasis is rightly placed upon helping the young offender to become a useful and law-abiding member of society, rather than on making him pay for what he has done by suffering retributive punishment. There is a much-quoted section (44), previously referred to, in the Children and Young Persons Act, 1933, in which are stated the principles to be observed by all courts in dealing with children and young persons, and the first part of this section reads as follows:

Every court in dealing with a child or young person who is brought before it, either as being in need of care or protection or as an offender or otherwise, shall have regard to the welfare of the child or young person and shall in a proper case take steps for removing him from undesirable surroundings, and for securing that proper provision is made for his education and training.

In the endeavour to decide what steps it would in all the circumstances be best to take, the court has the help of the report on the background and home surroundings of the juvenile which has been made by the probation officer (or, as in some areas, by the child-care officer), and also of the report on his education and any medical history known to the school. It often happens that these serve mainly to alert the Bench to the need to obtain more detailed reports from wider and more intensive investigations than it has been possible to make in the time available. There is power under the law for the Bench to do this, and the juvenile courts as a whole make very considerable use of this power. These are not powers which refer specifically to juveniles; they are the general powers of magistrates' courts, already referred to, and given under Sections 14, 26, and 105 of the Magistrates' Courts Act, 1952.

REMANDING FOR FURTHER REPORTS

In the case of a juvenile the further reports required are often those of a doctor, an educational psychologist, possibly a psychiatrist, and, if the offender is remanded in custody, a report from the superintendent of the remand home. Courts vary in the extent to which they require a psychiatrist's report, especially in areas where there is no full-time child-guidance clinic in operation, since there may well be no psychiatrist available except at intervals of several weeks. A remand in custody solves difficulties which might arise as to the availability of the child for investigation and makes it possible for an experienced superintendent to form a very good idea of the kind of person the defendant is at present, at any rate when away from his parents (and when with them, too, on visiting days), from his behaviour in all the circumstances of day-to-day life in the home.

The remand cannot be for longer than three weeks on any one occasion and many courts use shorter remands than this. This sometimes means that the period of remand is over before full reports can be made, especially if the investigations have involved medical tests, the results of which are awaited. At present an application for a further remand, which again may not be longer than three weeks, can be made, but the defendant must appear in court as the subject of the application. This may involve considerable travelling and expense, and the use of a member of staff

for half a day or more. A very large proportion of the
remands for full reports are remands in custody, and they
are made in this form to secure the availability of the
offender for examination and the advantage of what is
often a most illuminating report from the superintendent.
Except for the superintendent the reporting experts do not
usually live on the premises but hold weekly sessions there to
examine the juveniles on remand and to confer with the
superintendent and his staff.

These arrangements have developed from the provisions
in the Children Act, 1908, that juveniles who were remanded in custody at any stage in the proceedings were to
be sent, not to prison but to places of detention which it
was the responsibility of the police authority to provide.
The Committee on Young Offenders reported that very
little was being done in these places by way of medical
examination, and the courts had no regular way of securing
medical examination. It would be impossible to provide the
expert staff required at most of the places of detention, and
even in London the average numbers were too small to
make it anything but an extravagant proposition. Yet the
Committee was very impressed with the need for much
greater facilities for the examination and observation of
young offenders if the court was to discharge its function
of deciding the right treatment in each particular case, and
a study had been made of methods adopted abroad, especially at Moll in Belgium where there was a central observation school, established in 1915.

The final recommendation was that at least three central
remand homes or observation centres should be set up to
provide for the examination and observation, when
necessary, of all offenders under twenty-one. Such numbers
would justify the employment of the best possible expert
staff and these institutions should be provided, maintained,
and controlled by the State. Most juveniles who could not
be released on bail could, it was thought, be sent to such
institutions.

This recommendation was not carried out, but, as

already mentioned, provision was made in the Children and Young Persons Act, 1933, Section 77, as amended by the Criminal Justice Act, 1948, 9th Schedule, under which the local authorities were made responsible for providing remand home accommodation for the use of the courts where necessary. However, though this meant that a suitable place was provided for a juvenile to stay at while reports were being obtained, it was far indeed from the comprehensive provision suggested by the 1927 Committee. Under the provisions of the Criminal Justice Act, Section 49, facilities may now be provided in the homes for the observation of any juvenile on whose mental or physical condition the court requires a report, to help it to decide what to do. Alternatively, arrangements can be made for facilities provided elsewhere to be used. Thus some children's departments of local authorities use the services of psychiatrists and psychologists supplied to them on a full- or part-time basis by the local public health authority, while others may rely on the resources of the child-guidance clinic provided by the local education authority or the regional hospital board.

At present, when a court remands or commits for trial a juvenile who is not released on bail, it must commit him to a remand home, with certain exceptions. The exceptions include cases where a young person is too unruly or depraved, or has been committed to the quarter-sessions with a view to a borstal sentence, and these may be remanded in prison unless the court has already been notified by the Secretary of State that a remand centre is available to it, in which event they must be committed to the remand centre. A third exception, however, is that of children under fifteen years of age. The court may, if it wishes, commit these to a special reception centre, also under the children's department, if there is such a centre in the area (Children and Young Persons Act, 1963, Section 24 (i)). The latter may be provided with the necessary facilities for observation and report.

Remand centres were provided for in the Criminal

Justice Act, 1948, Section 48, as amended by the Prison Act, 1952, Section 43. They were to be set up for the detention of persons aged fourteen to twenty-one, who were remanded or committed in custody for trial or sentence, and facilities for observation and report were to be provided in these centres. The first centre was opened at Ashford in Middlesex in 1961, and nine centres had been opened by the end of 1965. It is expected that these will meet the needs of courts in the major part of the country. All the centres provide accommodation for boys under twenty-one who are remanded in custody to await trial or sentence; four also provide accommodation for girls aged under twenty-one in similar circumstances; and one, at Risley in Lancashire, provides accommodation not only for boys and girls under twenty-one but also for adults.

The remand homes continue to be used for most of the children and young persons who appear before the juvenile court, and who are remanded in custody for further reports in order that the court may determine the most suitable way of dealing with them. The following are examples of such reports to the court, and concern Shirley Y, aged fourteen, found guilty of stealing articles of clothing from a shop, and remanded for three weeks in custody for reports:

Extract from psychologist's report

Verbal Scale I.Q.   111
Performance scale   113
Full scale I.Q.   113
This result places her in the bright normal range.
Test: Wechsler Intelligence Scale for Children.

Shirley looked older than her years and very depressed and frightened. She is obviously very fond of her father and younger sister and, while having not the first idea of housework, has tried to do her best for them. She is in a very low state and will need considerable building up and support if she is to cope with her difficulties in the future. She is an affectionate and rather innocent girl who has gradually become increasingly desperate. She is very anxious not to be taken away from home and it might be worth trying probation if supervision can be fairly intensive at first.

Extract from superintendent's report

Shirley has now been here for nearly three weeks. She is a girl of good quality, intelligent, loyal and – under proper guidance – capable.

In spite of the filthy conditions found in the home there was no real sign of neglect on admission. She was not badly infested.

At first she was stolid and appeared apprehensive and rather sullen, but she seems to have settled down confidently. As she becomes more relaxed, she proves a girl with whom one could come to real terms of trust and affection.

She was not able to give any reason for the theft, but it is obvious that she is completely lacking in care and guidance. Nor can she account for her failure to attend school, but it seems very much a matter of the home situation so that she feels unable to face implicit comparison with her classmates. She has good standards.

She seems a wholesome character, sexually innocent. She may have some knowledge of the reason for her mother's committal to prison (drunkenness and soliciting), but it did not so appear. Shirley simply referred to her having been in prison several times for stealing.

There is a strong sisterly affection. When Shirley went out shopping she intended choosing something for the little sister's birthday and was not looking for anything for herself. She has reconciled herself to being unable to return home at present.

The difficulties in the home are so great that Shirley may well deteriorate there unless she has strong support.

Extract from psychiatrist's report

I saw Shirley when she had been in the remand home for ten days. She was extremely depressed and will become more so if she is not allowed to return home eventually. She requires psychiatric treatment. We could provide this for her as a patient at our occupational therapy department, where we could give her training and experience in housekeeping, etc. She and her father would profit from a period of supervision by a probation or child care officer with a view to returning her to the A class at school.

Remanded cases come before the court again at the end of the remand period; the reports which have been made are handed up to the Bench and, after these have been considered and discussed, the court decides on the method of treatment to be embodied in the order it now has to make.

METHODS AVAILABLE IN DEALING WITH YOUNG OFFENDERS

Some of the provisions available to the courts in dealing with offenders are common to both the juvenile and the adult courts, e.g. discharge, fines, and probation. Others, such as borstal, detention centres, and attendance centres, overlap, and statutory provision is made for their use for persons up to the age of twenty-one. Others again are specifically for use with juveniles, such as detention in remand homes (where used), fines on parents, approved schools. Still others cannot be used by juvenile courts at all, such as sentences to imprisonment, corrective training, and preventive detention. Even the methods which are equally open to both juvenile and ordinary courts were used in very different proportions for the different age groups in 1965, as the following tables indicate.

How the Magistrates' Courts (England and Wales) Dealt with Persons Found Guilty in 1965 (percentages)[3]

INDICTABLE OFFENCES

| | Age last birthday | | | |
	Under 14	*14–16*	*17–20*	*21 plus*
Absolute discharge	3·1	2·1	1·0	0·9
Conditional discharge	26·9	18·9	9·3	9·3
Probation	33·3	29·2	17·4	9·3
Fine	18·5	31·6	53·5	60·5
Other methods*	18·2	18·2	18·8	20·0
TOTAL	100	100	100	100

* Includes approved school committals, detention, etc.

NON-INDICTABLE OFFENCES

	Under 17	All ages (not including traffic offences)
Absolute discharge		1·7
Conditional discharge	16	3·9
Probation		1·8
Fine	79	88·4
Other methods*	5	4·2
TOTAL	100	100

* Includes attendance centres, approved schools, committed for trial, borstal and hospital orders, as appropriate.

PROBATION AND DISCHARGE

In the juvenile court, probation and conditional discharge were used much more and fines much less than in the adult courts.

In view of the extent to which probation orders are made in the juvenile court, some account of the development of the probation system will not be out of place in relation to that court. Probation came into being as an alternative to detention in prison and elsewhere. Its main contribution is in the supervision of an offender in his normal surroundings by someone who can help him to rehabilitate himself and to keep himself from further crime without institutional training. After 1925 all courts were required, under Part 1 of the Criminal Justice Act, to have paid probation officers; before that date some had no probation officers, paid or otherwise, and could not put offenders on probation.

Between 1907 and today the use of probation has increased very much in absolute figures, but has decreased proportionately since the last war. The percentage of persons found guilty of indictable offences who were placed on probation in the juvenile courts rose from twenty-six per cent in 1900[4] to fifty-four per cent in 1933.[5] In 1938 it was fifty per cent,[5] and by 1956 it had dropped to thirty-nine per cent,[5] and by 1963 to thirty-two per cent,[5] while in the same period the use of fines and of new methods provided under the Criminal Justice Act, 1948, increased proportionately. As in the case of other methods open to the court, there are variations in the extent to which probation is used between different juvenile courts. For example, in 1963 it was used in only 439 out of 1,641 cases in Birmingham, but in 485 out of 1,182 in Kent.[6]

The Probation of Offenders Act, 1907, included three different methods of dealing with offenders and these were: dismissing the charge, discharging conditionally on a recognizance for not longer than three years, and the conditional discharge on a recognizance which included a condition that the offender be under supervision. Perhaps the other most important feature of the Act was the provision that courts of summary jurisdiction (though not quarter-sessions or assize courts) might place persons on probation after the offence was proved, but 'without proceeding to conviction'.

At first the term 'probation' was often used in cases where there had been a dismissal or a conditional discharge without supervision. The Committee on Young Offenders objected strongly to this and re-emphasized the importance of the idea of supervision in the probation system. After 1914 it was possible under the Criminal Justice Administration Act to make conditions as to residence as part of a recognizance. This resulted in the use of such a condition to require probationers to live for the whole or part of their probation period in a Home or institution of some kind. These places were not subject to any kind of inspection and in many cases were not chosen by the court but by the probation officer under some such requirement as that the offender must live where required by the probation officer. A condition of residence not infrequently meant that the probation officer lost all touch with his charge. This undesirable practice seems to have developed in response to the placing of unsuitable people on probation by courts which had no knowledge of the home background of the

offender. This was commented upon by the Committee on
Young Offenders in 1927, but, even after the passing of the
Children and Young Persons Act, 1933, home inquiries
were not always being made, although under this Act
(Section 35), where a juvenile was to be brought before the
court for an offence or as in need of care or protection,
notice must be given to the probation officer and the local
authority. In other cases, offenders were placed on probation by the court in order to avoid proceeding to conviction
and as an alternative to sending them to a reformatory or an
industrial school or, later on, an 'approved' school as each, in
truth, acquired in the public mind the stigma of penal
treatment.

The Departmental Committees on the Treatment of
Young Offenders (1927) and on Persistent Offenders (1932)
and on Social Services in Courts of Summary Jurisdiction
(1936) all tackled the question of the selection of offenders
suitable for treatment 'in the open' or otherwise, among the
important matters they considered. The Committee on
Young Offenders (1927) took the view that offenders not
suitable for treatment in the open should not be placed on
probation, and if an offender able to benefit by open treatment was living under very undesirable conditions a
requirement to reside in a hostel or approved lodgings,
from which he could go out daily, would meet the case.
The Home Office took the view that it would be unwise to
make a rule that no probationer should ever be sent to a
Home as a condition of probation, and that a better course
would be to approve Homes suitable for this purpose,
which they did, while the Committee on Social Services
in Courts (1936) recommended that a condition of residence
in a Home ought to be limited by law to six months.

The Committee on Young Offenders (1927) also considered representations that a court should have power to
combine probation with other forms of treatment, such as a
fine or birching, but rejected the suggestion on the ground
that it was not in line with the principle of probation which
was that of an alternative to punishment.

They did not question the provision of the Probation of Offenders Act, 1907, that a summary court might make a probation order without proceeding to conviction, though they pointed out the inconsistency by which quarter-sessions and assize courts had to convict before making such an order and recommended that they be brought into line with the juvenile courts in this respect. In 1925 the Committee on Sexual Offences against Young Persons had commented on the same point and made a similar recommendation. However, the Committee on Social Services in Courts (1936) took quite another line.[7]

It appeared that in 1919 the case of *Oaten* v. *Auty*[8] had provided the occasion for judicial interpretation of the words 'without proceeding to conviction', and two judges had expressed themselves freely on the point. Among other comment, Darling, J. is alleged to have said that the words were 'merely a concession to the modern passion for calling things what they are not, for finding people guilty and at the same time trying to declare them not guilty'. Mr Justice Avory thought that the Section might be made sensible by reading the words 'without proceeding to conviction' as meaning 'without proceeding to record the conviction'. As a result of these considerations the Committee took the view that, when a person has been found guilty of a criminal offence, the fact ought not to be concealed by a technical pretence that he has not been convicted. It might reasonably be asked, they pointed out, 'why an offender who commits a serious offence and is placed on probation should receive more favourable consideration than one who commits a minor offence and is dealt with by a fine?'

On the other side, it was argued that *Oaten* v. *Auty* was the only known instance in which any inconvenience appeared to have been caused to the courts by a system which had been in force for the last thirty years, that two previous committees had argued for its extension to the higher courts, and that an amendment in the law along the lines now proposed would be contrary to the intention of the

Probation of Offenders Act, 1907, which sought to avoid 'branding an offender whom the court may want to help rather than to damage, with a mark which he will carry through life'. As a compromise, an alternative suggestion made was that a new system should be adopted whereby the original charge might be dismissed, on the offender's completing satisfactorily his term on probation. The Committee on Social Services in the Courts (1936) finally proposed, however (with two reservations), that, where the offence was proved, a summary court should be enabled to make a probation order 'without proceeding to impose punishment' instead of 'without proceeding to conviction'.

In 1948 the Probation of Offenders Act, 1907, was repealed by the Criminal Justice Act, and there was a general tidying up of the statutory provisions regarding probation. Since then neither the Ingleby Committee in 1960 nor the (Morison) Committee on the Probation Service, which reported in 1962, suggested any major changes. Probation must now be for not less than twelve months and for not more than three years. The court may not require residence in an institution for more than twelve months in all, and if a residence requirement is imposed the court must review the order at the end of six months to see whether the requirement should then be cancelled or reduced. The term 'probation' is applied to probation under supervision only and the need for a recognizance is removed, but the principle of voluntary cooperation is preserved in the provision that where an offender is fourteen years of age or more his consent is required before a probation order can be made. An important change was that, under Section 3, the words 'instead of sentencing him' were substituted for 'without proceeding to a conviction'. Neither the word 'conviction' nor the word 'sentencing' is used in the juvenile court since the Children and Young Persons Act, 1933, Section 59, but the court now finds the charge proved and then, instead of punishing the offender, puts him on probation by its usual procedure of 'making an order'. This removed the difficulty under the previous system of appealing to a higher court without having been convicted.

Probation is used nowadays in a wide range of cases in the juvenile courts, both for children and young persons. Experience appears to show[9] that only about thirty-six per cent of first offenders are reconvicted within three years of being put on probation. The rate for second offenders is about forty-five per cent, and that for recidivists fifty-eight per cent. This does not, of course, mean that recidivists should not be put on probation. Indeed, poor though their success rate may appear to be, it is actually rather better than would have been expected from the general tendency of young recidivists to commit further offences (see later, Chapter 10).

FINING IN THE JUVENILE COURT

Juveniles, like adults, are liable to be fined for offences or to pay costs and damages, and in non-indictable cases this is much the most common way of dealing with an offender. The question which springs naturally to mind in considering fines, etc., in relation to juveniles is 'Who is expected actually to pay?' Under the Children and Young Persons Act, 1933, the court must order the parent or guardian to pay if the defendant is a child, and it may do so also in the case of a young person; the exception to this is where the court is satisfied that the parent has not contributed to the offence by lack of proper supervision of his offspring, or that he cannot be found. There is, however, a limit in respect of children and these cannot be fined more than £10 by a magistrates' court (Criminal Justice Act, 1961, Section 8), while £50 is the limit for young persons aged not less than fourteen and under seventeen.

There are also special provisions relating to the enforcement of fines where the offender is under twenty-one, by which he may be sent to a detention centre or ordered to

attend an attendance centre (substitutes for being imprisoned) for non-payment. In the case of children and
young persons a similar provision has been in existence
since the Children Act, 1908, and defaults on fines are very
rare. Since 1914 (Criminal Justice Administration Act,
Section 1) it has been possible for courts to place offenders
aged between sixteen and twenty-one under supervision
during the payment of a fine where time has been allowed.
The Committee on Young Offenders (1927), commending
this provision, suggested that it should be extended to
children and young persons. In 1935 (under the Money
Payments (Justices' Procedure) Act) supervision became
obligatory where a person under twenty-one fails to pay a
fine, and this is the law today (Magistrates' Courts Act,
1952, Section 71). The Home Office has suggested on
many occasions that the suitable person to supervise in
these cases would be the probation officer. But it seems that
such supervision could, in the letter of the law, only refer
to the actual payment of the fine and not to the general
behaviour of the defendant. If that were not so it would
simply mean that, under cover of this Section, a person
could be both fined (i.e. punished) and put on probation for
the same offence, which is not at present the law. In many
courts such supervision is exercised by the collecting officer
from the money-payments side of the magistrates' clerk's
office or some other such person. The question is probably
not of very great importance since the fines are usually paid
quickly and there are very few defaults indeed. In many
cases the parents pay the fine either immediately or in a
few days. Some courts make a practice of ordering the
parent to pay the fine in the case of a young person who is
still at school as well as in the case of a child, expressing the
pious hope that the amount will be deducted from the
offender's pocket money over a period – supervision in the
home!

The Committee on Young Offenders (1927) suggested
that the court should be given power to order a parent to
pay costs or damages or a fine, and also to place the juvenile

on probation for the same offence. They made the point that as the punishment would fall on the parent and not on the child the proposal was not open to the objection that it was combining probation with punishment. This proposal did not become law. More than one opinion may be held on the advisability of combining punishment with probation, but as the law stands at the moment this cannot be done in relation to the same offence any more than it could in 1927. As far as the Committee's reasoning goes, however, it is difficult to see what the effective difference is between ordering a parent to pay a child's fine (which must in law be done) and fining the parent direct; if the child cannot be fined *and* placed on probation, it seems illogical to empower the court to fine the parent. Another objection is of course that, if punishment of the offender would be a poor start for the probation officer's efforts to rehabilitate him, it is not clear that punishing the parent would produce a cooperative and welcoming attitude in the home. Yet the cooperation of the family is essential in almost every case if the child is to receive lasting benefit.

The parents of a juvenile offender may be ordered by the court to give security for his good behaviour and to enter into such recognizance as the court thinks fit (Children and Young Persons Act, 1933, Section 55). If the juvenile is in need of care, protection, or control there is a similar provision (Section 62) to require them to exercise proper care and guardianship. Many courts hesitate to use this remedy in the case of an offender, since it is felt that it would be difficult to enforce it, and in many cases doubtfully just to do so, and that a fine on a juvenile if it falls on the parent is at least as effective. In fact, there are some grounds for thinking that a fine imposed on an offender of any age may be rather more effective than any other sentence, or than a probation order.[10]

DETENTION

After the Children Act, 1908, no child could be sentenced to imprisonment, and young persons could only be sent to prison if the court gave a certificate that this was necessary owing to their unruliness or depravity. These provisions reduced the number of those under sixteen received into prison on conviction from 572 in 1907 to eight in 1925. In 1933 the prohibition on imprisonment was extended to cover juveniles aged sixteen with an appropriate extension of the system of certification for exceptional cases. Under the Criminal Justice Act, 1948, the power of magistrates' courts to impose imprisonment on offenders under seventeen was finally abolished, although an assize court or quarter-sessions can impose imprisonment on fifteen-year-olds in certain circumstances. The Act restricted prison sentences on persons under twenty-one to cases in which the court, having considered all the circumstances and all other methods of dealing with the offender, holds the opinion that no other method is appropriate and (in the case of quarter-sessions or a magistrates' court) is prepared to state its reasons (Criminal Justice Act, 1948, Section 17). The next step came with the Criminal Justice Act, 1961, which provided, in Section 3, for the elimination of prison sentences on a person within the limits of age which qualify for a sentence of borstal training, except for sentences of 'not exceeding six months' or 'for a term of not less than three years'. The transition is complete with the provision, in Section 4, for detention centres to be used instead of imprisonment for short sentences.

As a substitute for prison both on remand and committal to custody the Children Act, 1908, provided that children should, and young persons generally might, be sent, for not more than one month, to a place of detention provided under the Act by the police authority. Although detention was at first used fairly frequently as a punishment, its use declined until by 1927 only about thirty cases were so dealt with each year. One difficulty was that the

places of detention were also being used for the custody of
children on remand or awaiting trial and it was felt that
there were serious disadvantages in associating children
undergoing punishment with the other categories. Except
in some large towns, the places of detention were, in any
case, not at all suitable for keeping a child under punishment for a month. In some places, workhouses were used,
and, in others, rooms on police premises. The Committee on
Young Offenders (1927) [11] thought it would not be possible
to take away from the court the power of ordering detention, but, except in the rare cases where it might be necessary as the ultimate means of enforcing a fine inflicted on a
child or young person, they could find little value in it and
recommended that, in general, other methods open to the
court should be used.

In the meantime one or two centres had opened remand
homes either in specially built premises (as in Birmingham
as early as 1910) or in existing houses adapted for the
purpose. Their experience showed that, because of the small
number of children concerned, the cost of provision was
very high and it would be difficult for local authorities to
establish properly equipped homes unless several authorities
made use of the same provision. The Children and Young
Persons Act, 1933, made provision for the council of every
county and county borough to provide an area home or
join with a neighbouring council in establishing one as
needed (Section 77). Under the same Act, however, custody
in a remand home was substituted for imprisonment (Section 54), so that the old difficulty of mixing different
categories still remained, although the new special premises
were much more suitable for the custody of juveniles.

This was the position up till 1948, when the Criminal
Justice Act (the relevant Act is now the Prison Act, 1952,
Section 43) gave the Secretary of State power to provide
detention centres in which people between fourteen and
twenty-one can be kept under strict discipline for short
periods. The offence committed must be one for which an
adult could have been sentenced to imprisonment. The

detention term for under-seventeens is normally three months. The court must first consider every other method by which it might deal with the offender and satisfy itself that they are all inappropriate before it can make an order committing him to a detention centre. Moreover, the offender must be one who has not previously been sentenced to borstal.

There are thirteen senior (for offenders aged seventeen to twenty years of age) detention centres and one more under construction; four junior (for offenders aged fourteen to sixteen years) detention centres and one more under construction; and one detention centre for girls aged sixteen to twenty. More detention centres for boys and another for girls are being contemplated.

Possibly the outstanding feature of these centres is that their intention is primarily deterrent and no one is there except as a punishment. This means that what was thought to be the major difficulty in the effective use of the old 'places of detention' and also the remand homes for punitive detention has been done away with. It may also mean that the inmates of the new detention centres are, as far as the reason for being there is concerned, a much more homogeneous group than was the mixed bag in the senior remand home, which might have contained at any one time, for example, a few children awaiting a court appearance, some more on remand for reports to be obtained before the court could decide what ought to be done, one or two undergoing a month's 'punitive' detention, and four or five thoroughly chastened youths awaiting their departure to classifying school under an approved school committal order. The new detention centres are administered by the Prison Commissioners, whereas the remand homes are administered by the local authority or, in a few cases, by voluntary bodies. Under the 1948 Act each court may be notified as a centre is opened and made available to it. Once a court has been so notified it no longer has power to sentence a young person to detention in a remand home under Section 54 of the Children and Young Persons Act,

1933. Some courts welcomed the new centres, while others, which had had, perhaps, a good and successful experience of using the remand home in their area (owing maybe to an outstandingly capable superintendent and staff), would have preferred to continue to make use of the facilities under the older Act. At first courts which might have been embarrassed by receiving notifications from the Secretary of State that one of the new centres was available for their use, and that they must now use it, might receive a preliminary inquiry as to whether they would wish to be notified that a centre was available. If they did not wish it they need not be notified but might continue to use the facilities of the remand home as before. Now, however, detention centres are in general use.

The fact that each juvenile court had to make a choice as to whether it would use the remand home or the centre exclusively was significant. It seemed to rest on the assumption that a detention centre serves the same purpose as detention in a remand home, that there is a clearly defined class of young offender for whom detention is appropriate, and that the only relevant variable lay in the choice made by each court as to where it would send all such offenders.

There is considerable evidence that such an assumption is not realistic. The Superintendent of Forhill House Remand Home, Birmingham, referring to detention under the Children and Young Persons Act, 1933, Section 54, states,[12] 'Boys who have committed three or more offences are not, in the main, suitable', while the authorities at the Home Office describe[13] detention-centre treatment under the Criminal Justice Act, 1948, Section 18, as being 'for the hardened boy in his teens'. The Superintendent of Forhill House did not advocate segregation in separate premises at all. In his view, the boy in detention compares his lot with that of his fellow awaiting transfer to an approved school and is stimulated by this warning to behave better in future. He saw no disadvantage in housing a mixed category of boys together since he regarded the element of punishment as consisting in the deprivation of liberty rather than in the nature of the régime. Forhill House, as compared with other remand homes, had considerable success with less-hardened offenders, but would have preferred the maximum period to be raised to three months in some instances.

The detention centres on their part are tending to move away from their rather repellent and unconstructively punitive régime. This development seems to be due partly to the difficulty in getting mature and intelligent staff to go on punishing youngsters for months on end, but also probably to the fact that the offenders sent form a very mixed group. Courts which have opted for the centres send some offenders who would formerly have gone for a month to the remand home. Others send the hardened offenders for whom it was intended. The unsettled state of such a population unfortunately makes it difficult for any very constructive work or planned training to be undertaken with the group. It is difficult to form an estimate as to how effective the centres really are in the task set for them. 'In terms of reconviction it appears that they have so far produced results which for all types of offender were within the range expected for the class of offender concerned.'[14]

It seems that it would have been advisable to make both forms of disposal available to each court so that those young offenders thought likely to benefit from detention could be sent for a suitable period to the place which was most appropriate. There are two different categories of offender requiring detention: the hardened case and the less-hardened. This should be recognized by the making available of two different categories of provision.

The provision of detention-centre places for boys is at present far short of the demand from the courts and is unlikely to become adequate in the foreseeable future unless there is a sharp drop in juvenile crime. As a result, courts which applied to the Secretary of State for notification of an available centre and which have been so notified are in some instances attempting to revert to the use of the senior remand home when, as is very often the case, no places are available at the centre. Thus two different categories of provision are sometimes being used, but on an inappropriate basis of selection.

Many magistrates think that the short, sharp shock of detention centre experience is unsuitable for girls. One hundred and ten girls have passed through the centre during the last year.[15] Most of them were sentenced for larceny and most of them had previous convictions, only eighteen being first offenders. Twenty-seven had had previous institutional training, sixteen in approved schools and eleven in children's homes. In our culture criminality would seem to be a masculine attribute and some magistrates feel that a quiet and relaxed atmosphere in which adolescent girls can gain knowledge of themselves, confidence in other people, and a friendly and more gentle attitude is a prerequisite to a more radical cure, of which the basis must be self-respect. It is not at all self-evident that the treatment of delinquent girls must or should be identical with that of boys. For example, as long ago as 1932 the Departmental Committee on Persistent Offenders found that, for the majority of women, the traditional type of prison was unnecessary and harmful. And today the Magistrates' Association views with grave concern the lack of appreciation of the different needs of the sexes shown in the provisions made for custodial treatment.[16]

Until 1958, and the decision in *R.* v. *Evans*, many juvenile courts had – where more than one offence by the same offender fell to be dealt with – made a practice, where an order for detention was made, of making a probation order on another offence. It had for some time been felt by many people that the experience in the detention centre might form a favourable prelude to a period on probation and that, in any event, some sort of continuing supervision was advisable for any young offender whose criminality was regarded as serious enough to justify a detention order. After *R.* v. *Evans* this means of providing compulsory post-detention supervision was removed. Later, however, under the provisions of the Criminal Justice Act, 1961, Section 13 and First Schedule, arrangements were made for compulsory supervision by a probation officer for a period of twelve months from the date of release. During this time the offender must comply with any requirements specified in the notice of supervision and if he fails to do this he may be recalled to the centre to serve out the unexpired portion of his term, or fourteen days, whichever is longer. Cases are reviewed when half the period of supervision has expired to assess the necessity for continuing supervision.

Turning to an examination[17] of the subsequent history of boys who have been in detention, the results appear to show that the centres were more 'successful' – as might be expected – with first offenders than recidivists, and with younger boys than older ones. Of junior boys (fourteen to sixteen), less than one-third of first offenders were reconvicted within two years, while the rate for second offenders was forty per cent and rose to sixty-four per cent for recidivists. In comparison detention in remand homes appears to have been rather less effective, at any rate as far as first or young early offenders were concerned.

CHAPTER 5

APPROVED SCHOOLS, BORSTALS, ATTENDANCE CENTRES, AND 'FIT PERSON' ORDERS

COMMITTAL TO APPROVED SCHOOLS; CLASSIFICATION AND AFTER CARE

A CHILD, asked in court what he thinks eventually happens to boys who go on stealing, will usually oblige with the reply: 'They get put away, sir', and it seems to be well understood by most offenders that there is a strong risk of being 'put away' in an approved school if probation has already been tried, especially if more than once, while the risk amounts almost to a certainty if one has already had a spell of detention before making the final fatal slip. In 1965 a total of 5,370 juvenile offenders were committed to approved schools in addition to 490 other juveniles committed as a result of care and protection, out of control, or truancy proceedings.[1] The system of institutional training embodied in the approved school system, which is now very often postponed to a comparatively late stage in the criminal career of the young offender, has grown directly out of the old reformatory and industrial schools. These schools, brought into being by the untiring, devoted and loving efforts of Mary Carpenter and others like her, provided the first alternatives to imprisonment for children.

The first Reformatory Schools Act was passed in 1854 and empowered the courts to send young offenders to the existing institutions. These were run by independent voluntary bodies, but there was already an administrative practice by which young people under sentence of transportation or imprisonment were pardoned on condition that they placed themselves in one of these institutions for the reformation of young offenders. Treasury contributions to the schools were authorized under the same Act, and parents could be made to contribute. Children could be committed by the magistrates for not less than two or more than five years.

Industrial schools were an attempt to provide elementary education and training for the children of the poorest classes, and in 1857 an Act was passed empowering courts to send children to these schools also. Both the industrial schools and the reformatories remained under voluntary management, but they received legal powers of detention and were subject to state certification and inspection, and the principles laid down in these early Acts were incorporated in the Children Act, 1908.

A Departmental Committee on Reformatory and Industrial Schools reported in 1913. This Report was followed by considerable reorganization, with financial aid from the state and local authorities, and in 1927 the Committee on Young Offenders described the schools as 'enabled to employ a well-qualified staff and maintain a high standard of efficiency . . . the schools are now generally well equipped and are carrying on their difficult work with marked success'.[2] However, already in the period following the Children Act of 1908 and the Probation of Offenders Act, 1907, and still more after the First World War, the numbers of children in the schools dropped very considerably, partly owing to a decrease in the number of charges proved against juveniles, and partly owing to the development of other methods of dealing with them.

The Committee on Young Offenders in 1927 considered that the distinction between the children sent either to reformatories or to industrial schools – the convicted offenders between twelve and sixteen years old to the one, and the younger offenders, neglected children (Children Act, 1908, Section 58), truants, and those who were out of control or refractory to the other – was in practice unsound. There was little or no difference in character and needs between the children and in many instances mere accident had determined the category in which a child found himself. The distinctive names of the schools were disappearing and the existing unreal classification of intake should be abolished; the schools should in future be known indiscriminately as schools approved by the Secretary of State.

The Committee recommended that, with the disappearance of the existing classification, there should be a reclassification of the schools, and this should be based upon training offered, age group served, denominational character, and geographical location. The Committee seem to have thought that geographical location was very important, since some courts took an interest in local schools and made a practice of sending children to them, while some parents might naturally object to children being sent long distances from home. It was important, in suitable cases, that the schools should keep in touch with the parents and 'secure their cooperation in the training of their children'.[3] It all has a rather cosy, intimate, and local touch. The Committee went on to recommend that the courts should continue to select the appropriate school (from over eighty available!) for each child, and based this recommendation on the ground that selection must be based on personal knowledge of the child, which it would be difficult to pass on to the Home Office. The Home Office, although they had much greater opportunities of getting to know the characteristics of the different schools, had none for direct knowledge of child or parents. Obtaining reports on the child and his circumstances from the home area would involve too much delay and too heavy a load of work on the Home Office. The Home Office should therefore supply the courts with the fullest possible information about the schools and, with this information on the one hand, and, on the other, with the much fuller medical, psychological, and social reports on the offender which the suggested new observation centre or central remand homes could supply, the court would be in a really excellent position to assess the sort of training required and make an order accordingly.

This is one of the most interesting parts of the Committee's Report. The observation centres or remand centres were to help the court to know which form of treatment would be most appropriate to the offender before making any order at all. If, in the light of the information thus supplied, the court decided on institutional treatment, it would be able, with the help of the information from the Home Office as to what each approved school had to offer, to make a well-informed choice of the right one for the particular offender and send him there. In other cases the court might feel that the choice lay between a particular school or else supervision 'in the open' or a month's detention.

The system of choice by the court is no longer in force. During the Second World War the pressure on approved school places became very great, and some children were obliged to wait for several weeks in the remand homes after a committal, while the court made urgent inquiry for vacancies at schools all over the country, often having to go far beyond the particular schools of which members of the Bench had personal knowledge. As a result of this situation, the Home Office set up a vacancies pool from which they were able to advise courts as to the current situation. Papers were sent to the Home Office in respect of the children for whom places were being sought, so that each child could be allotted a place in the nearest available school of his own denomination. During this period the Home Office must have received a very striking impression of the great variety of children being sent to approved schools, and the next stage appears to have been the setting up of classifying schools for all non-Roman Catholic boys and for non-Roman Catholic girls over the age of fourteen years. Today, following the recommendation of the Ingleby Committee embodied in the Children and Young Persons Act, 1963, Section 8 (1), the courts decide upon the suitability of institutional training for a particular offender 'in principle', so to speak, and make an order committing him to an approved school without knowing the identity of the school to which he will eventually be sent after investigations lasting four to six weeks at one of the Home Office classifying schools for boys. It is obvious that no court can today be as well-informed and up-to-date as the Home Office about the particular opportunities and specialized training, personal relationships, disciplinary tone, and physical amenities available at each of a very large number of schools. It should also, presumably, be true that a classifying school, which has skilled resident staff with a variety of professional and technical qualifications for assessing the boys and which has every opportunity for the closest possible observation from many aspects for a number of weeks, plus reports on the home and family, should know more about him as a person at the end of that time than the court did, even after several appearances (perhaps before different Benches). It is, nevertheless, still open to a committing court to recommend a particular school and the Home Office will inform the court of the reason if such a recommendation is not followed.

The present procedure is, however, not entirely satisfactory in some respects. The court decides on the appropriate treatment for the offender without having the full information, which becomes available only some weeks after the committal. It may, for instance, happen that a child who has already been committed by the court to an approved school is found at the classifying stage to be one who is unlikely to benefit from that type of treatment at all. From this point of view it would be much better if the classifying took place before any decision was made as to the appropriate line of treatment. But, in practice, many Benches would not think of committing any offender to an approved school without first obtaining the fullest reports after a three-week remand in custody. The offender may even, on a previous occasion, have suffered a period of detention as a punishment, and this may itself have followed an earlier three-week remand for reports. In many cases the offender was originally placed on probation after his first appearance in court, and the probation officer has a good knowledge

of his family background as well as of his personality and
potentialities. It is difficult to see what additional information the classifying school can obtain to justify its use in
such instances.

When a non-Roman Catholic child is committed, after
a remand in custody, a period of seven to ten weeks in
remand home and classifying school may well elapse between the trial of his offence and his arrival at his approved
school. This is a very long time for a juvenile, who may be
expected, in any event, to be in a state of apprehension and
strain, to be held in an unstable situation.

At present there are four classifying schools for boys, each
run in conjunction with a training school, and each serving
a quarter of the area outside London. They are at Aycliffe in
Durham, Redhill in Surrey, Kingswood in Bristol, and
Red Bank in Lancashire, and serve respectively the north-
east, south-east, south-west, and north-west areas. They
are available for all boys, other than Roman Catholics,
whose homes are in the areas served by them. There is also
a classifying centre for boys, and this is at Stamford House
Remand Home in London; it classifies London boys of
twelve or over, including Roman Catholics. London boys
under twelve, other than Roman Catholics, are classified
at Redhill.

There is only one classifying school for girls, and this is
likely to close if a classifying remand home can be established elsewhere. It is at the Magdalen Hospital School in
London, and takes girls of fourteen and over (other than
Roman Catholics) from the southern part of the country
but excluding London. There are two girls' classifying
centres. One is at Cumberlow Lodge Remand Home in
London, and takes all London girls of fourteen and over.
There is another classifying centre at The Moss Girls'
Remand Home in Sheffield, and this takes all girls of
fourteen and over from the north-east.

These arrangements are based on the principle that
children for whom classifying facilities are available should
be sent initially to the classifying school or centre that

serves their home area. Children for whom classifying facilities are not at present available are allocated to training schools by the Home Office. There have been recent discussions with the Roman Catholic authorities and, if Roman Catholic boys were to be brought within the general arrangements for classification for boys outside London, further classifying schools or centres might well be needed.

The formal classification of the training schools is mainly based on age groups and religious persuasion, and the assignment of a boy or girl to a school within the appropriate age group is determined by such considerations as the type of vocational training to be provided, the environment of the school, and the probable reaction of the child to the individual personalities of the staff which are matters which do not lend themselves to formal classification. Three boys' schools specialize in nautical training, but they also give training in other subjects; and two boys' schools cater for those of higher intelligence. No approved school is classified specifically as catering for educationally subnormal children, but some do specialize in dealing with the very dull or retarded child. The vocational training covers a wide field, including farm training (which is now provided at twenty-nine schools including two for girls) and training in such subjects as building, mechanical engineering, automobile engineering, electrical installation work, and horticulture.

There are at present eighty-six schools for boys and thirty-five for girls. There are no 'closed' or 'secure' schools. A special 'secure' unit has, however, been attached to Kingswood School, Kingswood, Bristol (one of the classifying schools), for the treatment and training of boys who have shown, by persistent absconding or disruptive behaviour, either that they will not respond to training in an open approved school, or that their behaviour in such a school is having a seriously disruptive effect on the training of the other boys in the school. This unit which provides accommodation for twenty boys, was brought into use on 1 October 1964. Two other similar units, each for thirty boys, are being provided at two of the other boys' classifying schools.

Other recommendations on the subject of the schools were made by the Committee on Young Offenders (1927) and were carried into effect by the Children and Young Persons Act, 1933. Children under ten were not normally to be sent to approved schools; the maximum period of detention should be three years or till school-leaving age, whichever is the later; and committal should always be for this period in the first instance, leaving it to the Home Office and the schools to give earlier release on licence, where appropriate. On the question of length of detention in the schools, the Committee had some interesting points to make.[4] They felt that in recent years the whole theory of the value of very long detention had lost much of its support and, as a result of reluctance on the part of some courts to send young people away for long periods, some offenders were being placed on probation who really needed institutional training. This led the members of the committee to wonder whether there was a case for a much shorter institutional sentence, varying, say, from three to six months. Relying on the experience of people who had had the institutional care of young delinquents the Committee came to the conclusion that training and short detention are really incompatible. If the object is training, then detention cannot be short. There might be exceptional cases of people suitable for short training, but 'it would be impossible for the court to pick out such cases', and it should be left to the Home Office to pick out cases for exceptionally early release. These remarks are of great interest in the light of experience since 1927.

Before the last war two short-term approved schools for boys had come into being; these were Banstead Hall in Surrey and Shawbury Approved School near Coleshill in Warwickshire. Both received boys of all denominations exclusively for short-term committals. When the classifying system came into being with its advantages of intensive investigation, short-term cases were not produced in the same numbers as previously under the system of direct choice and placings by the courts, and Shawbury School has now been made available for approved school admissions for as long as the managers think desirable within the ordinary rules. Facilities for exceptionally early licence may, as before, be granted by the Home Office if the school wishes to license a boy in a suitable case before the expiry of the ordinary twelve months' minimum laid down in regulations. The average length of stay in an approved school is twenty months for boys and eighteen months for girls, and this has varied very little from year to year; the greater proportion of boys and girls are released after a stay of between one and two years.

The rate of committals of boys to approved schools has increased steadily over recent years – for example, from 6,700 in 1959 to 7,560 in 1964. The number of girls has, however, decreased over the same period from 1,322 to 1,138.[5] Present indications are that the rate of committals is likely to increase during the next five years, and a number of schemes are in hand for extending and improving the amount of accommodation available in order to provide sufficient places.

The Committee on Young Offenders in 1927 recommended that after-care should remain at the choice of the schools themselves. They quoted with approval the dictum of a previous Committee that 'mere obtaining of information is not after-care' and the schools should provide for each boy or girl a local friend. The Ingleby Committee in 1960 were less sure about this and recommended that the school managers' choice should be limited to the probation service and the local children's authorities, and that 'the welfare officer service should be allowed to run down gradually', mainly 'because of its isolation from other social services concerned with the family and because of the difficulty of supervising its work'.[6] The Advisory Council on the Treatment of Offenders (A.C.T.O.), reporting in 1963 on the Organization of After-Care, went further and recommended that 'a date should be set up by which the approved school welfare service would finally be wound up.'[7]

In that year approximately 4,200 boys and 800 girls were released from approved schools. The probation service undertook the after-care of about one-third of the boys and two-thirds of the girls, approved school welfare officers undertook the after-care of about one-half of the boys, and the child-care service mainly undertook the rest. Until 1 January 1964 children's authorities had a power but not a duty to undertake approved school after-care. A duty was laid on them from that date by paragraph 26 of the Third Schedule to the Children and Young Persons Act, 1963. Steps are also being taken to wind up the approved school welfare service depending on the availability of trained staff in the probation and child-care services and the final date has not yet been fixed.

The welfare officers' districts did not at any time cover the whole country, and were for the most part concentrated in the more heavily populated areas. At the end of 1963 there were about fifty approved school welfare officers in post. During the eighteen months following the publication of the A.C.T.O. report, about thirty of these either reached retirement or left the service to find other jobs (including probation and child-care). It was hoped and expected that the special skill and experience of many of the remaining twenty could also, as far as practicable, be made available to the probation and child-care service.

The present position is that boys are usually released after a period of between eighteen and thirty months' training; most girls somewhere between fifteen months and two years. The minimum possible without the special permission of the Home Secretary is six months. After-care continues for two years after release. Recall renders the offender liable to serve out the unexpired period of his detention or six months from recall, whichever is the longer. When supervision is at an end, voluntary after-care can continue at the offender's own request as long as he is under twenty-one years of age.

BORSTAL

A committal to borstal training can only be made by a juvenile court in the case of a person who is fifteen years old and has been shown to be a persistent absconder from an approved school or guilty of serious misconduct there. This is a provision which causes many magistrates to hesitate a very long time before committing to an approved school any child who has not committed a criminal offence – for example, a truant or a refractory child – since, if he absconds, he runs a serious risk of ending up in borstal, though in no way a criminal person. However, if a fifteen-year-old has been found guilty in the juvenile courts of an offence for which a person aged more than twenty-one could be imprisoned, and the court is satisfied that, having regard to his character and record and to the offence, it would be best for him to go to borstal, they may commit him in custody to quarter-sessions for sentence. They must first, however, obtain a report from the Prison Commissioners on the offender's physical and mental condition and his suitability for borstal training, and they may remand him in custody for this purpose for not longer than three weeks at a time. There is, of course, no certainty at all that quarter-sessions will in fact commit the offender to borstal.

A young offender who is sent to borstal may be detained for a maximum period of two years or a minimum of six months, according to his individual requirements. Release is followed by a period of supervision for up to two years – usually by a probation officer acting as an agent of the Central After-Care Association. If, while under supervision, the offender fails to comply with requirements, he may be recalled and detained until the end of the period of supervision, or for six months after his recall, whichever is longer.

ATTENDANCE CENTRES

One of the means open to the juvenile court in dealing with an offender is the attendance centre. The Secretary of State is empowered to provide these for offenders less than twenty-one years of age, under the Criminal Justice Act, 1948 (as amended by the Criminal Justice Act, 1961, Section 10), and he may arrange with the local authority or the police authority for the use of premises. The centres are for use where the defendant is not less than ten years of age and has failed to comply with the requirements, or some of them, of a probation order, or has committed an offence or defaulted on a fine, for which an adult could have been committed to prison. The attendance which may be required must normally be twelve hours in all, at times as specified in the order, and which as far as practicable do not interfere with working or school hours. This method may not be used for offenders who have already been to a detention centre or an approved school.

The first junior attendance centre for boys under the age of seventeen was opened at Peel House, Westminster, SW1, on 8 July 1950. There are now fifty-five junior centres, serving between them most of the main centres of population. None have been provided for girls, mainly because there are, nowhere, enough girls dealt with by the courts who are likely to be suitable for this form of treatment.

The Home Secretary has the statutory responsibility for providing attendance centres, and local agents supervise the running of them on his behalf. At Hull, the local agent is the county borough council acting through its children's committee, and at Reading it is the chief education officer; elsewhere it is the chief officer of police. The staff of attendance centres, from whatever service they are drawn, are volunteers to the work and do it in what would otherwise be their free time. One centre is in the charge of a retired approved school welfare officer, another in that of a schoolmaster; elsewhere a police officer is in charge, usually of the rank of chief inspector or inspector. Some centres have civilians (usually instructors in evening institutes) on their staff as well as police instructors and there are wide differences of régime. Of the fifty-five centres now open, thirty-two are held in schools by arrangement with the local education authority; eleven are held in police premises, usually in headquarters buildings or training schools, rarely in police stations, and then in a part of the premises out of sight of the public and of persons in police custody; five in youth clubs; and seven in halls and other places.

There are proposals to establish additional junior centres, but it is unlikely that these will be in rural areas as it is not possible to organize a centre with only one or two boys attending and the committal area cannot be extended beyond a reasonable journey from the town in which the centre is held. In 1963 attendance centre orders were made in respect of 49,411 boys aged between fourteen and under seventeen, and of these 17,547 were guilty of motoring offences. The corresponding figures for boys under fourteen years of age are 1,869 and 3. There are two senior attendance centres, one at Manchester run by prison officers from Manchester prison, and one at Greenwich run by the police. They are both for boys aged between seventeen and under twenty-one, and are therefore not available to the juvenile court. The principle of giving treatment or punitive functions to the police is very controversial and it might seem desirable that senior centres should be run, as at Manchester, by prison staff as part of the Penal System.

The results of sentencing young offenders in the various ways outlined give little ground for regarding any of them as effective ways of dealing with criminality. First offenders do better than recidivists under any treatment, as might be expected. The failure rates of recidivists, in terms of reconviction within a given period of years, are more than discouraging. A study of an admittedly small sample reported in *The Sentence of the Court*[8] gives figures of seventy-eight per cent, eighty-two per cent, and ninety per cent juvenile recidivists reconvicted within five years of release from approved schools, attendance centres, and borstals respectively. The general situation thus revealed is not confined to courts dealing with juveniles nor is it affected by the intentions of the court in sentencing – be they reformatory or punitive. The very grave problem which it presents is taken up again for discussion in Chapter 10. In the meantime one further alternative at the disposal of the juvenile court remains to be discussed.

COMMITTAL TO THE CARE OF 'A FIT PERSON'

In some cases where a juvenile is found guilty of an offence it seems to the court that his home circumstances and the general undesirability of his surroundings are such as to make it advisable to give someone other than his parents the responsibility for his guardianship, in order that proper provision may be made for his education and training, in observance of the principle laid down in Section 44 of the Children and Young Persons Act, 1933. The offence of which he has been found guilty must be one which, in the case of an adult, would be punishable by imprisonment (Section 57), and, if that condition is satisfied, the court will probably make a 'fit person' order, that is, they will commit the offender to the care of a person fit to assume the guardianship which they are removing from his parents. In 1965 a total of 1,370 young offenders were the subject of such orders.

A 'fit person' order may also be made in the case of persistent truants, juveniles out of the control of their parents or guardians, or who are shown to be in need of care or protection, and in 1965 there were 2,270 juveniles who were committed to the care of fit persons in this way.[9]

A person to whose care as a 'fit person' a juvenile is committed will have the rights and powers in regard to him, and the same liability to maintain him, as his own parents had previously. The 'fit person' must be of the same religion or give an undertaking to bring the juvenile up in that religion. Even though the parents have lost all parental rights over the juvenile who has been committed to care, nevertheless, they must make contributions to the 'fit person' to be applied to the benefit of their child, unless he has reached the age of sixteen. A juvenile who is working and is sixteen years old or more is liable to make these contributions himself. The 'fit person' order comes to an end at the age of eighteen, i.e. one year after the juvenile court has ceased to have general jurisdiction over its subject. A 'fit person' order may be appealed against and the appeal is heard by quarter-sessions.

The 'fit person' to whom the juvenile is committed may be a relative or friend or anyone who is willing and suitable to undertake the care of him. A local authority may also be a 'fit person' and nearly all 'fit person' orders are made in respect of local authority committees. The courts have had powers to commit to a 'fit person' for a long time. Under the Children Act, 1908, Sections 27, 58, and 59, a juvenile could be so committed if the parent or guardian had been convicted of certain offences; if the child was truant, refractory, or beyond control or convicted of his first offence (or of any offence if he was under twelve); and if the juvenile came within any of the categories of neglect or ill-treatment listed in Section 58 (1). A rather similar provision under that Act was that made in Section 53, by which children under eight who were sent to industrial schools could be boarded out until they reached the age of ten.

The Committee on Young Offenders which considered these methods 'very valuable' found[10] that the average number of juveniles made the subject of 'fit person' orders in a year was under twenty; yet the L.C.C. was taking advantage of the provision to enable industrial schools to board out, by having about three hundred children, nominally attached to industrial schools, boarded out each year. The Committee thought that the failure to make more use of the 'fit person' procedure was probably due to the unwillingness of friends or relatives to undertake responsibility especially where there was no financial assistance. Another difficulty was that, if friends and relatives did not come forward, there might be no one else available; and it was no one's business to find such people, and the court itself could not be expected to do it. The Committee noted that the Poor Law Guardians, under the Poor Law Act, 1899, had power to adopt certain classes of Poor Law children, and this had proved a very valuable system, so there seemed to be no difficulty in principle in arranging for some authority to accept responsibility for children who were in need of protection, although they had not actually come within the Poor Law. This would make it possible to give financial aid also, which had already been suggested twice previously. It was suggested that the local education authority would be the most suitable body to carry out these functions and to be enabled to act as a 'fit person'.

Under the 1933 Children and Young Persons Act, power was given to the court to name the local authority as a 'fit person' to assume guardianship through its education department if it was willing. A local authority acting as a 'fit person' had power to board out and maintain the child. These provisions remained undisturbed until 1948. In the meantime many courts discovered that bringing the horse to the water was a different matter from being able to make it drink. They might decide that the local authority would be the suitable 'fit person' and that the child ought to be removed to its guardianship, but if the local authority was not willing to take on this function it could not be compelled to do so.

This situation was altered by the passage of the Children Act, 1948, following the Report in 1946 of the Curtis Committee which inquired into the arrangements being made for the care of children deprived of a normal home life. Under this Act (Section 5) the assent of a local authority is no longer necessary to enable the court to make a 'fit person' order committing a person to care under the Children and Young Persons Act, 1933 (unless the juvenile is already the subject of a probation order or a supervision order). However, there is a safeguard which helps the court to look before it leaps, in that it must allow the authority to make representations to it as to the making of the order, and that it must consider any representations so made before it does proceed to make an order – unless to do so would, in its own opinion, cause undue delay. This provision is a very important safeguard, since the making of a 'fit person' order does not automatically follow upon, for instance, the court's finding that a juvenile is in need of care or protection. The court has the alternative of deciding to order the parent or guardian to give recognizances, making the child the subject of a supervision order, or sending him to an approved school. Again it does not follow that a child who is committed to the care of the local authority as a 'fit person' will then be removed from his home, or, if he is so removed, that he will be placed in a foster home. As the law stands at present, the effect of the 'fit person' order – whatever hopes may have been nursed by the court which made it – is simply to take the choice of where and how the juvenile shall live out of the hands of his parents and place it in those of the local authority. The court takes a decision as to who shall be responsible for the juvenile in these cases and thereafter the responsibility is exercised by the 'fit person' into whose care he goes. As that 'fit person', the children's department may even decide to leave the juvenile in his own home or to return him there on trial after a very short period in one of their homes. If they do so, they do it on their own responsibility as legal parents, and it is no longer the concern of the court, although it was the court which took the rights away from the natural parents and gave them to the local authority.

In practice a 'fit person' order has usually, in the case of juveniles in need of care or protection or out of control, been preceded by a supervision order (or a probation order in the case of an offender), and thus a certain amount is known as to the possibilities of working with the family and making suitable arrangements for the child before the case finally comes before the court again for a 'fit person' order to be made.

Where a child or young person is thought to be in immediate need of care or protection, for any reason, there are special provisions to enable him to be taken care of at once, until the matter can be gone into before a court. Under these provisions (Children and Young Persons Act, 1933, Section 67) a constable or a justice of the peace or anyone authorized by any court may take the juvenile to a place of safety until he can be brought before a juvenile court. When he comes before the court, it may be that the case cannot be heard at once for some reason such as further inquiries having to be made, or if it can be heard, the court may not be in a position to decide what order ought to be made. In such event the court may make an interim order for the juvenile to remain in a place of safety or for his committal to the care of a 'fit person' who is willing to look after him. The maximum period for which such an order may be made at any one time is twenty-eight days, but at the end of that time a fresh application may be made. The working of this procedure of remand on an interim order is, except for the longer period, very similar to the procedure in regard to a remand of an offender. A place of safety is defined in the 1933 Act, Section 107, to mean 'any remand home, workhouse, or police station, or any hospital, surgery, or any other suitable place, the occupier of which is willing temporarily to receive a child or young person'. Remand centres are included among the places of safety for the purpose of interim orders made in respect of young persons too unruly or depraved to be kept in a remand home pending appearance before the court, or where the court, having heard the case, requires reports on a juvenile who is not an offender in order to decide how to deal with him, and if it is satisfied that facilities for investigation cannot conveniently be provided in the place of safety to which he might otherwise be sent.

A 'fit person' order may be varied or revoked upon application, usually by the parents, and often the course of events may then go through the previous stages in reverse, so that the child who was in the care of the local authority returns to the care of his parents, at first under a supervision order or recognizances, and then, later, absolutely.

There are, however, a very large number of children in the care of local authorities who are not the subjects of 'fit person' orders. Under the Children Act, 1948, Section 1, the local authority has a duty to assume the care of juveniles who are orphaned, abandoned, or lost, or whose parents are prevented from providing for their proper accommodation, care, or upbringing, provided that their intervention is necessary in the interests of the child. (If, however, there is a parent or guardian, a relative, or suitable friend, the authority must try to place the child with him.) The power may also be exercised under the Children and Young Persons Act, 1963, Section 48, where it appears to the local authority that the parent or guardian is unfit to have the care of the child either because of a mental disorder or because he has persistently failed, without reasonable cause, to discharge the obligations of a parent or guardian.

An authority which takes a child into its care as above may, by a committee resolution, vest all the rights and powers of parents in itself. If the written consent of the parent or guardian has been obtained, the resolution stands, and the juvenile remains in care. If that is not the case, the parent or guardian must be told in writing that the resolution has been passed, and that if he wishes to object he must do so in writing within one month. If he does object, then the resolution will lapse within fourteen days, unless the authority complains to the juvenile court and the court prevents it lapsing before the case is heard and decided. The court can prevent a resolution lapsing if it is satisfied that the objector has abandoned the child, or was unfit to have care of it. If, under this subsection, the order does not lapse, then the parent or guardian has a right of appeal to the juvenile court (Section 4).

The rights of appeal from decisions of a juvenile court are the same as for the adult court. The constitution of the appeals committee or court has, however, been modified as follows. Under the provisions of the Criminal Justice Administration Act, 1962, Section 4 (7), arrangements must be made to secure, as far as practicable, that not less than half of the justices on the appeals committee hearing an appeal from a juvenile court must be justices qualified to sit as members of a juvenile court. Arrangements for the hearing of appeals from a juvenile court by a recorder have been modified by the Children and Young Persons Act, 1963, Section 19, which provides that, as far as practicable, the recorder shall be assisted by two members of a juvenile court panel, who shall sit with him and act as assessors.

The provisions have brought about a new situation in the recorder's court, since he had previously been used to sitting alone to hear appeals from the juvenile court as from any other court. Nothing appears to have been laid down as to the weight to be attached to the opinion of an assessor in the event of a difference of opinion between the assessors and the recorder. Practice may vary from one recorder's court to another, but it is becoming clear that, in many cases, while the recorder may hear the assessors' opinions with greater or less respect, he regards the final decisions as being matters for himself alone and not as a sharing of responsibility.

Until recently, in contrast, however, the lay justices at many quarter-sessions and appeals committees were accustomed to sitting under the chairmanship of a non-lawyer, one of their own number, and – in this situation – to having their individual opinion asked as a member of the court and considered as being in itself of equal weight with that of any other member including the chairman. The now almost universal election of legally qualified chairmen, many of whom sit elsewhere alone as recorders or deputy recorders, may in many areas, for good or ill, be bringing a change of practice in its train.

CHAPTER 6

THE JUVENILE COURT AT WORK

I T now remains to take a closer look at the actual working of the juvenile court today. A visit to such a court in operation is indispensable for a real understanding of what it is doing, and the court may permit a visitor to attend if application is made, either direct to the justices or their clerk, or through a probation, education, or children's officer, or some other responsible and friendly person who works with the court.

The emphasis on education and welfare in the Children and Young Persons Act, 1933, seems to have tended to obscure in the minds of at least some sections of the public, the fact that the juvenile court, as at present constituted, is still a court of law and not a kind of welfare clinic. The first essential to a proper understanding of the juvenile court is to understand its place in the administration of justice, and this presupposes some familiarity with the procedure of the adult court and of the distinctive features of British justice. Visitors who come to the juvenile court knowing nothing of ordinary court procedure are likely to do themselves and the juvenile court more harm than good by carrying away a lively crop of misunderstandings as to what the court was supposed to be doing and what was actually happening.

In Chapters 1 and 2 of this book we therefore gave some account of the business, procedure, and atmosphere of the adult court. Against this background were discussed in Chapters 3 and 4 the development of the special summary court for dealing with charges against juveniles and applications relating to them, and the modifications, such as they are, which have been made over the years in the effort to adapt the procedure of the adult court for use in dealing with children and young persons. It is very necessary to keep the origins of the juvenile court firmly in mind, since they have so much bearing on the procedure. The rules of evidence must be observed here, as in any other court. Witnesses must be sworn, and the record of the defendant must not be made known to the court until after the charge has been found proved. It must not be assumed that a defendant is guilty, but a plea must be taken and the charge either admitted or proved. The magnitude of the 'punishment' usually bears some relation to the crime and the record of the defendant. A finding of guilt for a first offence of a minor character is, for example, seldom held to justify any order heavier than a small fine, even though the members of the Bench may be unanimous in feeling that the defendant is a person who, on other grounds, ought probably to go away from home to an approved school or into care. In such a setting, then, how do the modifications in the ordinary procedure work out, and how is the injunction laid down in Section 44 (see Chapter 4, page 95) carried out?

BEFORE THE HEARING

As far as the court is concerned, the proceedings start when the magistrates take their seats on the bench, but this is not the beginning of the visit to court for the juvenile defendant. He has been separated from adult defendants at the police station, while in custody, while being conveyed to the court, and while waiting for trial; or, more probably, he has not been in custody but has been brought straight from home by his parents. In practice, this separation from adult defendants brings its own difficulties. In the group of persons waiting to go into the juvenile court there are usually more youngsters than adults, sometimes twice as many, since there is often, alas, more than one defendant per parent. This congregation may remain in the ante-room to the court for some time, since it is extremely difficult to forecast how long each case on the list will take.

Some justices take much longer to hear a case than others – a difference which does not necessarily relate at all to the thoroughness with which the case is investigated – and some cases take an unexpected course. A plea that the charge is 'not true' may disturb the time-table far more in the juvenile court, in which such pleas are much scarcer, than in the adult court.

The mixed group of persons in the ante-room (most of them in a state of some anxiety and tension) is quite likely to need careful handling. The position is in theory complicated by the fact that, while some of the children are about to be tried for breaches of the law, but may be innocent, others have already admitted charges, and yet others are the subject of care, protection, or control proceedings and are technically at least in the class of the 'more sinned against than sinning'. It is the practice in some courts to arrange for defendants to arrive near the estimated time at which the case is likely to be heard. The advantages and disadvantages of such arrangements are of the same kind as those pertaining to an appointments system in the out-patients department of a hospital, and, if the court is at all busy, most defendants find they still have to wait for some time. The court usher, who may be a policeman, generally manages to keep things orderly in the ante-room, and this point is important, since it is most desirable that children and parents should enter the court in a state of proper respect and with their minds focused on the matter in hand.

THE COURTROOM

The general provisions to ensure that the juvenile court shall be separate from the adult court should facilitate the creation of a less-formal atmosphere and surroundings than for the trial of adults. In some instances, however, the result may be that the juvenile court is held in premises which are not really suited to the procedure of a court at all, or even to that of a formal inquiry, and whose only advantage would appear to be that they are indeed separate. The atmosphere of the juvenile court should be both dignified and informal, each in a suitable degree. This is a very difficult balance to strike in view of the age range for which the provision is required, but in general it is safe to say that the courtroom should not be so large or so arranged that the Bench cannot talk confidentially with the defendant, or that he is too far from his parents to consult them easily where this is advisable. On the other hand, the room must not be so small that a child sees it as crowded. The shape of the room can be advantageous or otherwise, and probably the most awkward is a long, narrow shape with a table running most of the length of the room. If the magistrates are at one end and the defendant at the other, he will certainly be facing his judges, but from the farthest possible point and separated from them by everyone else present. If, on the other hand, he and the magistrates face each other across the width of the table, communication is easier in some ways, but the situation may be confused for the defendant if the magistrates are to him indistinguishable from a number of other similar personages sitting on the same side, the view from his side somewhat resembling the traditional picture of the free bench in the park at Aberdeen! An alternative sometimes adopted is for the magistrates to sit alone at the end of the table with the defendant seated or standing half-way down one of the long sides, but turned so as to face the Bench. However, unless the magistrates are taking a very active part in the proceedings, the defendant will almost certainly find his attention being drawn across the table and he may even have to turn his back on the Bench in order to 'listen to what the officer is saying' when evidence is being given.

A combination of a relatively large number of people with an informal atmosphere in a small and unsuitably shaped room makes it easy for the proceedings to get a little out of hand, so that the rules of evidence are in danger of not being observed, or even that the young defendant feels intimidated by the proximity of hostile witnesses. It is especially difficult for a child to know who are the judges, in view of the large part taken often, unavoidably, by the clerk in such circumstances. Indeed, such a scene may compare unfavourably with that in an ordinary court which has been cleared, under the provisions of the Children and Young Persons Act, 1933, Section 37, for a child to give evidence. However informal the tone of the proceedings, it is surely self-evident that any kind of disorder, hysterical or exhibitionistic behaviour, or shouting by anyone is out of place in a court. Especially in a juvenile court it is to be avoided if the young defendant is to receive a true impression as to the nature of a court and to understand that all the issues involved have received calm, just and dispassionate consideration. An experienced chairman will foresee indications of a rising storm and adroitly avoid encouraging these. It is usually possible for such a chairman, himself a reasonably mature personality, to do this without depriving parents or defendants of the opportunity to voice protest or express themselves bluntly and forthrightly. But a court which is not open to public view and which may be less formal than usual, lacks some of the usual restraints, and the quality of the chairman (or failing him the clerk) will determine how well the court is run from this point of view. Where an upset does occur, even if it may seem to have been unavoidable, the Chairman may do well to consider how far his own or his clerk's conduct of the proceedings may, even unwittingly, have been a factor contributing.

FORMALITY OR INFORMALITY

This is not to say that there ought to be more formality in juvenile courts generally. Formality is, in itself, neither an advantage nor a disadvantage, but its value is to be assessed in relation to the purpose of the occasion. In the adult court it helps to ensure an orderly procedure, and encourage respect for the law – two essentials, if justice is both to be done and to be seen to be done. Many juvenile courts, however, achieve the same objects with only the very minimum of formality. Held perhaps in a committee room or in an office on local authority premises, the general atmosphere suggests an inquiry rather than a trial. There are present only the three justices and their clerk, the defendant with one or both parents, the representative of the local authority and/or the probation officer, the prosecuting officer, and the court usher – no more than ten or eleven people in all. Thus these courts very often combine informality and intimacy with good order and dignity.

Some of the London juvenile courts seem to achieve the same sort of result in quite another setting. While there may be more people present than are concerned in the particular case being dealt with, this seems in no way to affect the demeanour of the defendant or his parents, who are directly in front of the Bench. It is true that many children seem not to notice other people in court as long as there is no one between them and the Bench. They seem to relate themselves easily and directly to the Bench or to what appears to them to be the focal point of the proceedings, but less easily to the whole group of strangers, and often they do not seem to be aware of themselves as the centre of the attention of all present. This is less true of adolescents, however, and there may be additional reasons in their cases for carefully observing the statutory limitations upon the persons allowed to be present in a juvenile court.

'AS PRIVATE AS POSSIBLE'?

In spite of the apparently narrow restriction, the number present in a juvenile court may, in practice, be quite large. In a case of larceny there may be, for instance, one or both parents of each defendant member of a little gang, one or more witnesses, the prosecuting solicitor (and the defending solicitor if any), a police officer in charge of papers and records and acting as an usher, two or three magistrates and their clerk, and one or more members of the press. In addition, it is found useful in many courts to have present a representative of the children's department, a school attendance officer, two probation officers (man and woman), and an additional clerk from the magistrates' clerk's office. In some courts these extra people may have no personal connexion with any of the cases coming before the court, though it may very well turn out to be advisable to consult them about the facilities available for carrying out an order which the Bench wishes to make after a charge has been found proved. The children's officer or his representative may produce the school report and the report on a child's home background, but the handing of these to the clerk may turn out to be the only contribution required from him or his representative during the sitting. But in some areas, especially the smaller ones, such officers may be the actual men and women who have had contact with the defendant, and are in any case likely to know a great deal about him and his family, and their intimate knowledge may be of much assistance when it comes to deciding what to do with the offender. In these smaller areas, too, there are fewer social workers available for court duty, and it is quite usual for a considerable amount of inter-departmental cooperation to go on in suitable cases, so that an officer represents other departments besides his own.

As a further addition there may be in some courts persons in training for each branch of work indicated above, e.g. child-care students, law students, probation trainees, police cadets, and visiting or new magistrates. Other candidates for permission to attend include persons in training as teachers, youth leaders, health visitors, ministers of religion, social case-workers, general social science students, visitors from abroad, and other interested persons. Most courts which receive many requests for permission to attend put a limit on the number of visitors to be allowed on any one occasion. This is in the spirit of the Act, since, however important it may be that these people shall understand what goes on in such a court and how charges against children are dealt with, the fact remains that they are complete strangers to the defendant and only serve to swell the size of the crowd before whom his affairs are to be investigated. The problem is a difficult one, and perhaps all that can be said is that the claims of such people to be present in cases in which they are not concerned and not likely to be concerned are not the most important consideration. Against them must be weighed the interests of the defendant, which the relevant part of the law was intended to safeguard.

In cases in which it is alleged that an adolescent girl is in need of care, protection, or control, or is in moral danger, part of the evidence for the prosecution may include an allegation that the girl has had sexual intercourse, and has made a detailed statement to the police, not only admitting her seduction but also giving a minute description of the physical details. Such a statement has usually been made in the comparatively intimate conditions of an office at the police station, and to women police officers; but in some courts it may be read out during the proceedings in front of the girl and her parents and in the presence of whoever is in court, of whom perhaps as many as twenty or twenty-five persons are total strangers to her. If it is felt to be essential that such a statement should be read out, these are occasions on which the chairman is certainly justified in clearing the court of all but the persons actually connected with the particular case, and *bona fide* representatives of the Press. This can be done, and ought to be done, as part of the policy of having regard to the welfare of the young person. Otherwise she may well be robbed of the last vestiges of her self-respect, feelings of personal worth, decency, and privacy, although these are the very factors on which her rehabilitation, if it is to be achieved, must be built. An alternative procedure adopted in well-run courts is for the statement to be produced by the woman police officer giving evidence on oath and handed to the chairman of the Bench, copies being given to the other magistrates, the clerk, the defendant, counsel, etc. The defendant

is then asked to read through the document (and identify it as her statement) and is given an opportunity
of challenging it in any respect before it is admitted in
evidence.

Some of the same considerations apply where adolescent
boys are charged with having exposed themselves before
women. These boys are often sensitive, intelligent youngsters, deeply ashamed of the behaviour complained of, and
thoroughly frightened about the possibility of its recurrence.
They are under a considerable disadvantage in answering
questions about the incident or about their feelings, motives,
intentions, etc., if these are put in front of a number of
curious and interested spectators.

In general, the main immediate disadvantage of numbers in the juvenile court is that it makes it difficult to keep
the simple, less-formal atmosphere originally intended. It
takes more experience and more confidence on the part
of the chairman to take as active and direct a part in the
proceedings, or to get into the same contact with the juvenile, than when there are only seven or eight people present.
From the defendant's own point of view, especially if he is
stationed rather towards the back of the room, the proceedings are not likely to give the impression of being 'as
private as possible' (as recommended by the Committee
on the Treatment of Young Offenders, 1927) if the place
appears to be full of people. It has to be remembered that,
while most of those present are familiar to the Bench and to
each other, and their functions make them all part of the
team, as it were, to the juvenile who is there for the first
time they are simply a crowd of strange adults, a species of
person with which he is not, at the moment, on good terms.
The appearance in court is not intended to be a punitive
experience in itself, but publicity and strangeness can easily
make it so, and it is undesirable that this should happen
if the defendant is to form a proper picture of the administration of justice. This is even more important if he is before the court, not as a defendant on a criminal charge but

as the subject of an application alleging, for instance, that he is in need of care and protection.

RESTRICTIONS ON PUBLICITY

Some people feel that the privacy of the juvenile court, and even the prohibition on the publication of identifying particulars, is a mistake. It is argued that the shame involved in publicity would be a deterrent to future wrongdoing by the culprit himself and by others, and would also ensure that the parents were held up to deserved public reproach.

There are a number of things which may be said against such a view. It is not clear that shame is precisely the emotion which would always be felt by a youth who saw his name in print, with perhaps a photograph, as the leading figure in a court case. For the same reason the effect upon other potential wrongdoers might be quite the opposite of deterrent. There is no doubt, however, that in many cases publication of identifying particulars would be a punishment to the parents, and the argument is that this would goad them into keeping better control over the child in the future, thereby preventing any repetition. But in many cases the parents could not possibly have prevented the offence by any means short of an impracticable minute-by-minute supervision, nor is it clear what specific preventive action they ought to take in the future. In other cases the offence seems to have resulted in part at least from the whole *milieu* in which the child lives, the way of life of his family and friends. These are, perhaps, the cases in which publication would be least of all likely to be effective or felt as a deterrent.

Many of the offences with which children are charged are very small – for example, stealing one and sixpence at the swimming-baths – and some are the result of reports to the police by the parent unaware that the thief is at home. Something under two-thirds of charges are against first offenders who do not come before the court again. The publication of names in such instances might bring disproportionate shame, antagonizing the neighbours, and creating the very situation in which a young offender might indeed be expected to develop into an anti-social adult.

Probably the strongest argument in favour of the present prohibition is that it would be unwise and unjust that a child should be heavily handicapped by being branded publicly as a thief or other criminal, particularly among schoolmates and at the very outset of his life. It is part of the modern view of the significance of juvenile behaviour and its appropriate treatment that this should not be done. A change in this part of the law would certainly add greatly to the gravity of bringing a juvenile before the court, and it seems at least likely that, in such an event, many cases would not be brought at all and the offenders would not be dealt with.

Some people, while in general agreement with the foregoing, think, nevertheless, that there are some crimes – for instance, sexual offences by adolescent boys against young children – in which the names of the offenders should be published, in order that parents may be able to safeguard their own children against such youths. It is possible for the court to dispense with the prohibition on publication in certain circumstances, and an instance is reported in *The Magistrate*[1] of a petition being sent to the members of a particular Bench asking them to give permission for publication in all such cases. But the writer of the article points out that whereas the Act gives the court or the Secretary of State power to dispense with the requirements of Section 49 of the Children and Young Persons Act, 1933, if satisfied that it is in the interests of justice to do so, there is no power to do this in the interest of the welfare of possible victims. Nor is there power to make a general dispensation applying to 'all cases of a particular kind'.

JURY TRIAL?

During the conduct of the trial in the juvenile court there will be a number of points of special interest to watch. Parents usually stand near their child while the charge is read. Not only does this often reveal a highly suggestive resemblance between parent and child, seeming to imply that the accused is after all nothing more or less than a chip off the old block and as unlikely to yield to treatment, but also it enables him to consult his parent if necessary. If the charge is indictable and the defendant aged fourteen years or more, he will be informed by the clerk of his right to be tried in a higher court and before a jury if he so wishes and invited to make his choice. It may be said at once that he invariably asks for summary trial. In the rare cases where he electrifies the court by announcing that he wishes to go to a higher court, the consternation of all present is obvious. It is not without its effect on the defendant. After receiving an angry nudge from his parent and possibly a further inquiry from the clerk, he usually corrects himself and hastily requests 'to be tried here today'.

In regard to young persons this situation has changed in no way since it was noted and discussed by the Committee on Young Offenders in 1927. The right to go for trial before a jury is an important part of the administration of justice in this country. In so far as the young defendant is to have the same rights at law and to be dealt with in the same way as an adult, there would seem to be a case for retaining this right. On the other hand, the whole procedure for dealing with young defendants is one which has been modified, in the light of modern views about young people, *precisely because they are young people*. The fact that, in practice, juveniles almost never do elect to go for trial to the sessions suggests that the case for retaining this part of the ordinary procedure is very academic, to say the least. It may seem that were it dropped entirely the course of justice would, for all practical purposes, proceed entirely as now. The position might, however, alter considerably if any change came about which led to a greater number of juvenile defendants being legally advised – a point worthy of serious thought in this and other connexions.

KNOWING THE ACT WAS WRONG

The modified wording used in the juvenile court is on the whole suited to a child's understanding. To many children 'true' or 'right' is clearly understood to refer to a matter of fact, viz. whether it is true (or right) to say that the act was committed. But to ask whether a person is 'guilty' is to inquire about his feelings in relation to the fact. This difficulty came out clearly in discussion with an intelligent boy of ten after a charge of wilful damage had been found proved. The word 'guilty' was inadvertently used and the boy politely corrected the Bench, saying that, while his co-defendant had been guilty, he himself had not. This, he explained, was because the other boy had been caught in the act, while he had run away before the policeman actually reached the scene and therefore he had not had any guilty feeling. In another instance, an eighteen-year-old pregnant girl, already on probation, was about to come before the ordinary court for stealing cot sheets, blankets, and a pillow from the mistress of the house where she worked as a domestic. She announced to her probation officer that she most definitely would not be pleading guilty, 'as I don't feel guilty at all because Mrs X has such a lot of things and I have hardly any'.

This is an exceedingly important and relevant point in regard to the whole question of the age of criminal responsibility, and especially to the use made of the juvenile court in dealing with children who have broken the law. In regard to knowing an act was wrong the matter appears to be somewhat as follows. Children very early become aware that there are a large number of acts and situations which are not approved of by adults. Only a minority of these are, however, against the law. There are a number of other things, for example, playing with old railway sleepers on railway premises, which are against the law, though only policemen and a few other people disapprove of them. One therefore does not necessarily disapprove of these latter things oneself, but it wouldn't be common sense to do them if there was a policeman standing at one's elbow. Sometimes one doesn't know whether a thing is against the law or not, but if a policeman is coming, and especially if he shouts, one knows it is and one runs. When a policeman is coming, it is better to stop whatever one is doing and do something else – or better still, do nothing. Curiously enough, this latter course isn't too clever always either, as it makes them ask questions about what one has been up to lately, and it's pretty likely something or other will turn out to have been wrong, or if it doesn't one begins to feel as if it had been.

While the outline above may be somewhat over-simplified it is possible and even probable that a proportion of the children coming before the court did not know that what they were doing was wrong in the same sense that an adult would have known this. It did not appear wrong to the child to do it, and he did not have the appropriate feelings about doing it, though at the same time he would have known, if he had thought about it, that an adult would think it wrong. At a later stage he does have appropriate feelings against doing things that adults think are wrong, and this gradually changes into a feeling that the things themselves are wrong things to do. In short, he has reached the stage of internalizing the moral standards of the adults round him, beginning with those closest to him. If he is fortunate in his family background, he will now find himself in line with society generally. If not, he may nevertheless conform with most of the requirements of the law as soon as he is intellectually aware of what they are, and of the advantage of conforming, though in his own personality he makes no real response to them.[2]

Since there are wide variations in rates of development

as between different children and as between different aspects of the same child, and as growth and development do not proceed steadily but in uneven stages, it has to be accepted that, even in normal circumstances, children do not all succeed in internalizing the moral values of their society at the same age or stage, and it is exceedingly difficult to know exactly where any given child stands in the process during the short time he is in court, and even more difficult to know where he was two months ago when the alleged offence was committed.

It must be remembered that the appearance in court and the careful recital of what happened, the discussion with the parents and the complainant, and finally with the child himself, all build up into an experience which will become part of his life. A child who comes into court with no feeling about having done something wrong, in spite of knowing that he has done it, sometimes seems to acquire such a feeling during the proceedings, as if the gap between his private view of life and that held by society had suddenly diminished. Such a child was recently charged with having picked up a number of boxes of pencils and taken them away from a locked warehouse into which he had climbed. After a finding of guilt he was called up to the Bench and the following conversation took place:

CHAIRMAN: What is a person who takes things belonging to other people called?

CHILD (slightly self-righteous): A thief, sir.

CHAIRMAN (after a pause): Is that what you are, then?

CHILD (after a long pause): No sir . . . I just wanted the pencils . . . (Further pause, followed by a visible internal struggle and the beginning of tears . . .) Yes sir!

Only the subsequent behaviour of the child will show whether this was anything more than the same intellectual perception with which he entered the court, or whether he had at that moment succeeded in finally accepting a little bit more of reality for himself. In these cases the subsequent attitude of the parents or, if necessary, of a probation officer to the offence is probably the paramount factor in consolidating or arresting any movement which may have been made.

If the above discussion has any validity at all in terms of the development of the personality towards social maturity, some doubt may be felt as to whether the age of ten years is the right one at which to hold a child criminally responsible and whether the safeguards which the law provides quite fit the realities of the situation. In the writer's view it is unlikely that the actual appearance in court and the trial proceedings themselves, if the court is run well, do most children any harm whatever. They are probably even helpful to both him and his family. Unfortunately they also mean, for what it is worth, that for the rest of his life he will be a person against whom there was, on at least one occasion, a finding of guilt in a criminal court. The fact that it was the juvenile court does not for many people quite remove the special feeling of moral judgement and condemnation with which they are accustomed to view a conviction for a criminal offence.

'TRUE OR NOT TRUE'

A striking fact noticeable in any summary criminal court is that the very great majority of defendants plead guilty, and the juvenile court is no exception, whatever form of words is used in putting the plea. Very often the young defendants have been caught in the act, though not necessarily by the police. Even so, some children may say that the charge is not true simply because some detail is not quite accurately stated – for example, because an alleged theft of 35*s*. was in fact a theft of only 33*s*. 6*d*., as if there were some hope that while stealing 35*s*. was admittedly a crime, stealing 33*s*. 6*d*. might not be. It is therefore always worth while in such cases for the clerk to make a further inquiry, such as 'Do you say you didn't steal the money?'

in order to avoid confusion and to amend the charge if necessary.

A child will also say that the charge is not true because, although he helped to steal the goods, he did not get a share of them afterwards – or alternatively because, although he kept watch, helped the others in and out of the window, and had his full share of the proceeds, he was not inside the building with the others when they actually took the things. In these cases it has to be explained what is involved in being concerned with others in doing an unlawful act, if the defendant is not to labour under a feeling of injustice or feel that the charge is being stretched in some way on purpose to include him.

On the other hand, a child may say the charge *is* true because he has not understood exactly what the charge is. Stealing in law is usually taking the thing away with the intention of depriving the owner permanently of its possession. A child who has, without permission, taken a ride on a bicycle belonging to a friend may feel extremely guilty about the whole situation *after* he has been questioned by a policeman, and fail to be aware of any difference between this situation and having stolen the bicycle. In a recent case a child arriving late at his club decided, instead of going in, to have a ride around on a friend's bicycle which he saw leaning against the wall outside. In the nearby park his attention was taken up and he stayed away much longer than he had intended. In the meantime the club leader, feeling unwell, had closed the club early, and on finding that a bicycle was missing reported the matter to the police on his way home. The child, finding that the club had closed and recollecting that the owner lived some way off and that he himself would have to walk home in the dark if he returned the cycle that night, decided instead to take it to his own home and return it in the morning. Unfortunately the police officer arrived before he had made the journey. The child's plea in court was at first one of guilty, but this was later changed, and after hearing what was said on both sides the Bench dismissed the charge.

In another case, however, a child said that the charge was 'not true', after having first held a whispered colloquy with his father standing behind. The evidence was such as to leave little room for doubt of guilt from the start, and it was a very depressing experience to hear the child continuing with his emphatic denials on oath in the witness-box. The charge was found proved and the record of previous offences turned out to be quite considerable. This, together with a home background of a depraved and criminal character, topped off by the horrifying performance in court, combined to convince the Bench that the time had arrived for removal from the undesirable surroundings of home and for provision to secure proper education and training. An approved school order was made, and the court did not omit to discuss the situation with the father in very plain terms.

A child or young person who pleads that he is not guilty may, as in the case of an adult defendant, indeed be innocent. However important it is in the ordinary court to see that an innocent defendant is not found guilty, it is even more so in the juvenile court, which is equally a court of justice. A child's faith in the value of telling the truth and his hopes of justice in the future can be very severely shaken by a wrong finding, and, if he is not represented or the charge is a comparatively minor one in the eyes of the law, it is unlikely that he (or his parents) will appeal, and thus the matter will not be put right.

At least the same standard of proof must be required in a charge against a juvenile as in the case of an adult defendant. Where necessary there must be corroboration. When a child is giving evidence on his own behalf it must be made clear to him that the court is paying as much attention to what he or his parents are saying as it is to the evidence of the police. It is just as true in the juvenile court as in the ordinary court that the accused person is presumed to be innocent until there is a finding of guilt and 'there is no presumption at all in favour of the police witness . . . who is appearing in the case'.[3] This, to some minds, is a very odd feature of the juvenile court indeed, and it may be felt by some people that a child and an adult should not stand on the same footing in this matter. But from this point of view the fact that the defendant is a child is irrelevant, and it does not in law create a presumption in favour of the witness for the prosecution simply because the latter is an adult.

In a case of larceny five boys aged between ten and twelve were charged with having stolen a quantity of a certain sweet-stuff during the dinner hour by means of running behind the delivery lorry as it was being driven up a long, narrow entry, and slashing at the sacks with razor blades. Four said the charge was true, but one denied it. The police officer had seen the boys running away into the school, was sure he had seen five, and had identified five panting boys a few minutes later in the classroom. The fifth boy said that he had left the school at the end of the dinner interval to go to the nearby clinic, but, finding it closed and no one there, had run back and re-entered the school just behind the other four. He gave his evidence on oath, but had no witnesses. However, the fact that he had not been with the party was corroborated on oath by one of the other four boys, and, against the uncorroborated evidence of the police, the charge was found not proved. The demeanour of the children throughout was such that the Bench had no doubt whatever that a mistake had, in all honesty, been made by the police officer.

QUESTIONING WITNESSES AND GIVING EVIDENCE ON OATH

After a witness for the prosecution has been called, the defendant has a right to question him. Adult defendants in court for the first time often find this difficult and are inclined to try to make a statement or are unable to frame their questions. A child is almost certain to need help if he is not represented, and considerable latitude in helping him is allowable. The bewildered statement 'You couldn't have seen me because I wasn't there' can usually be re-framed by the clerk in some such way as 'Are you asking him whether he is quite sure it was you he saw and how he knows it was you?', without objection.

A juvenile court may, under Rule 9 (2) of the Summary Jurisdiction (Children and Young Persons) Rules, 1933, go even farther than this where the defendant is not legally represented or assisted by his parent in conducting the cross-examination of witnesses for the prosecution. If a defendant in these circumstances makes assertions instead of asking questions the court 'shall then put to the witness such questions as it thinks necessary on behalf of the child or young person and may for this purpose question the child or young person in order to bring out or clear up any point arising out of any such assertions'. This is an extremely important provision for the protection of a juvenile as a defendant. The conscientious discharge by a judicially minded chairman of the duty here laid on the court also serves a most valuable purpose in bringing home to the child that the magistrates are sitting as judges to assess what is said by either side, and not as instruments of the prosecution.

The point was discussed by the Ingleby Committee in connexion with the provision of legal aid in the juvenile court. The Committee rather reluctantly urged the magistrates to exercise more readily their power to allow free legal aid in criminal cases although they thought legal representation to be less necessary in juvenile courts on the ground that the court itself is required to help an unrepresented juvenile. Moreover 'the justices are in a closer relation with the parties and depend on having a child's full understanding of his situation for making the right impression on him: the salutary effect of appearing in court may be diminished if legal argument, however well justified as such, obscures the substance of the proceedings'. In fact, of course, the 'closer relationship' if not illusory is very much a matter of chance and varies from one Bench to another. In many divisions the picture would be true to a much greater degree of the domestic court which is often far more private and more intimate, and where it is just as important to the justices that the parties shall fully understand their situation. Yet the provisions of the Legal Aid and Advice Act, 1949 have now (Legal Aid (General) (Amendment) Regulations, 1961) been extended to these proceedings as well as to affiliation and guardianship proceedings. It has, of course, for many years, been common practice in summary courts generally for chairman or clerk to help an unrepresented defendant in his examination of witnesses if necessary and to ask him questions on points which it appears to be in his interest to bring forward. The Rule 9 (2) as above simply makes this common practice an obligation in the case of an unassisted juvenile. It does not carry the implication that the practice is either non-existent or unsuitable in the context of other summary courts or unrepresented defendants.

It is also not clear why the Committee thought that legal aid should be foregone in order to preserve 'the salutary effect of appearing in court'. If there were anything in this extraordinary argument why should it apply only to juveniles? And why has the innocent defendant, as well as the guilty, to be exposed to a 'salutary effect'? The defendant, whether guilty or innocent, is in court solely in order that charges may be heard and determined and the sentence decided upon. The court appearance and the proceedings are not in themselves intended to be either reformative or punitive. One wonders whether the Committee would also prefer the court appearance to exert its salutary effect on a child brought before the court in care, protection or control cases, as the victim of a First Schedule Offence.

It may be true that, as the Committee said (paragraph 250) 'The methods and procedure of a juvenile court even in criminal cases differ from those in other courts', but the differences are very slight. None of them is of a fundamental character. The Committee's attitude seems to rest on an unspoken assumption, both fallacious and inappropriate in this context, that 'father always knows best'. But the procedure in juvenile courts as in adult courts is accusatorial and not inquisitorial; the matter in hand is a trial of charges or allegations, not an inquiry into them. It is not the duty of the Bench to find out who did what. It is the duty of the parties each to put his own case in the best light, and for the court then to make a decision between them on *the evidence which has been placed before it*. Although the court is under an obligation to help the unassisted juvenile, it cannot behave like a professional advocate and try 'to show the justice of his case and the fallacies of his opponent's' (see Egerton *Legal Aid*, reprinted 1946, p. 2.). It would be technically impossible to do so since the court is not fully informed of the defendant's case at that stage, and furthermore its inquiries cannot be allowed to develop into an actual battle with the prosecution.

Some of the most difficult points of law in criminal cases are precisely those which are likely to come up in the juvenile court, as, for example: the difference between stealing and borrowing *on the reasonable assumption that permission would have been given*, the identification of the offender, signed statements taken in the absence of parents and later disputed, questions of *mens rea*, receiving *knowing the goods to have been stolen*, stealing *by finding*, or being concerned with others (in committing an offence), etc. These are only some of the most common instances in which the represented defendant has a much better chance of being found 'not guilty'. Very often the unrepresented child and his parents do not even know that he has a defence. It should be obvious that the Bench cannot, even under the specific provisions of the Rules, be expected to substitute adequately for professional representation on points such as these. It is probable also that professional representation of the child defendant has the effect of making the Bench more conscious of the possibility of an appeal against sentences which are 'disproportionate' in the sense implied by the Ingleby Committee. In short, it may rightly be thought that legal representation is in the interests of justice (as indeed it is intended to be) in the juvenile court as in any other.

As in the adult court, the defendant in the juvenile court is offered a choice between making a statement or giving evidence on oath. It is usually assumed that an adult is able to grasp the difference between the two procedures, but a child appears often not to have understood the implications even after the difference has been explained as clearly as is possible without appearing to be urging one course rather than the other. If the child chooses to make a statement he cannot be questioned on it, and although the Bench may ask him to repeat or amplify parts of it the result is often very inadequate as a defence or even an explanation. Neither the Bench nor the clerk must get into a position where they are in effect acting as an advocate for one side, i.e. the child; yet not the least of the difficulties is the fatal tendency of some children to assume that the court is already in full possession of all the facts and all he need do is to add a few rather irrelevant comments. It seems very doubtful indeed whether persons below the age of twelve or thirteen are all necessarily capable of properly and knowledgeably exercising this choice between making a statement or giving evidence on oath, and children sometimes unknowingly put themselves at considerable disadvantage by choosing to do the first, and then omitting to mention facts and topics which are vital to their defence.

The problem is how to get the significance of the difference across to the child. It sometimes helps to put the choice somewhat as follows. 'Now just listen again before choosing. The police officer has given us his side of the story on oath. Now it's your chance to tell us your side. You needn't say anything at all if you don't want to, or you can just say what you want from where you are standing now. If you do either of these nobody can ask you any questions. If you come over here as the police officer did and tell us your story on oath you can be asked questions just as he was. Whichever you do we have to decide afterwards who to believe, you or the police officer. *He gave his evidence on oath* and we were able to ask him questions. Which are you going to do?'

It is always worth while explaining to a child what is meant by swearing upon oath, and that the book he has in his hand is the Bible. From articles which appear in the press from time to time, it might be thought that among children generally there is an appreciable proportion who do not know what the Bible is, and have never heard of Our Lord. As far as children appearing in court are concerned, such cases seem to be so rare as to be almost non-existent. It is not quite so unusual to find a child within the age of criminal responsibility who cannot properly read. If he nevertheless understands the nature of an oath, and the meaning of telling the truth, he can repeat the oath phrase by phrase as it is read over to him by the clerk. It would be very ill-mannered of the Bench or their clerk to give the slightest sign of surprise or reproach at a witness's inability to read (e.g. 'Well, we are surprised, a big boy like you!'), and it is best to treat the matter easily as if it were quite usual and all in the day's work. As in the ordinary courts, the evidence of a child witness 'of tender years', who is thought not to understand the nature of an oath but to be sufficiently intelligent to understand the duty of speaking the truth, may be received in spite of not being given on oath. If for the prosecution it, must be corroborated in material particulars by some other evidence in support which implicates the accused.

It is sometimes felt that the system of asking witnesses to swear on oath is unsuitable for the juvenile court. Discussion around this point is frequently bedevilled by points which are in no way especially relevant to juvenile courts; for example, some people have a general objection – based on religious or other principles – to the procedure of swearing and the wording of the oath in any court at all. Such a general objection cannot reasonably be advanced in support of a contention that swearing should be abolished specifically in juvenile courts. The fact of the matter is that most of the witnesses in juvenile courts are adults, and no special difficulties would appear to arise out of the fact that they are being sworn or giving their evidence in a juvenile court. But, as far as juvenile witnesses are concerned, there are grounds for thinking that the ordinary procedure may not be suitable because of their intellectual limitations and emotional immaturity. The word 'swear', for instance, has inappropriate associations for most of the juveniles who appear in court, while it is most doubtful whether the term 'evidence' is understood by many children. The Ingleby Committee recommended that a simpler form of oath should be prescribed for children in all courts and also taken by adults who give evidence in juvenile courts. They suggested[4] that the oath might be – 'I promise before Almighty God to tell the truth, the whole truth, and nothing but the truth.' As a result it was provided under the Children and Young Persons Act, 1963, Section 28, that the words 'I promise before Almighty God' should replace the words 'I swear by Almighty God', when the oath is taken by any person in a juvenile court or by a child or young person in any court. No change was made in the remainder of the wording. Where either form is used instead of the other, as long as the oath was otherwise duly administered and taken, it shall in such circumstances 'nevertheless be deemed to have been duly administered and taken' (Section 28 (2)).

Another solution might have been to abolish the oath in juvenile courts altogether. This would appear to have its dangers, since some of the witnesses who most frequently appear to give evidence in juvenile courts also appear frequently in the adult courts, namely, the police. If such a change were made it would be a little difficult to see why it should be necessary for such witnesses to swear to the truth of their evidence in one summary court, if this were not necessary in another. If their evidence was to be regarded as of equal weight in both courts, why swear in either?

It sometimes happens that a child or young person – more usually a child – who has already made a statement admitting the offence, retracts all or part of this statement when the case comes before the court. Three eleven-year-old boys were charged with breaking and entering a certain warehouse and stealing some boxes containing roll film which they later threw unopened into the canal. All three had made statements admitting the charge to the police, but in court only one said the charge was true, while two said it was not. The charge related to an incident alleged to have happened well over three months previously, involving a particular warehouse similar in appearance to any one of a number of warehouses in various districts bordering on a canal. The two boys maintained on oath that although, along with the third defendant, they had been in the habit of playing near the canal and climbing about among the buildings, and although they had forced an entrance in several instances and had taken articles in boxes, some of which they later threw into the canal – yet they had never been in or near the particular district mentioned. They could not say whether any of the boxes they threw into the canal might or might not have contained roll film. On the subject of their signed statements they said they had thought the taking of the statements would be 'the end of it', so it hadn't been worth bothering about exactly what went in.

The third boy, after consulting his mother, had declined the invitation to reconsider his plea if he so wished, adding as he did so, 'Everything I said was true.' Nevertheless, as the clerk mentioned various detailed points, e.g. possession and use of a screwdriver, he equally emphatically denied a number of these. The only explanation of this discrepancy which the boy seemed able to offer was the cryptic one that 'those things aren't true but my statement was true'. Although it was said that this boy had actually identified the warehouse (after over half an hour's supervised searching up and down one stretch of the canal), in the circumstances the charges against all three were dismissed.

THE JUDGES' RULES AND THE
JUVENILE DEFENDANT

Children's minds do not appear to work in quite the same
way as those of adults. It is doubtful whether the caution
administered under the Judges' Rules conveys to them
what it is intended to convey. The further safeguard that,
where a statement has been taken down, the person making
it shall be asked to read it and to make whatever corrections,
alterations, or additions he wishes, does not always seem to
allow for a child's peculiar view as to what points matter and
what do not. From the court's point of view, a most valuable part of the Administrative Directions published with
the new Judges' Rules (1964) reads as follows: [5]

As far as practicable children (whether suspected of crime or
not) should only be interviewed in the presence of a parent or
guardian, or, in their absence, some person who is not a police
officer and is of the same sex as the child. A child or young person
should not be arrested, nor even interviewed, at school if such
action can possibly be avoided. Where it is found essential to
conduct the interview at school, this should be done only with the
consent, and in the presence of, the head teacher or his nominee.

These and other points are important not only to the
young defendants but also to the police, since no one wishes
to bring into court evidence which may fall apart. As any
teacher knows, the questioning of children is quite a skilled
job, and the taking of a voluntary statement which may be
used in evidence must be a task requiring very considerable
experience, patience, restraint, and understanding of the
child mind. It also requires a strong sense of justice if the
Judges' Rules are to be observed and a statement which is
both true and relevant obtained from the child without
what amounts to a cross-examination. It is a great tribute
to the ability and understanding of the police that events in
court so seldom take the course described above.

Very occasionally a child or a young person will say in
court that he was either threatened, hit, or shaken at the

police station in the course of questioning. This is always very disturbing, since, on the one hand, it is denied and therefore either the defendant or the prosecution witness must be lying, and, on the other, if such an incident did occur it might well be impossible to verify. Here again, the point is as important to the police witness as to the defendant or to the court. If there was no one else present with the defendant and himself when the incident is alleged to have occurred, the officer may be left with the feeling that though no attempt was made to prove the allegation, a suspicion which he has no way of counteracting may nevertheless linger in the minds of some of those present in court.

It may be felt that the whole procedure (by which the questioning of suspects and of persons in custody, and the treatment of accused persons at the police station, is regulated by Rules framed evidently with reference to adult citizens) is quite unsuited to the handling of children. It may be so, but if children's misdemeanours are to be dealt with by the courts (and, still more, by the police) at all they must be dealt with according to the provisions of the law. Possibly the best way of protecting child defendants, and people who have to do with them, against difficulties which may arise through their intellectual and emotional immaturity is to have the parent present, as is done in court for this and other reasons. This has obvious disadvantages in that the parent may be at work or otherwise difficult to contact without revealing the situation to outside parties. Sometimes, also, the attitude of a parent to the alleged commission of an offence leaves much to be desired before the court appearance, and there may in some instances be more chance of a child making a clean breast of the matter immediately he is tackled about it by the police than after consultation with the parent. This, it may be argued, is only similar to the situation of the adult who refuses to answer questions except in the presence of his solicitor, but it again points to the doubt as to whether these procedures related to the administration of justice in criminal cases are really appropriate to children at all.

EVIDENCE OF PARENTS IN CARE, PROTECTION, OR CONTROL PROCEEDINGS

It was suggested earlier in this chapter that the actual appearance before a well-run juvenile court and the procedure of trial itself is unlikely to do positive harm to any juvenile and might, indeed, do good. Before the Children and Young Persons Act, 1963, there were, however, two classes of case in which such a statement might well be untrue. These were where the juvenile was the subject of applications alleging that he was in need of care or protection, or else that he was out of his parents' control. In the first instance the case would be brought by the local authority, the N.S.P.C.C., or the police, and, as it was necessary to prove lack of proper guardianship, the juvenile who was the subject of the application was likely to hear very painful, unpleasant, and damaging statements made against his parents purporting to show that they were bad parents and did not look after him. It might be thought that, if matters had reached such a pass as to necessitate court action, nothing that was said would be news to the children or would be felt as hurtful by them. This was not so. Anyone working much in the courts is aware of the extraordinary tenacity with which children go on assuming that, underneath everything, they are loved by their parents and matter to them and that the parents themselves are lovable and trustworthy. Even the difficult adolescent girls or boys, who may themselves have done everything to justify a complete rejection by the parents, are often deeply ashamed, not about their own behaviour but about the implied relationship with the parents if these do not turn up at court; they seem to feel that whatever they themselves have done it could not explain or justify such a lack of interest. The parents, for their part, may have behaved in a way from which any reasonable adult would draw the conclusion that they cared little or nothing for their children, but this conclusion is not necessarily drawn by the children, particularly if the evidence is based upon such matters as poor school attendance, lack of suitable clothing and cooked meals, dirt and squalor in the home, no attempt to get work, arrears of rent, etc. There may be strong emotional ties between children and parents even if these are expressed without apparently involving the parents in exercising the most elementary foresight in making provision.

In cases where it was the parent who had initiated proceedings by bringing the boy or girl before the court as out of control, it was the parent who gave the main evidence. In these cases the boy or girl might have to listen to the parent denigrating him before strangers in very rejecting and hostile terms. This was not always so, since such a case might be brought by a widow or deserted wife who needed help in dealing with a son or daughter, did not know where else to go, and hoped to get a supervision order made. In these cases the evidence might often have been described as mournful rather than hostile in character, but it was still likely to come down to a recital of misdeeds. Possibly the most painful cases were those, fortunately few in number, in which the parent was determined to get rid of the boy or girl if at all possible, on any terms, and could not be stopped in time from saying such things as 'I don't care what happens to him, I don't ever want to see him again.' Sometimes, where the girl or boy had a good answer to all the allegations, the situation revealed might be such as would appear to justify care or protection proceedings, and such proceedings might later be instituted if the out-of-control case failed, though not, of course, by the parent.

It is difficult to know whether, or how much, emotional damage was caused to the subjects of such applications by the court situation itself and what it involved, but it is pleasant to record that, under the 1963 Act, it has now become possible to avoid such misery in many cases. What has now to be proved in care, protection, or control cases is not the unfitness of the parent in itself but that – whatever the quality of the guardianship the parents maintain that they are 'exercising' – the child or young person is nevertheless not *receiving* 'such care, protection and guidance as a good parent may reasonably be expected to give' (Section 2 (1) (*a*)). Similarly, the provision (Section 3) that the parent may no longer bring a juvenile before the court as out of his control, but must instead request the local authority to do so, has meant that the children's officer, having the parent's cooperation, can usually deal with the case without it coming before the court at all. In these cases recourse to the court is only necessary if powers additional to those already available by parental consent are needed in dealing with the refractory youngster, for example, committal to an approved school.

CHAPTER 7

AVOIDING THE STIGMA OF A CRIMINAL CONVICTION

ALTHOUGH the legal disqualifications attaching to a conviction for felony were removed under Section 100 of the Children Act, 1908, and a similar provision was made in the Children and Young Persons Act, 1933, it has not always proved possible to mitigate the social handicaps. In 1927 the Committee on Young Offenders noted that some juveniles were actually being placed on probation in quite unsuitable cases for the sole reason that the court would thereby be enabled to avoid proceeding to a conviction, but this possibility was removed in 1948, as already described. Since the Children and Young Persons Act, 1933, Section 59, it has been incorrect to refer to a finding of guilt in the juvenile court as a 'conviction', but the alteration of the technical wording has, as the Committee feared, done little to conceal the actual fact. If the defendant should appear in the courts on any further occasion before he is twenty-one years of age, the previous finding of guilt will probably form part of the answer to the question 'Any record?' before sentence is passed. If he applies for employment to some of the large employing bodies, he may be asked the direct question, possibly in writing, as to whether he has ever been found guilty of an offence in a criminal court. His alternatives are to lie, to admit, or to refuse to answer (much the same as admitting). The superintendent of a well-known remand home quite frequently receives telephoned inquiries direct from prospective employers asking for references in regard to his former residents.

All this is quite out of line with a realistic and balanced appreciation of the moral ups and downs which normally occur during the development of a young personality, or of the effects of an unhelpful environment in exposing a child to situations in which the risks of coming into conflict with the law are greatly increased. Even so, relatively very few children come before a court before the age of eleven or twelve, and, on the most pessimistic view, little harm could be done by delaying the use against a child of the machinery provided by the criminal law for the protection of the public against crime, until a rather later age. This is not to say that nothing whatever should be done by anyone outside the child's immediate family. The latter may themselves be at fault and the situation may be one calling for some outside intervention. But there is much to be said for exploring ways of dealing with the matter outside the penal system.

One way of avoiding the conviction of all but persistent offenders is provided by the juvenile liaison officer schemes now being operated by the police forces in a number of urban areas.

JUVENILE LIAISON OFFICER SCHEMES

This is an extension of police activities from the simple caution to a system which is intended to be a positive approach along preventive lines. A distinctive feature of the schemes is their recognition by the police forces concerned and by the Home Office.

Official recognition of schemes under which it is assumed that it is part of a policeman's duty to 'supervise' people – even people under seventeen – who have not been convicted of any offence might have been expected to arouse a certain amount of public uneasiness. Doubts have, indeed, been expressed by the Magistrates' Association from time to time, and the Ingleby Committee on Children and Young Persons, which reported in the autum of 1960, found itself 'unable to recommend that the Government should encourage their general adoption'. In a special article on delinquency prevention in *The Times* of 19 October 1961, Dr Gordon Rose referred to the courts and the probation services 'complaining . . . vehemently that their rights and duties are being infringed'. The truth is, however, that the comments of the Magistrates' Association have been extremely cautious, and the probation services, feeling themselves likely to be regarded as interested parties, have on most occasions refrained from public comment. However, the very existence of the schemes is unknown to most people and it is likely that those who are most familiar at first hand with their working, i.e. the parents of young offenders (for whom a court appearance is thus avoided), see the advantages very much more clearly than any objections in principle or potential dangers in practice.

The best known of the schemes is probably that which was started by the Liverpool police force in 1949 on the basis that the solution to the problem of juvenile delinquency lay in preventing its development rather than in improving the methods of dealing with the delinquent after conviction. The working of the scheme has been described in booklets issued from time to time. A liaison officer was appointed to each division. These officers were carefully selected and were to devote themselves entirely to the prevention of juvenile crime. They were to take no part in the normal procedure by which children caught by the police, or handed over to them after committing an offence, are dealt with. The official caution was to be administered in the ordinary way. Not until it had been decided (by the divisional superintendent) that there should be no prosecution, should the liaison officer, in suitable cases, step in.

In 1954, when particulars were circulated to the Central Conference of Chief Constables, the emphasis was on the liaison set up by each officer with schools, youth clubs, churches, businesses, parents of offenders, other children, and, in fact, everyone in close contact with children or in a position to observe and report signs of delinquent tendencies. Special study was made of places which appeared to offer a particular temptation to children. A major feature was the visiting of parents. In 1956 the method was referred to as 'a period of supervision on the child', and an example was given where this period was still continuing after

nine months. In October 1957 'supervision' appears to
have become a tainted word, and Sir Charles Martin,
originator of the scheme and Chief Constable of Liverpool,
was at pains to explain in a letter to the *Sunday Times* that
what another correspondent had referred to as 'supervision' was 'really a number of visits by a police officer to
the home of the child'.

The 1958 booklet issued by the Liverpool police force
reaffirms the category of children dealt with as those who
commit a minor first offence to which they admit, but on a
later page we learn that 'much of the work . . . is among
children who have not actually committed offences'. This
work, in which women members of the police force play
a major role, particularly concerns children who are out
of the control of their parents, or adolescents who are falling into bad associations or moral danger. These children
are by definition those for whom the plain caution is
thought to be not enough, though it could not be said that
in every case court proceedings would have followed a re-
fusal to accept supervision. The numbers dealt with by
those police forces with a formal scheme seem to be equal
to between fifty per cent and a hundred per cent of the
numbers brought before the juvenile court.

It is not known how many police forces have followed the
early examples of Birmingham, Leeds, Dudley, Hudders-
field, Birkenhead, Bradford, Blackpool, Bristol, North and
South Shields, and Greenock, and have themselves developed schemes more or less similar to the Liverpool
pattern. Such schemes do not need the formal approval of
the Home Office. It is known that some chief constables
simply do not wish to have a scheme while others take the
view, expressed by the Commissioner of Police for the
Metropolis in evidence before the Ingleby Committee, that
the clear intention of Parliament, as expressed in the
Children and Young Persons Act, 1933, 'was to provide in
the juvenile court system a means of dealing with young
offenders in the interests of their own welfare and in a way
that would prevent them from taking to a life of crime'. It

would be wrong, they argue, for the police, however coura-geous and good their intentions, to withdraw some children from the operation of the system to be dealt with in a different way.

Each scheme has its characteristic features – the specially chosen full-time officers in plain clothes in Liverpool; the sergeants and inspectors in Birmingham in their ordinary uniform making 'casual' visits to only one or two cases; and, in some areas, the clubs or recreational evenings run by the police. In other areas there is pressure for a police representative on the committee of each of the local boys' clubs; in other areas, again, the distinctive feature is the way supervision is exercised – the child may visit the police station instead of the officer visiting the home.

Each of the schemes acts as a preliminary sieve to the juvenile court; they should not be looked at simply as a displacement of the probation officer. In one sense the system is one of trial by inquiry instead of prosecution and defence, with the police acting as judge and prosecutor, hearing the evidence, deciding on the guilt, and making the order. In this way, however, they do by-pass the probation officers and any other professional experts who might assess the child's needs before an order is made by the juvenile court, and in supervising they again do the job which would presumably otherwise be done by the probation officer.

A case may be argued for doing away with the system of criminal trial for children, but the question remains whether the police force is the agency best suited to take the place of the courts. The Ingleby Committee gave no more than a glance at this particular solution and instead suggested a civil jurisdiction for all children below the age of twelve. This is interesting, because one of the advantages urged for the schemes is that they also avoid the stigma of a criminal conviction for the child, though it is, of course, far from clear that no stigma attaches to having been 'supervised' by the police after admitting an offence.

Among other claims made for the schemes is that they have everywhere had a good reception and this is certainly true of the press reports.[1] They are said to have been particularly well received by the multiple store managers and the schools. Store managers are said to be reporting far more cases of theft because the child will no longer 'get away with it' through the alleged leniency of the juvenile court and they themselves are not put to the expense of sending a witness to waste a morning in court; and, on the other hand, they can report children to the police knowing that this no longer means that they have been the cause of a child incurring a criminal conviction. Schoolmasters apparently punish children at the instance of the police for offences outside the school, and call the officer in to deal with offences which have taken place inside the school; indeed, 'it is now the practice for the liaison officer to follow classes from one school to another, and when a class transfers . . . he explains to them that a higher standard of behaviour is now expected . . . .'[2] The police officers are said to have an advantage over probation officers in that they can go into districts where no one else would dare to go and can enter houses which would be closed to other people. They are said not to overlap with the probation service since they retire in the few cases in which they find that the probation officer is already 'in' the home. The police claim upwards of ninety per cent success and compare this with the sixty-five per cent or so success in probation and with the fact that about forty per cent of children appearing before the juvenile court as first offenders are subsequently reconvicted.

On the other hand, the schemes raise certain problems. There is a difficulty in deciding how an offender's previous encounters with the police should be referred to in court (and the figure of ninety per cent success is sometimes difficult to reconcile with the incidence of such references in juvenile court business). If they are referred to, they should, of course, be put to the offender and either admitted or denied, but this is not always done. The writer has also seen cases where a written report contained a list of previous offences, one of which was 'larceny [date]' with a note of the 'sentence' as 'police supervision'. On another occasion the list included an 'offence' of larceny with the outcome shown as 'case dismissed'! On a further occasion the body of a report contained a remark that the offender had been 'placed under police supervision for larceny' and in reply to a question from the court it was stated that 'he was placed under supervision by the chief constable – he has powers, you know'. If this kind of muddled thinking can flourish among people who have had at least some experience in legal matters and are constantly in touch with the courts, it is not surprising if it is sometimes assumed by untrained people that the position and powers of the police are something other than what in fact they are in this country. It has not been part of the function of our police to take part in the actual punishment or other treatment of offenders. This principle may perhaps be regarded as having been infringed by the setting up of police-run attendance centres for the punishment of the ten- to seventeen-year age group (under the Criminal Justice Act, 1948, as amended by the Criminal Justice Act, 1961). The senior attendance centre at Manchester for young adults is staffed not by police but by prison officers. A second senior centre, opened in London in 1964, is, however, run by the police.

One wonders why the police, especially those forces which are under strength, should want to run such schemes. It is not known, and, in the fluctuating conditions of crime and the difficulty of validating and comparing statistics, it cannot be known with certainty, how the schemes affect the incidence of juvenile delinquency. The success rate means little, since those 'supervised' are a highly selected group not thought to need court action. Moreover, in spite of their large numbers, their absence from court has apparently left the reconviction rate for the court group – now presumably containing the more hardened characters only – unchanged, or at any rate not demonstrably different from areas where there are no schemes and children are more commonly brought before the court. The probation officers do an immense amount of voluntary work in the shape of un-official supervision where families are getting into difficul-ties, but only at the pressing request of the parents and not as the alternative to a court appearance. The shortage of pro-bation officers is not the reason, since schemes are run in areas which are just as short of police. Incidentally, one might have thought that the police would glean a great deal of useful information from such a wide network of contacts in areas of high delinquency; but this does not appear, in fact, to be the case.

Some senior police officers, and here perhaps we come to the heart of the phenomenon, see the schemes as a public relations exercise. In country and small urban areas, casual supervision of known bad risks among both children and adults goes on as a matter of course all the time. The village constable is accepted for what he traditionally is. In densely populated urban areas, the police activity which probably makes the most favourable impact on the public mind, and more especially the juvenile mind, is the traffic and safety lecture in the secondary schools. Here the officer presents himself and is accepted by the children as a per-son who looks after you, finds you when you are lost, takes you across the road, breaks the news of your accident gently to your family, and finds and restores your lost dog. He is, by definition, kind, fatherly, and protective. It is this pic-ture which the police force hopes to carry right into the homes, especially in the fight against crime, so that children and their parents come to see the police as friends who, offering help and guidance, deserve loyalty and support. The schemes are said to be of great help in this important uphill work and particularly valuable in fixing the police-man's idea of himself and his protective role in society.

The cost of training a probation officer is above £1,000 and it would be absurd to maintain that police officers selected for quite another purpose can do the same job with no training at all. However, with a case-load maxi-mum as high as Liverpool's has been (of 150 per officer) and a contact which lasts only for three or four months, it seems obvious that the police are not attempting to do the work of a trained social worker. They may, and do, fail to diagnose deep-rooted personality disturbances showing themselves through the delinquent symptom. The probation officer is also likely to have some people on his case-load who obtain all they need from one straight talk and a weekly 'chat'. In a large number of other cases he will have advised the court that probation is unnecessary as the offender is unlikely to reappear. But the probation officer may say, in other cases, that fuller reports are needed before any opinion as to the future can be given. It is a tragedy if many – or indeed any – children whose circumstances contain the seeds of persistent criminality or real distress of other kinds are deprived of the chance of early diagnosis and trained help. Delinquency is only one of the problems faced by many families and it is essential that social workers who have personal contact with families should, as often as possible, be trained workers if problems are not to be perpetuated. The probation officer leaves his probationer not just less inclined to criminality (though this is of obvious importance) but with greater self-awareness, more control of his own behaviour, and more understanding of his own social surroundings. With luck, he will also be better understood by his family, and will emerge to some extent a new person. The hope is that his development has been encouraged and guided in a steady and sometimes even close relationship with someone who uses to the best advantage his or her specialist training.

The plain answer given by the police to the simple question of what they have that the probation service has not is 'Authority' – and this is true as far as the child's view goes, however slender the basis for this proposition may be in law. The probation officer's role is seen generally as educative and therapeutic; that of the policeman as authoritarian. No attempt has yet been made to face squarely the difficulty of reconciling the therapeutic and authoritarian roles in the same police figure.

It may be remembered that the Committee on Social Services in Courts of Summary Jurisdiction, which reported in 1936, laid it down that the statement of antecedents given by the police would not be a sufficient substitute for the probation officer's home inquiry, even if the police had visited the home. The approach is that of two different professions serving different purposes and each is, in the court situation, complementary to and not interchangeable with the other. A quarter of a century's further experience led the Streatfeild Committee, which reported in 1961,[3] to the same conclusion.

The police supervision schemes are no rival to the probation service, and they may well seem to undermine the intentions of Parliament in regard to the provisions relating to the juvenile court, for they cut straight across the importance normally attached to such matters as adversary procedure, the presumption of innocence, the rules of evidence, the Judges' Rules, the public court, and the protective presumption of *doli incapax*. They may tend to blur in the minds of the police the limitations on their own powers and functions. It will be interesting to see what happens if the age of criminal responsibility is raised to twelve or sixteen and offenders below such an age are dealt with under a civil jurisdiction, when much of the alleged *raison d'être* of the schemes will disappear.

OTHER SUGGESTIONS FOR AVOIDING THE STIGMA OF CONVICTION

Other solutions to this difficult problem have been advanced and have proved popular in some quarters. One[4] was that the criminal jurisdiction of the juvenile court should be completely done away with and replaced by a 'jurisdiction of guardianship'. Raising the age of criminal responsibility automatically does this for those who fall below the new age, if by a jurisdiction of guardianship is meant the procedure for dealing with children in need of care, protection, or control under the civil jurisdiction of the court. The Ingleby Committee recommended along these lines that the minimum age of criminal responsibility should be raised to twelve and, possibly at some future date, thirteen or fourteen. But in the event this recommendation was not acted upon by Parliament, and Section 16 of the Children and Young Persons Act, 1963, raised the age only to ten.

However, the civil procedure for bringing to court children who are out of the control of their parents has been available in suitable cases since the Children and Young Persons Act, 1933, Section 64, though, under the Children and Young Persons Act, 1933, Section 3, it is now the local authority and not the parent who brings the child before the court. In fact, a persistent offender of any age up to seventeen can be brought before the juvenile court under the civil jurisdiction as out of control and, if the allegations are proved, found to be in need of care, protection, and control regardless of the quality of guardianship he is receiving. Alternatively, if proceedings are brought under the criminal jurisdiction of the court and there is a finding of guilt, a 'fit person' order instead of a penal order may be made precisely as might have been done in civil proceedings. In practice, however, neither the civil action nor the attempt to obtain a 'fit person' order under the criminal jurisdiction is useful, for obvious reasons, except in the case of fairly persistent offenders. It is, in any event, far from clear that proceedings which involve proof of offences, even in a 'guardianship' court, would carry no stigma.

Another solution, which has been advanced by John Watson, J.P.,[5] and was also put forward by the late Sir Basil Henriques, J.P., another magistrate of immense experience, was that, where a child subsequently behaves well over a given period, the record of any earlier conviction should be wiped out. This point was put to the Ingleby Committee by several witnesses. One of the most serious criticisms of any system of expunging records, if it meant that these would not be available to the court in the event of any future offence, is that it negates the whole idea that the court needs to know as much as possible about the offender before it if the right measures are to be applied. The Committee make this point in their Report and also that any social handicap 'does not arise from entries in police or other records, but from the facts . . . employers . . . seek for such information as they want by asking the applicant himself and his referees'. There is much common sense behind their conclusion: 'Any substantial alteration in nomenclature may lead to a change in the formulation of questions'[6] and they made no recommendation. It seems, however, that parliament did not entirely agree with this reasoning and under Section 16 (2) of the Children and Young Persons Act, 1963, it is now provided that, in proceedings after the age of twenty-one, findings of guilt under the age of fourteen are to be disregarded 'for the purposes of any evidence relating to his previous convictions; and he shall not be asked, and if asked shall not be required to answer, any question relating to such an offence, notwithstanding that the question would otherwise be admissible under Section 1 of the Criminal Evidence Act, 1898'.

It must have become abundantly clear to the reader, from the points raised in the foregoing pages, that the whole subject of how to deal with the criminality of children needs to be discussed in a much wider context than that of the courts if it is to be seen in its true perspective, and if some of the more obvious difficulties are to be avoided. In the meantime it should be remembered that a very considerable amount of advice and voluntary supervision of children is given to families by probation officers at the direct request of parents, and they may also have occasion to refer such parents or their children to other advisory and treatment services. In addition, although the age of criminal responsibility was raised only to ten, and not to twelve as recommended by Ingleby, the Home Office, when bringing the provisions of the 1963 Children and Young Persons Act into operation, suggested[7] to police forces that they should make arrangements for informal consultation with the children's department of the local authority before they institute criminal proceedings against any person under twelve years of age, or in any case where they have reason to suppose that the local authority or a voluntary organization are doing preventive work with the child's family (in view of the duty laid upon local authorities by Section 1 of the Act to do preventive work to avoid the necessity of bringing children before the juvenile court). It is most unfortunate that this suggestion has not so far led to the anticipated results, owing to the lack in many areas of trained staff available for such work and of the social services they would need to have at their disposal.

A later suggestion was embodied in a government White Paper 'The Child, the Family and the Young Offender', published in August 1965,[8] and intended 'for the purposes of discussion before legislation is prepared'. Here the proposal was that the great majority of offenders below the age of sixteen should be dealt with outside the courts altogether. These would be the children who, with their parents, were prepared to follow advice and accept treatment under the provisions of the social and educational services. Where parents or child were uncooperative, an action might be brought before a proposed 'family court'. These matters will be referred to more fully in later pages.

CHAPTER 8

THE FINDING AND THE ORDER

WHEN a hearing in the juvenile court reaches the point at which the court must consider its verdict, it becomes important to remember once again that these courts were not set up on any different principles from the adult courts. The reader may be reminded that, after reviewing the experience of nearly twenty years, the Committee on the Treatment of Young Offenders reported (1927) that, although they had considered whether or not any change should be made in the fundamental legal principles underlying the juvenile court, they had come to the conclusion that no such change should be recommended. This is still the position today. As in the case of a defendant in the adult court, therefore, the defendant charged with an offence in the juvenile court is there, not simply because his behaviour is regarded as anti-social or he himself is looked upon as a generally unsatisfactory person, but because it is alleged that he has done something which is against the law. It is this which must be conclusively shown by the evidence if there is to be a finding of guilt.

NOT A COURT OF MORALS

Even this elementary principle may be the cause of confusion to a child. It has often been pointed out that the courts of justice are not courts of morals and that immoral or anti-social behaviour does not necessarily constitute an unlawful act. On 4 February 1956 the Lord Chief Justice, giving a judgment in the Divisional Court in the case of *Moynes* v. *Coopper*,[1] is reported in *The Times* as having said 'that while the defendant was guilty of grave dishonesty in their Lordships' opinion he was not guilty of any criminal offence'. This distinction is one which is not always easy for a child to grasp. One may wonder what is the effect upon a child's developing moral sense of a case such as the following.

An eleven-year-old boy, loitering one night in the deserted car park of a greyhound-racing stadium, picked up a dilapidated cigarette carton. This proved to contain not the hoped-for cigarettes but two one-pound notes and a ten-shilling note. Hundreds of people, many of whom had come long distances, had been in the car park. The carton, being very light, was being blown along the ground when picked up and may well not have been dropped in the car park originally at all. The boy gave one of the pound notes to a nine-year-old friend. The ten shillings was spent on candies, jointly consumed, after which the boys buried the two pound notes for the night in some allotments near their home.

At school next day a pound note was found in the playground during the mid-morning break and handed in to the head teacher. A little later the eleven-year-old boy appeared before the head teacher to claim the money. On being questioned as to how such a large sum had come into his possession, he at first told several obvious lies, and finally the police were informed.

In court both sides were legally represented. The head teacher told the court that she had questioned the boy for a considerable time before getting him to admit that he 'had done something wrong'. The general tone of her evidence left the court with the impression that for some reason she had at once suspected that the boy had come by the money dishonestly. She said that she had not been surprised that he had made no effort to report the find, but was, in fact, only anxious to conceal it.

The boy himself appeared to have no doubt that he should have told somebody about his find. He knew the money was not his and that it must have belonged to someone, and he had not stopped to consider whether it would or would not be possible to find the owner. His nine-year-old friend went farther and agreed that they had buried the money to avoid discovery. On being asked from whom they wished to hide it, however, he replied engagingly, 'From our mums; we didn't want them to get it' – a very reasonable reply.

In the end the case turned on whether it could reasonably have been believed that the owner could have been found and whether the boys had thought so. After much legal argument on both sides the case was dismissed – to the evident astonishment of the two boys – on the ground that the charge of stealing by finding had not been proved. The magistrates discussed the feasibility of a chat with the two boys so as to be able to leave them with the feeling that an honest person who picks something up will usually attempt to find the owner. However, in view of the possibility of an appeal by the prosecution, and on the advice of the clerk, nothing further was said. It is difficult to imagine what the boys could make of the distinction between the moral code of their schoolteacher and the position in law.

SOCIAL NEEDS NOT NECESSARILY IN PROPORTION TO CRIMINALITY

In other cases the children concerned may be in considerable social need of some kind or other, and if there is a finding that the alleged offences are proved, these social needs will be borne in mind when the appropriate order is being considered. The probation officer or child-care officer who prepared the report on the home background may be confidently expecting that, as a result of the appearance in the juvenile court, little Johnny will at last be removed from his undesirable surroundings and given the benefits of proper provision for his education and training in an approved school. But first there must be a finding of guilt, and this will not be arrived at in our courts merely on the ground that to do so would enable the court to cause the defendant to receive suitable treatment. If the guilt is not in the evidence, the charges will not be found proved and no order can be made, since it is a major feature of the criminal jurisdiction that it protects the innocent not only from punishment but also from compulsory treatment of any kind. But the Committee on Young Offenders found that, even in countries where the trial of young people for offences was separated from criminal jurisdiction, the offences had nevertheless in most instances to be proved. They had noted the situation in New Zealand, where the statute provided that the court need not hear and determine the charge, but might proceed to act 'after taking into consideration the parentage of the child, its environment, history, education, mentality, and other relevant matter'. The Committee had decided that this example was not to be followed and in their Report took, instead, the line that the action of a court in dealing with delinquents must be based on the offence, and offences must therefore be proved.

It might be thought that, in cases of social need, it must always be possible to bring care, protection, or control proceedings and in this way to achieve the removal of the child from home. The provisions of Section 2 (1) (a) of the Children and Young Persons Act, 1963, have eased the way, in that the complainant is no longer faced with having to prove that the parent or guardian is unfit or unable to exercise or is not exercising proper guardianship but only with the lighter task of showing that the child or young person is in fact not *receiving* such care. Nevertheless, it is sometimes very difficult to prove the case in these proceedings. Unless the child or young person can simply be shown to be beyond control, the complainant must show two things. He must show first, that lack of parental care and guidance is likely to cause the child unnecessary suffering or to seriously affect his health or proper development; or that he is falling into bad associations or is exposed to moral danger; or that he is the victim of a First Schedule offence or is a member of the same household as a person convicted of such offence against a juvenile in the same household; or that, if a female, she belongs to a household of which a

member has committed or attempted an offence under
Section 10 of the Sexual Offences Act, 1956 (incest by a
man); and, *in addition*, it must be shown that the child is not
receiving such care, protection, and guidance as a good
parent may reasonably be expected to give.

Some people think that it should not be necessary thus
to have to prove two allegations. For instance, it was
suggested in the Memorandum of Evidence submitted by
the Magistrates' Association to the Ingleby Committee in
1958[2] that, where it is shown conclusively that a juvenile is
in moral danger or is falling into bad associations, it could
be and it ought to be presumed that he or she is without
proper care and guardianship. Similarly, it is felt that,
where a child has been the victim of an incestuous relationship with her father, the court ought to be able to presume
by that fact that she is in need of care, protection, or
control.

Against these suggestions, it must be admitted that most
people whose work brings them into much contact with the
courts have knowledge of cases where such presumptions
would not have been justified. The mother of the victim of
incest may have had no means of knowing that such a thing
was going on and may be perfectly capable of looking after
her small daughter while the father serves a prison sentence. It can by no means always be assumed that a girl
who has been indecently assaulted on the way home from
school was necessarily not receiving such care, protection,
and guidance as a good parent may reasonably be expected
to give. In cases of rape, also, the happening could not
always have been foreseen by the parents or envisaged as
likely, and in many such cases no ordinary parent could,
before the occurrence, have been expected to take any steps
in care or guardianship of their child other than those
which were in fact taken.

The procedure suggested by the Ingleby Committee[3]
included the obtaining of proof that the child or young
person 'needs care, protection, treatment, control, or discipline which is likely to be rejected or unobtainable except

by order of a court'. The difficulty of proving such a probability except by reference to the past or present situation is obvious, and it is doubtful whether any real change in the burden of proof could have been brought about by this means.

As the law stands at present it is, except in cases of offenders or juveniles beyond control, necessary to prove that good parental guardianship is not being received, as a separate issue, before the court can take away the parental rights. The law assumes that the boy (or girl) is receiving guardianship until it is conclusively proved that he is not.

If the law were changed in this respect, then the onus of proof might no longer be on the prosecution but on the parents if they wished it to be accepted that they were not, by inference, at fault. There might often be difficulty in producing evidence to the satisfaction of a court which was in the position of being wise after the event. It does not follow, of course, that, where it was not possible to produce such evidence, the boy or girl would necessarily be removed from home or that the court would make a 'fit person' order, and it may well be that, in most of the instances in which such proceedings are brought, the advice, assistance, and friendship of a probation or child-care officer under a supervision order would be of great benefit.

If such a change in the law as envisaged did come about, and more especially if it were accompanied by an extension of this jurisdiction, the definition of the phrases 'in moral danger' and 'falling into bad associations' would be doubly important. They might need to be defined more clearly if, with no need for lack of guardianship to be proved, the courts were to have power to remove young people (possibly up to eighteen years of age) from home on finding such allegations proved.

There are other cases where children, living with parents who are mentally unbalanced, are thought to be suffering harm although there is no actual ill-treatment or neglect. These are not cases which fail through inadequate evidence so much as cases where it is difficult to find grounds for bringing proceedings at all, and where different departments of the local authority or different social agencies may well hold divergent views.

In spite of the frustrations which may result, most people who have to do with courts of justice would agree that, whatever the charges or allegations on which even a juvenile is brought into court, these ought to be proved to the satisfaction of the court before they are regarded as justifying compulsory treatment of any kind. Once a finding has been made, however, the scope for disagreement is much greater. Widely differing views are held upon the relation, if any, which ought to exist between the gravity of the defendant's offence and record and the weight or otherwise of the subsequent order.

Some rather indirect guidance on the subject is offered by the law in, for example, the provision that the court must not make orders for punitive detention unless it has first considered every other method of dealing with the offender (except imprisonment) and found them all inappropriate. But, in contrast, a juvenile offender may be sent to an approved school on the commission of a first offence if it is an offence for which an adult could be imprisoned, e.g. larceny, while, on the other hand, an offender with a long record may, as in the ordinary court, be put on probation for the umpteenth time if the court thinks fit.

The juvenile defendant's own view of the probabilities is strictly related to legal justice as he sees it. He seems to have a scale running from a fine on his first appearance through probation to a period in a remand home or detention centre and finally one in an approved school. In the remand home there is considerable discussion about the place of individuals on this scale. The discussion is realistic; the forecasts err on the gloomy side. There is usually no suggestion, certainly none among the younger boys, that any considerations other than justice on the one hand and mercy on the other enter into the decision. The different possibilities are seen in terms of different degrees of punishment.

The clerk to the court, too, has something similar in mind, but in a more modified form, with 'justice' setting the limits of 'welfare' as it were, and a strong leaning towards equality of treatment for the same offence.

The door to inequality of treatment is, however, fairly opened to the Bench by Section 44 of the Children and Young Persons Act, 1933, namely, 'Every court . . . shall have regard to the welfare of the child.' The Section continues: 'and shall in a proper case take steps for removing him from undesirable surroundings, and for securing that proper provision is made for his education and training.' It is for the court, however, to decide what is a proper case. On the one hand, there are the nature of the charge and the defendant's record and, on the other, the undesirability of his surroundings.

JUSTICE AND WELFARE IN SENTENCING

The main question at issue, however, is not that of equality or inequality of treatment for the same offence, which is only part of a general question common to all courts of justice. The main question is that of the function of the juvenile court in making an order. According to some views the correct interpretation of Section 44 is that it indicates that justices in the juvenile court have a different function from that which they have when sitting in the adult court. It is thought that a justice sitting in the juvenile court has, in addition to or instead of his ordinary function, a 'welfare' function which operates, so to speak, as soon as a finding is reached. From then on the welfare of the defendant is the primary or only consideration in making the order and therefore the offence itself may for practical purposes be ignored. There need, for instance, be no relation between the weight of the order and the nature or seriousness of the offence and record. This view is well put by Dr J. D. W. Pearce in his book *Juvenile Delinquency*:[4] 'This Act [the Children and Young Persons Act, 1933] laid down clearly that the welfare of the child or young person is the first consideration.'

Other people interpret Section 44 as meaning only that 'the welfare of the child or young person', etc., shall be kept in mind when the Bench is reviewing the methods of disposal which are appropriate to a particular case. C. J. Collinge, M.A., J.P., then Chief Clerk of the Metropolitan Juvenile Courts, states:

This Section is often cited as the corner stone of English juvenile court law, yet it contained nothing that was new to the practice of the courts . . . [which] . . . were already accustomed to have regard to the welfare of the offender, whether adult or juvenile. Nor does it [the section] require the court to have regard only to welfare, or even to regard welfare as the paramount consideration (as does a parallel provision in the Guardianship of Infants Act). The importance of Section 44 is that it recognizes, and gives the force of law to, a principle which was already widely accepted, and that its explicit statement of that principle is a perpetual reminder to the courts of their duty in this matter.[5]

Justices taking this view would probably not describe their function in the juvenile court as being concerned exclusively, or even primarily, with the defendant's general welfare but – as in the ordinary court – with the protection of the public against crime. Justices holding such a view would nevertheless usually be the first to agree that in dealing with a young offender this function involves his reclamation. This involves having regard to his welfare and to his need for proper education and training if he is to be turned from his criminality and prevented from developing further delinquent tendencies. But the Bench's interest in the defendant's welfare, in their capacity as magistrates, is related to his delinquency. It is only this which empowers them to interfere in his affairs at all and, if the delinquency is a first offence of a very trivial kind, justices thinking along these lines would not regard themselves as authorized thereby to make any very drastic order. The extent of a young defendant's needs on the welfare side and the degree of radical action required to meet these needs do not necessarily bear any relation to the gravity or heinousness of his offence – or indeed to his offence at all. The existence of the two views outlined above means therefore that, even though the justices have had the benefit of expert opinion about the nature of the defendant and his needs before making an order, the kind of recommendations which would involve serious interference with personal liberty, or the gravity of which appear disproportionate in relation to the triviality of the offence or the record, may be acceptable to some justices and not to others.

It must be admitted that the functions which the juvenile courts as at present constituted are to fulfil – in so far as these are to be deduced from the various acts, rules, recommendations of royal commissions and departmental committees, Home Office circulars advising on the qualifications and training thought desirable for justices serving on the juvenile court panel, etc. – are far from clear. As a result, the degree to which the juvenile court regards its function as being related to the child's delinquency, or to every aspect of his welfare, seems to vary from court to court.

These two different views as to the proper function of the justices in the juvenile courts have been stated in an over-simplified form and pushed to extremes for the sake of making a clear distinction between them. It is nevertheless not at all difficult to find among justices, as also among the general public, people representing each of these viewpoints roughly in the form outlined.

Whatever view the justices take as to the nature and scope of their function in making an order in the juvenile court, they must follow the procedure laid down under Rule 11 of the Summary Jurisdiction (Children and Young Persons) Rules, 1933. Where the child or young person is found guilty of an offence, whether this is after a plea of guilty or not, both the defendant and his parent must be given an opportunity of making a statement before the order is made. In districts where it is the custom for the inquiries about the defendant's school record and home surroundings (in pursuance of Section 35 of the Act) to be made before the trial has taken place, the reports on these inquiries will be produced to the court immediately after the finding. In that event the members of the Bench will read the reports either at once or after hearing anything the offender or his parent may wish to say at that stage, and then discuss with them any points arising.

THE PURPOSE OF THE REMAND PERIOD

If such inquiries have not already taken place it will probably be necessary to adjourn the case for further inquiries, under Rule 11 in the case of an offender or under Rule 21 if the juvenile has been the subject of an application. The court is obliged, excepting only in cases of offence which appear to be of a trivial nature, to

obtain such information as to the general conduct, home surroundings, school record, and medical history of the child or young person as may enable it to deal with the case in his best interests, and shall if such information is not fully available consider the desirability of remanding the child or young person for such inquiry as may be necessary.

In the case of an offender the remand may be for any period up to three weeks and may be in custody. If the remand is in custody, the court will have the advantage of the superintendent's observations in addition to any other reports, and arrangements can be made for special examinations by psychiatrists, educational psychologists, and doctors, if such are felt to be necessary.

Where reports under Section 35 are available to the court immediately after a finding, the court may or may not think that still further information is necessary before they can decide on what order should be made. Whether they do remand for further reports will depend upon the nature of the information they have already obtained from the evidence during the trial, from parent or defendant in their statements after the finding, from the reports already supplied, and from the police record of previous offences. It will also depend upon the view the justices take as to the seriousness of particular offences or the significance of any of the information which they may have been given. The probation officer's report is often of crucial importance, as, for example, in a case where a youth was found guilty of a homosexual offence against a four-year-old child. There was no previous record of any kind. The boy's personal character and school report were good, and he was deeply ashamed of his offence. The child's doctor had felt it his duty to write to the public prosecutor to point out that the contact had been very brief indeed and that in his firm opinion the child would suffer no lasting physical or psychological damage of any kind. The probation officer, however, in his report on the home background, described what appeared to him to be signs, especially in the relationship between father and son, of gross maladjustment in the latter, possibly indicating a deeply disturbed personality, which might lead to serious trouble in the future. He strongly recommended a remand in custody for full investigation and reports.

It must never be forgotten that a remand in custody is a deprivation of liberty. A person cannot legally be remanded as a punishment, but as far as a young offender, especially a child, is concerned the reason for the remand does not greatly affect the nature of his experience of it as a deprivation of liberty. The point is obvious to common sense where the remand home is also used for detention as a punishment, under Section 54, especially if the few boys in residence for that purpose are under a régime differing little if at all from that for the boys remanded by the court for reports. However well run the remand home may be, however well fed the boys, however imaginatively work and leisure are organized, most boys prefer to be at home. The shiny corridors, the suitable pictures, the tidy airy dormitories, the large rooms, the central heating, the excellent ventilation, the general cleanliness – in fact, the whole pattern of regulated living – strike a note which is unfamiliar in relation to the home life of the boys. A good superintendent and staff can do a great deal on the side of personal contact with their charges to compensate in some ways for the sudden deprivation of familiar things, but it is not the same as home.

Some remand home superintendents think that three weeks, the maximum period for which a court may remand an offender without a further appearance in court, is not long enough for observations on which to base reports which may seriously affect the whole future of a young delinquent. One solution might be to raise the maximum period to four or six weeks and fix a minimum period of three weeks. Against this it may be argued that, since further remands for continued observation are in fact seldom asked for, it is reasonable to suppose that the proportion of cases in which the longer period would be thought to be needed is very small. In those few instances reasons for a further remand can, and perhaps ought to, be given at a court appearance. An argument against a fixed minimum period of three weeks is that, as many courts are at present in the habit of remanding for a week or a fortnight only (although it is open to them to remand for three weeks), it looks as though the fixed minimum suggested might tend to deter some conscientious magistrates from remanding children in custody at all.

It is said, reasonably enough, that the doctor, psychiatrist, psychologist, etc., cannot hope to assess a boy on one interview. However, it is often the case at present that even where a boy is remanded for the full three weeks in custody he is still seen only once by each of the experts, although these may be paying weekly visits to the home. There would be little case for longer remands unless these were accompanied by a more intensive supply of expert services. Doubtless the superintendents, too, would have a better chance of making a more exact assessment over a longer period, but this could in a sense be argued however much the period was extended, and there seems to be no consensus of opinion at present as to what the optimum period would be. In passing, it may be remarked that it is not clear why the maximum period for a remand should be one week less than, or indeed different at all from, the four-week period provided for an interim order in a civil case. But the new remand centres may eventually provide more adequate facilities in some respects for observation and diagnosis, and it seems likely that, the longer the period of remand demanded, the greater the hesitation some magistrates may feel in remanding in custody, except where the offence is serious, or the record long, or the indications of personality difficulties related to the delinquency are very marked.

In urban areas, where comparatively adequate psychiatric, psychological, and medical services are available in connexion with the schools service, it might be thought that it should not be necessary to remand in custody at all unless the superintendent's report is considered particularly relevant, e.g. where institutional treatment is being considered. It is, however, administratively convenient since the offender will at least be available for examination when required. Though some courts would be glad for an offender to undergo prolonged observation and thorough investigation by a psychiatrist, which is seldom possible at present, most experienced Benches tend in any event to rely heavily upon the superintendent's observations for an assessment of the offender's personality, and a prognosis as to his future development, whether he appears to be suitable for institutional treatment or not.

It is probable that a child hardly ever – and a young person not always – understands the procedure of remand. Some children seem to think that it is the police who get them put into the remand home, merely passing them through the court as a matter of form *en route* so to speak, and that being sent to the remand home is a form of punishment. Where the children act out their own experiences with puppets, etc., it is not unusual to hear the puppet policeman shouting such threats as 'I'll send you to the remand home', or 'You'll have to go to the remand home if I catch you again.' Others grasp that it is not intended as a punishment (whatever it may feel like) but seem to regard it as a sort of trial run, so that if they behave well over the period they may escape a further spell and be allowed home – a sort of indeterminate sentence. Unfortunately the relation between 'good' and 'bad' behaviour at the remand home and a subsequent order based on treatment needs is not always very obvious to the offender. The 'good' behaviour may serve to show how well he would respond to treatment in an approved school, and some forms of 'bad' behaviour may be seen as indicating a deep insecurity requiring a long period of probation while the probation officer works intensively with both boy and family. Few seem to grasp the idea that the remand is an honest attempt by the court to find out what sort of person the defendant is, and that this is done with a view to treatment of a helpful kind, and not as a punishment.

RECEIVING REPORTS IN THE JUVENILE COURT

The same Rule (number eleven) regulates the procedure under which the juvenile court receives reports, whether these are the reports on the home background and the school record offered under Section 35, or the further reports obtained after remand under the provisions of the Magistrates' Courts Act, 1952. It is not the court which takes the initiative in deciding that reports under Section 35 should be obtained, but when these are produced the court is obliged under Rule eleven to receive them and to take them into consideration. Perhaps the most controversial provision under this Rule is Section iv, referred to previously, which provides that any written report, either of a probation officer, local authority, or registered medical practitioner, may be received and considered by the court without being read aloud. As a result of this provision, practice varies from court to court. In some courts, for example, the probation officer gives his own report verbally, after being sworn, while in others he is not sworn. In others, again, he or another probation officer hands in a written report, and it is read aloud word for word by the clerk; in yet others, his written report is not read aloud at all but considered in silence by the Bench. Where the magistrates read the reports to themselves they have under the Rule a legal obligation to communicate the substance to the defendant and his parents, since in whatever form reports are given to the court the defendant and his representatives must be given an opportunity of disputing what is said if they wish to do so. The principle is that reports concerning a defendant are not, and cannot be, considered private to the Bench. A system by which they could be considered private would, to put it mildly, contain greater danger of abuse.

The Ingleby Committee ran into fairly deep water in considering the oft-discussed and thorny problems arising from the procedure for the reception of confidential reports by the juvenile court. They point out the harm that may result from indiscriminately reading aloud all reports whatever their content. This is illustrated by instancing cases in which a child has heard 'in public', i.e. in court, for the first time that he is illegitimate or that his mother is a prostitute or that his father is in prison, or other cases where one parent has heard for the first time of some circumstance which the other had kept secret. This leads to a discussion of the difficulties if nothing at all is disclosed, or if the material parts are not disclosed, or even if the reports are not read aloud but given to the parents to read.

A great deal more is commonly made of the difficulties connected with receiving reports – and the Ingleby Committee is no exception – than in the writer's view the facts give ground for. For example, there is nothing in the Rules which requires, or would justify, telling a child any of the matters mentioned above, since they do not bear on his own character or conduct. The parent must be told of factors which the court thinks make a difference to how the child ought to be dealt with and have reference to the parent's character or conduct, or to the child's character or conduct or home surroundings or health. It does not follow that everything that is told to the parent must also be told to the child.

In the writer's experience, covering seventeen years in one of the busiest juvenile courts in the country, it is very difficult indeed to call to mind any occasions on which reports contained matters which really were 'material to the manner in which he [the offender] should be dealt with' and which could not be passed on without damage either to him or to his parents. This may be a matter of luck, but in some of the courts where most reports are received the reports, especially those of the probation officer, have already been discussed with their subject and this seems to raise no difficulty in the way of necessitating the omission of essential but dangerous matters.

The writer had the opportunity of reading evidence being submitted to the Ingleby Committee by fifteen or sixteen of the professional bodies whose members' work brings them into contact with the courts. This particular evidence may not, of course, have been representative, but it is noteworthy that some of those who had had the most experience in the matter actually suggested that, while reports should not be read aloud, the court should allow the parents to read any written report submitted. In the writer's experience, matter of which the parents cannot be told is generally speculative and non-factual in character, and in practice, though fascinating to read, it is not material to the manner in which the offender should be dealt with by a court. A great deal depends, of course, on what view the Bench takes as to matters which are 'material', but one may certainly ponder on why anything which is not material to how the offender shall be dealt with is included at all – which is a strong argument for letting the parents read the actual report and for including nothing in it that they ought not to be told.

The Ingleby Committee may truly be said to have searched its soul on this whole question. Although

Some of us thought it would be necessary wherever a report contained a 'confidential' section for the court to inform the parents of its existence (although not of its contents unless the child was to be sent away from home) . . . we did not feel sufficient confidence in it [i.e. 'a scheme on these lines'] to make it the subject of a recommendation.[6]

The final paragraph [7] in this section appears to be the result of yet another attempt to sit on several stools at once. The Report suggests that the best solution is the skilled summarizing of reports by the chairman as permitted by the existing Rules. Improvement in present practices can be achieved best by administrative guidance and more training for magistrates. These should be reminded that, while relevant information is not to be withheld, 'great care' is to be exercised over 'confidential matter'. To facilitate this, it is suggested, there might be a separate section of the report appropriately marked and with reasons stated why particular items *should not be disclosed* (italics ours) or should be disclosed only with circumspection. This seems to be where the Committee came in. If the confidential items are relevant they must be disclosed. If they are not relevant why are they included at all?

The manner in which the report is to be received by the court has, not unnaturally, a great deal of effect upon what is put into such a report, and how it is phrased. Reports expected by the writer to be read aloud word for word are likely to be more strictly factual and also to contain nothing which would be likely to damage the writer's future relations with the defendant or his family. This is a danger to which the probation officer and the schoolteacher, into whose care the defendant may subsequently be returned, are particularly exposed. A sensitive person writing such a report in the expectation that the whole of it will be read aloud may be inclined so to wrap up the more painful parts of his observations to avoid giving offence that neither the Bench, the defendant, nor the parent can make out what he is getting at.

Where reports are not read aloud there is, it must be admitted, considerable danger that not everything which the defendant or his representatives ought, strictly speaking, to know is being alleged about them will be passed on by the Bench or their clerk, even in an extensively bowdlerized form. The schoolteacher, for example, may inform the Bench that he has for some time 'been pretty certain' that the child is pilfering in school, but has never in fact caught him at it. The probation officer may express his strong suspicions of sexual malpractices in the home and state that he would very much like to see the child removed from further risk.

The position is further confused by the prevalence of widely differing views as to what should rightly be included in, for example, the report given by the probation officer on the home surroundings. The statutory provisions relating to the duties of probation officers in giving reports are to be found in the Criminal Justice Act, 1948, 5th Schedule, paragraph 5:

. . . to inquire, in accordance with any directions of the court, into the circumstances or home surroundings of any person with a view to assisting the court in determining the most suitable method of dealing with his case.

What this instruction means seems, in practice, to be a matter of interpretation. To one writer[8] it seems to mean that 'in practice each court can suit itself as to the kind of report it wants and it is well that this should be so', while to another[9] 'it seems to make it clear that the report must be purely factual as to the circumstances or home surroundings of the subject'. Probation officers and others soon discover what kinds of reports will be welcomed by particular Benches and how far they may go with different magistrates, but from every point of view it is desirable that the position in law should be clarified.

The school report usually gives a very useful account of

observed behaviour in the school, though the writer may tactfully refrain from comment upon the fact that the child seems to have been a candidate for special educational provision for many years, and typically end by placing all responsibility for the delinquency firmly in the home. Among the most useful parts of these reports are the notes upon the child's relationships with his school-fellows and with staff, and the estimates of his innate ability compared with his achievement in school. It is sometimes at this stage, too, that the Bench learn for the first time that the offender they have had before them is apparently of very low intelligence. Aged ten or eleven, he is perhaps at the bottom of the C stream – or the D stream if there is one – for his age group. Had this been known to the Bench earlier they might not so easily have assumed from his answers, or from the account of his behaviour after the act, that he knew that he was doing wrong. But at any rate, by the time the school report is received by the Bench, he really does know that what he did was wrong, if only because he is convinced of this by the attitude shown towards his offence by people in the court.

The probation officer's report giving an account of the home background and circumstances will be received and considered with the school report. When the parent is asked whether he wishes to tell the court anything, he will very often start with the announcement that the offender 'is a good boy at home', adding an assurance that 'he won't do anything of this sort again'. This is often more in the nature of a preliminary skirmish than anything more serious, before Bench and parents settle down to a closer discussion on the rather more realistic basis of points raised in the school and home reports.

Psychiatrists' reports seem to have a bad reputation in some courts and are often the subject of informal comment at meetings where justices from various Benches are gathered together. The psychiatric report seems sometimes to make the least positive contribution, offering either a set of opinions based apparently upon some theory of personality development with which the Bench are not familiar (and would regard with the greatest suspicion if they were), or else a short description of the physical appearance of the juvenile, which the Bench know already only too well, plus what appear to be the defendant's own views on his case as previously explained by him also to the Bench.

The educational psychologist's findings as to the child's abilities are often useful and the comments on his behaviour in the test situation are revealing. Nevertheless, it must be agreed that the psychiatrist, the probation officer, and the educational psychologist are each to a greater or lesser extent handicapped in their efforts to help the court if they have to make their assessment on the basis of one interview only.

The view held by the justices of their own function in making an order in the juvenile court will affect the nature of their demands upon the reporting experts. Their understanding of the experts' professional functions will affect this too. It is useful if the magistrates and the experts who are being asked for reports can have discussions together from time to time. The latter then have an opportunity of explaining to the Bench exactly what the area of their competence is, what information can, and what cannot, be expected from them in their professional capacities. The justices can then consider in the light of this the points upon which they will wish to ask for information in all cases or in any particular case.

It is reasonable to expect that each of the experts is able to assess the offender in the terms of his own particular professional competence. Thus the remand home staff can describe the boy's behaviour with staff and other children in most of the situations of ordinary life. The teacher can give the justices a comprehensive picture of the boy at school, the psychiatrist may offer an opinion on his mental and emotional state, the doctor on his medical condition, the probation officer may show the child in relation to his family background, and the educational psychologist give an up-to-date reading of the factors which indicate his educational potentiality and of the inter-relation between his situation and his attainment. Each one can say whether or not a condition exists which needs treatment of some psychiatric, medical, social, or educational kind, respectively, and whether it can be treated by the professional methods available in his own field.

A further question on which most courts will require an opinion is whether or not the delinquency is related to the condition, and if so what are the prospects as to the likelihood of further offences during treatment. This is particularly important in regard to certain forms of personality disturbance. It does not follow that the justices will, on being informed that there is a risk of further offences at least during the early stages of treatment, at once make an order confining the offender in an institution. But they will usually prefer to know the degree and nature of any risk in making an order which allows for the arrangement of treatment in open conditions.

Justices who see their function as being to make an order dealing with the general welfare of the defendant without reference to the offence may well expect to be advised by the experts as to what order to make. Indeed, if this view of the justices' function is accepted in its most extreme form, it would seem to lead to the conclusion that the order itself should be left to the experts, since they are by definition the people who know best how the welfare of the child would be served. There would seem to be no purpose in requiring formal endorsement of such recommendations by a Bench of magistrates who are themselves not welfare experts and are therefore in no position to differ, if there are no factors other than the defendant's welfare to consider. If this is the situation there would seem to be no objection and every advantage in handing the defendant over after the finding to a committee of experts, who would decide upon his welfare needs and have the power to enforce their decisions as to treatment openly rather than under cover of a so-called 'judicial' process.

Justices who regard their function in making an order as being related to the offender in his role as a delinquent, to the protection of the public against crime, and to a duty to hold the balance between the offender and the community, will see the decision as to the content of the order as their own responsibility and no one else's. Justices holding this view would regard it as not within the experts' function to give advice to the Bench as to how the delinquent *ought* to be dealt with. It would be regarded as within their function to describe his physical and mental condition, and to say as far as they can what his needs are and how he might be expected to react to various situations, so that 'the method of dealing with him' can be determined in the light of this knowledge and 'in a proper case' steps can be taken 'for removing him from undesirable surroundings and for securing that proper provision is made for his education and training'. According to this view, for instance, the medical officer would be within his function in saying: 'This boy needs regular food, exercise, and sleep, which he cannot get in his present home', or the educational psychologist within his function in saying: 'This boy is under-functioning intellectually and would enormously improve his attainment with regular schooling', and perhaps in adding: '*For these reasons* an approved school order might be beneficial.' The needs indicated are something that the Bench will bear very much in mind when considering whether the appropriate order in that particular case under consideration would be conditional discharge, fine, probation, detention, committal to the care of a fit person or to an approved school.

We have here to take up again a point already referred to on page 35 in connexion with reports upon offenders required by the magistrates in the adult courts, and to repeat that none of the reporting experts is, as such, an expert in penology nor is his professional responsibility in any case the protection of the public against crime. In short, as experts in psychiatry, psychology, medicine, and education, their opinions upon the subject of how to reduce crime, or any advice based upon these opinions which they may offer to the Bench, are of no more weight than those of any other person.[10] A certain amount of statistical information as to the general effectiveness of different sentences in terms of reconviction rates[11] is now available. Each category of offence, and of offender in terms of his age, offence, and record, has a known reconviction rate in past experience of such cases and this general information is one of the realities of which both reporting experts and sentencing courts should be aware. But it does not tell us how to treat criminality effectively. We do not yet know how to affect criminality. Nor does it constitute knowledge of a kind which enables a forecast to be made as to the future course of a particular offender's criminality. Unless the reporting expert has conducted serious researches and produced valid conclusions in the field of penology, his professional standing in some other field such as medicine or social work does not entitle him to make penological recommendations as to the use of one method in dealing with the offender rather than another.

If these considerations are considered to be irrelevant in the case of reports upon offenders before the juvenile court, on the ground that once the finding is arrived at the offender is not to be dealt with as an offender at all but simply in his total aspect as a child, it must be objected that in that case it is not clear why he should be dealt with by a court – especially a criminal court – or why the measures taken should be restricted to those available under an apparently irrelevant penal system.

COURT ORDERS AND SOCIAL SERVICES

The range of general provision for medical, social, educational, or psychiatric treatment which may be made under the statutory social services in the welfare state is now very wide. In contrast, the powers of the juvenile court to secure what it, on expert advice, or otherwise, may consider to be the treatment appropriate to the needs of a young offender are very limited in some directions. Practical examples of this situation are not difficult to find.

In areas where there is inadequate provision for special educational treatment and large classes abound in the ordinary schools, it is not unusual to read in the school report offered to the court about some lad of thirteen or fourteen that he is rated as 'very low' for both ability and attainment and that he 'seems to be the butt of the other boys and cannot hold his own'. If such a boy comes from a bad home, arrives at school for each day's failure, dirty, tired, hungry, and inadequately clothed, and is never given any pocket money, it is not surprising if he falls into temptation when it comes along. Such children are especially vulnerable to suggestions to go along with the gang, since they enjoy so little popularity, and have no pocket money in the normal course of events.

In such a case it may appear to the Bench, and be confirmed by reports, that the boy ought to be receiving intensive remedial education in the short time which remains before he reaches the age of fifteen and is launched upon the world with his inadequate defences and equipment. In a special school under the local authority he would continue to receive education and training until the age of sixteen. The court, however, has no power to arrange for his transfer to such a school under the local authority nor to send him to a residential special school. These are part of the educational system and not part of the penal system. The local education authority may act when their attention is drawn to the situation by the court, but if they do not wish to, or have no vacant places, the court cannot force them to make provision. Similarly the court cannot, on receiving the psychiatrist's report upon a disturbed child, make an order committing him to a school for the maladjusted, or to any other boarding-school provided by the education authorities. If the doctor reports that a boy is an epileptic the justices have no power to commit him to a suitable hospital or colony, or to compel such places to accept him.

These are matters for the social services. Such problems can sometimes be solved by making the offender the subject of a probation order embodying an appropriate requirement, but this is usually feasible in such cases only if all parties are willing, in which event there can hardly be said to be a problem. Where the need appears to be for some kind of special schooling, the problem is often dealt with in a rough-and-ready way within the penal system by a committal to an approved school, in the hope that appropriate provision exists or can be made within the approved school system, with the classifying school being left to sort out the finer details.

Quite apart from the fact that such a procedure implies a duplication of special educational provision which may not exist in reality, there are other objections to the system.

Approved school committal now usually comes at a much later stage in a criminal career, judged by the record, than formerly, but if regarded as a penal measure, which in law it is, very few of the boys so committed have records which would in themselves justify a three-year 'sentence'. Some of the approved school orders made can be justified only on the grounds of educational needs in the widest sense, i.e. the boys are to be re-educated in social living. In view of this fact it might seem that the court ought to be given power to commit to any suitable school within the ordinary system of education, since boarding-school education, rather than punishment, is what is intended by the court. The responsibility, however, of deciding what form of education is needed in a particular instance normally lies at present with the education authorities. Magistrates do not become expert in educational matters simply by reason of becoming magistrates, yet at present it is possible for a Bench to commit an offender to an approved school without making any inquiry of the education authorities as to whether this will meet his educational needs. If powers to commit directly to schools within the ordinary educational system were to be given to the courts, the education authorities would almost certainly demand a provision that such powers should only be exercised upon the recommendation of the education authority and after a thorough examination of the child's educational needs and circumstances. The fact is, of course, that there already exist general powers to compel any child within the ages of compulsory education to receive education according to his need and suited to his age, ability, and aptitude, and recourse to a court would only be necessary where parents refused to comply. In theory there is no reason why the ordinary procedure should not be employed in the case of a child who has been found guilty of an offence, if his needs and circumstances appear to be such as to call for his extensive re-education to fit him to take his place as a law-abiding member of the community. As a matter of experience, however, it is doubtful whether the education authorities would attach much importance to a child's tendency to commit offences against the law in assessing the urgency of his need for special education, even if these did not mean, as now, that he could be dealt with by another department and under a special system. While education authorities continue to have long waiting lists for residential special schools, they are likely to give only a doubtful welcome to delinquents as a class. Other children's parents, also, often object to the presence of delinquents in schools which their children attend.

At present it is often the case that the only way the Bench can ensure that 'proper provision' will, in fact, be made, and made within a reasonable time, is to make that provision themselves as far as they can either under cover of a penological measure (e.g. a period of detention or committal to an approved school) or under the requirements of a probation order. There is, for example, provision under the 1944 Education Act for children who need a boarding-school education to have it. But this provision is being interpreted exceedingly narrowly in most areas. Children who need residential special-school education – including the maladjusted – are dealt with separately under another section, and there are waiting lists at nearly all recognized special schools for the maladjusted. On the other hand, a child committed to an approved school will be removed, at least to the remand home, at once. But in some parts of the country, even if the court does not commit the juvenile offender to an approved school, he is still likely to have a considerably better chance than the next child of getting to one of the schools for the maladjusted (or of jumping the queue for the attentions of the child-guidance clinic) by the very fact that one of the symptoms of his disturbance happens to be the commission of illegal acts and that there have been findings of guilt against him in a criminal court. In this sense those social workers who sometimes appear to regard the juvenile court as a diagnostic clinic through which treatment may be secured are perfectly right. By being convicted the juvenile has been *ipso facto* diagnosed as a delinquent – a condition with a high nuisance value. Under the present scarcity of social provision it seems as if some children have to be convicted as criminals in order to obtain suitable education and training.

The origins of the juvenile court in this country and the form taken by its development over the last half-century seem to have resulted in a system of diagnosing and treating children's needs being grafted on to one designed originally for protecting the public from crime by punishing the criminal. The present hybrid institution is one in which the needs of the child are balanced in a rough-and-ready way against the demands of society – and the balance arrived at is different in different courts according to the view taken by the Bench of the nature of their functions.

In practice, there is something to be said in favour of this situation. The courts of justice are much older than the social services of the welfare state, and it is probable that they inspire more public confidence than some of the social services have yet had time to do. Many social workers think that the public generally, and especially that section most affected, i.e. the defendants and their relatives, feel much greater confidence in the court system as a means of deciding what measures are to be enforced against a person, as being in his own best interests, than they do in the method of administrative decision taken, upon expert advice, inside a department. As an example, it is suggested that parents object less to an approved-school committal – which follows a hearing and finding in a court of law – than they do to an administrative decision to send the child to a school for the maladjusted, following examination at the child-guidance clinic.

A proposal sometimes put forward is that there should be a separation between the procedure for trying charges and that for making an order, on the ground that, whereas the present procedure is well adapted to establishing guilt or innocence in a criminal trial, even of a child defendant, it is less well suited to ensuring that the order made will be primarily in the interests of the defendant's welfare. As already pointed out, some such proposal is implicit in the view of the juvenile courts' function in making an order, discussed on page 188, as being related exclusively to the welfare of the young offender in all its aspects. The trial would proceed as now up to the finding of guilt, but the order would be made by the experts in child welfare and education, to whom the offender would be handed over for examination. To meet situations in which there might be a difference of opinion between the welfare experts and the child or his family it would be necessary for the experts to have powers of enforcement, since a reference back to court in disputed cases would mean a return to the system of weighing the offence against the proposed treatment. These and other proposals will be discussed further, but there is a considerable body of opinion against the exercise of such powers administratively and outside the purview of the courts. For example, 'No persons of any age,' the Lord Chief Justice is alleged to have remarked, in the case of *Rutty*, 'were to be confined in institutions merely because doctors and officials thought it would be good for them.'[12] As lay people the justices may not be qualified very well, if at all, to consider welfare matters, but it is thought that the inadequacies of the courts in this respect may be regarded as being to some extent offset by the advantage of having any decision that is made arrived at in a judicial way, in open court, and subject to appeal, rather than in the private offices of the local authority.

CHAPTER 9

THE CHILD AND THE COURT

THE oft quoted principle that 'justice should not only be done, but be manifestly and undoubtedly seen to be done'[1] is upheld by the presence of public and press in the courts of this country. Each fully reported case contributes towards a more realistic picture of the administration of justice in the public mind. Those members of the public actually present in a court hear the charges and all the evidence; they also hear the verdict and the sentence. If the Bench pronounces a sentence which might appear to be out of line with the gravity of the offence some explanation is frequently offered, for example, 'This is an offence for which we could have sent you to prison for six months and we have seriously considered doing this, but in view of . . .'

For very good reasons the public are not present at hearings in the juvenile court. In addition to this, the restrictions on press publication mean that it is often difficult to give a complete account of such hearings without running the risk of including particulars which may identify the defendants. Furthermore, the practice in some juvenile courts of receiving written reports on offenders has in many instances the result, if these reports are not read aloud, that, even where the Press were present and do report the case, the relation between the offender's delinquency and the particular order made by the Bench is not always at all clear in the account which appears later in the newspaper. The juvenile court is thus deprived of some of the means by which it might otherwise have hoped to inform and educate the general public. Its work and policy, the kind of issues which come before it for decision, and the factors which its Benches take into consideration in their efforts to reclaim the young offender for society remain, for the large majority of the general public, a matter of surmise based upon assumption.

It is not unknown for otherwise responsible people to make public criticisms of the work of the juvenile courts without having troubled to obtain first-hand knowledge by visiting one. Lack of such knowledge is undoubtedly one of the main causes for such criticisms as that juvenile offenders are treated with sloppy sentimentality, or, on the other hand, that justice is dispensed far too harshly in juvenile courts. The juvenile court is one of those subjects upon which people seem ready to form strong opinions based only upon their own preconceptions. The juvenile defendant himself, even the young recidivist, is no exception in this respect.

THE CHILD'S VIEW OF THE COURT AND ITS FUNCTIONS

In the social circles from which most of the juvenile defendants come the 'police courts' are a familiar feature. The functions of these courts as places of trial and sentence and their purpose of protecting the public against crime are well understood. Most of the juvenile defendants seem to have accepted the court before which they themselves appear as a modified version of the adult courts – acting a little less predictably, and perhaps a little more arbitrarily, in choosing the appropriate sentence. Children seem to have a very clear and definite idea that the juvenile courts' function is to punish, and in one way this is not surprising since, in view of the rarity of pleas of not guilty, the trial of a charge plays usually a very minor and purely formal part in the proceedings. 'Sentencing' on the other hand – which seems to be equated in the child's mind with the award of punishment – takes up most of the time the court spends on each case.

While it is important that the public generally should have a correct picture of the work of the juvenile courts, it is even more important that the defendant himself, if he is to be assumed to have fundamentally the same legal rights and civil liberties as other citizens, and is to be treated upon the basis of this assumption, should also understand how the court works and what it is trying to do. This remains equally true whether the court sees itself as protecting the public from crime by punishing the wrongdoer or by reforming him, or whether it regards its responsibility as directed towards the defendant's welfare in a much more general way.

The child, however, is no blank sheet waiting to receive impressions. Before the magistrates set eyes upon him he has already formed a view as to what the court is for. This view cannot be easily modified on an intellectual basis or in terms suited to the needs, experiences, and perceptions of adults. What actually happens to the defendant will make much more impression on him than what is said to him about it. What he feels will be more important than what he hears. A great deal of what he feels will be dependent upon the views he held before he came to court, but some of it will be determined by his experiences in connexion with the court appearance. The child's-eye view can never be taken for granted, and it is always difficult to be sure of the meaning which a particular experience has had for children of different ages and backgrounds. The points raised in the remainder of this chapter are based upon observation and experience of children of various ages, and upon discussion with them and with the people who deal with them in school, at home, at play, and at all stages of court proceedings.

However informal the atmosphere of the juvenile court, the situation is one which appears essentially authoritarian to the child. He has been arrested, taken to the police station, questioned, and charged. He has sometimes, after being formally cautioned, made a statement at some length and has signed it after it has been read over to him. In court everything seems to him to emphasize that he is in the wrong, as the charge is read over and evidence is given.

However gently and benignly everyone concerned may have handled him, from the police constable to the magistrates' clerk, he knows he is there because he has done something wrong and so he expects to be punished for it. The defendants not only expect to be punished and regard this as fair, but, as has been pointed out previously, they expect particular penalties (implying particular degrees of severity) to be applied according to the stage the criminal career has reached, as measured by present offence and past record. They are shocked by the 'unfairness' of court decisions in cases in which other boys who have committed the same offence, or been in court the same number of times as they have themselves, receive different and possibly lighter penalties.

Generally speaking, the only alternative to punishment of which the defendants are aware is that of 'mercy' – a letting off, either wholly or in part. The concept of treatment is understood only in a strictly medical context. The possibility of social or educational treatment is not envisaged at all, though social causes for the offence – e.g. 'it's the district that's done it, sir, we've put in for an exchange' – are often put forward by the parents of the offender in court. Junior boys (ten to fourteen) remanded in custody for full reports under the Magistrates' Courts Act, 1952 (to enable the court to determine the best method of dealing with them) often appear to have no conception of the purpose of such a procedure. They view the reasons for their removal from home only in terms of their offence and record. In this sense they do understand that the remand for reports is considered by the Bench to be for their good, i.e. to make them better boys – but they see this as being done by means of the punishment of being taken away from home. Many young offenders, when asked on their return to court why they think they were sent to the remand home, reply that it was because they stole such and such – and apparently mean just that.

PROBLEMS OF COMMUNICATION

The Bench, on the other hand, may be regarding the offence as being of quite minor significance in the offender's total situation and may have in their minds no idea of punishment whatever. They only want to deal with the child in his best interests and may be united in the opinion that punishment is not the way to effect his reclamation to good citizenship. The Bench's idea and the child's idea of what constitutes punishment may well differ but this is not the important point. The real difficulty stems from the fact that the child and his parents believe in punishment as such. The Bench and their advisers, on the other hand, very probably do not. They are concerned with reform. This point is well and vividly made by Dr Eileen Younghusband writing[2] of the attitudes of parents in the juvenile court. 'The whole idea of reform . . . is usually alien from their thoughts . . . in the juvenile court are two sets of people talking to each other from within two different worlds.'

Where the members of the juvenile court panel have been carefully chosen and have taken the trouble to read relevant books, attend lectures, and make visits, they may be very well informed upon the various methods available for helping children and equally determined to see that the children get that help. On the other hand, most of the parents are those who are least in touch with the channels by which many parents are encouraged to move with the times, i.e. the parent–teacher associations, the wireless and television discussions, the weeklies and monthlies offering advice by staff especially trained in parentcraft and domestic matters. Thus while the magistrates see themselves as 'wise and good parents', the child sees them as 'dark avenging gods'. He and his parents expect him to be punished and accept this as the proper means of turning him from his delinquency.

The child usually appears to see the order which is finally made as the direct consequence of his misbehaviour. He does not seem to grasp that the home background is regarded as conducing to his behaviour or that his fault is largely ascribed to the outlook or behaviour of his parents. Whether it is possible or desirable for most children to understand the whole picture as seen by the court, including the nature of the basic factors thought to underlie the delinquency, and the reasons why it is thought impossible for the offender to develop properly at home, is questionable. What such a child does accept is the pragmatic test – i.e. the test of what in fact his behaviour has been – as the test of whether he can manage at home or not. The further the court appears to get away from the offence in making an order, the less understandable, in the court setting, the whole proceeding may become to the young offender, and the more likely it is to appear as an irrational and irresponsible exercise of arbitrary power at his expense.

There is a difference between younger and older defendants, and between defendants of the same age but widely differing intelligence levels or social experience, in regard to grasping the concept of reformation as opposed to punishment. Where the offender has previously had the experience of being put on probation, or has been attending a child-guidance clinic over any length of time, both he and his parents may have come to a realistic appreciation of what it is that the juvenile court is trying to do for their child. This is in itself a good reason for trying probation in every suitable case. It is a reason which may properly tip the balance towards probation in cases which do not otherwise seem altogether suitable. Even where the offender fails to make good on probation and is later subjected to some other form of treatment, the period of probation, under really good supervision, may have begun to lay the groundwork for the rehabilitation which takes place later.

If the court is held in premises ordinarily used for the sittings of the adult court and built for that purpose, it must be admitted that the surroundings are more likely to suggest that punishment awaits the guilty defendant, rather than concern for his welfare. The Committee on Young Offenders wisely suggested that this human tendency to interpret the meaning of the environment should be used positively – for example, the room should be specially furnished and arranged so as to suggest an inquiry rather than a trial. Such arrangements, however, can also bring their own complications. If what is in process is, in fact, meant to be a trial it is probably better that it should look like one. The child is far more likely to grasp the trial procedure if the room is arranged like a courtroom than if it looks, for example, like an office in which a head teacher and his staff are interrogating trouble-makers and meting out arbitrary punishment, regardless of the rules of evidence or of any other procedure laid down for the conduct of proceedings in courts of law. This is not to say that the rules of procedure are always meticulously followed even in a formal atmosphere, or that they cannot be adhered to in an informal one, but only that in the latter it is more difficult for a juvenile defendant to perceive them. Some may think that it does not matter whether a juvenile grasps the procedure or not, and that much of it, e.g. the rules of evidence, would be better dispensed with on the ground that it interferes with the court's efforts to get at the real truth of a human situation. It is arguable that a juvenile up to say thirteen or fourteen years of age is not equipped mentally or emotionally or in experience of life to benefit from the rules and procedures of formal justice. The important point in the present context, however, is that, as long as the juvenile court remains a court of law administering justice, it ought to act and appear like one. It is, to say the least, confusing if it looks like a court of justice while acting like a welfare clinic endowed with arbitrary powers both of treatment and punishment.

Many boys aged ten to twelve years do not have the same appreciation as an adult would have of the dishonest quality of certain acts and this is shown particularly in the most frequent offence of all, viz. larceny. A child's interpretation of the situation in which an offence took place may be much nearer that of a little animal than of the adult human being. For instance, where no effort has been made to guard against theft, many children seem to interpret this almost as a form of sign language indicating the owners' intention not to protect his goods from theft. Thus, to such children, taking money or articles left about in a house where the door is ajar is hardly wrong at all, though the owner might be annoyed. The question of morality is not thought to be relevant. Similarly, shopkeepers who display easily movable and highly attractive goods on unprotected counters are presumed to have taken into consideration the probability that quite a lot will be stolen. The situation is one for quick wits and sleight of hand rather than any considerations of a moral kind. In the same way goods taken from deserted houses or sheds on demolition sites have often been assumed by the child thief to have been abandoned, even though the things may have an obvious value, because no one has been seen to be looking after them. In such a case a child's reply to such questions as 'How would you like it if someone came in and took your things?' may be 'The door wasn't locked' or 'Nobody went there'. Doubtless the appearance in court has a very strong educational value in such cases but, as has already been pointed out, it also has the grave disadvantage of giving the offender a criminal record.

From informal discussion with children in remand homes, it seems that an appreciable number do not understand the significance of offences taken into consideration by the court as requested by the police on behalf of the defendant. Even on a first appearance in court there may be a number of such offences to consider and there is almost everything to be said for making a clean breast of it and clearing the decks in this way. But some children do have the feeling that they are pressed by the police to admit offences which they have not always committed, and on other occasions they have not understood what the offence was supposed to be. There is always a risk with a child that he may not pay enough attention to exactly what the alleged offences are but may admit them more in a spirit of cooperation than with a proper understanding of what he is doing.

Most children seem to accept the common picture of the policeman as, in general, a helpful and respect-worthy figure. As a consequence they expect a high standard of behaviour in every way – for instance, swearing is to be deprecated in anyone, but in a policeman it is a shocking thing. A bluff which might be taken for granted in other situations is regarded with very strong moral disapproval when employed by the police, as, for instance, if police who come to a boy's home to question him about a house-breaking offence tell him that they have found his finger-prints in the house, whereas, in fact, they have never taken his finger-prints, and cannot know whether those in the house are his or not. On some children, the sight of a policeman seems to have the same effect as an over-active conscience. In the words of a fourteen-year-old boy writing an essay on 'The Policeman', at a secondary modern school: 'I think everyone has a fault [sic] about a policeman and mine is that he makes me feel uneasy. When he walks along the road his eyes seem to hypnotize me and make a shiver down my spine.' A girl's version of the same feeling is: 'I don't like the way they peer at you till you feel you have done something wrong, when you haven't.' Little girls sometimes express surprise and a certain amount of priggish disapproval of members of the women's police force who wear make-up or paint their nails. But it was pointed out by a group of girls that although policemen are nicer than policewomen – who are 'strict' and tend to be 'sarcastic' – yet, on the other hand, it was much easier to talk about 'intercourses' to policewomen and this was thought to be important – as indeed it is. In general, the policeman and policewoman seem to be regarded as brave and protective figures by most children, and, on the whole, those who have appeared in court charged with offences seem to think that they have been fairly treated by the police.

Few children who have been to court appear to know who or what persons are represented there beyond the magi-strates and the police. As one fourteen-year-old boy put it:

'There were a few people sitting in some desks reading papers and writing.' A girl asked in discussion: 'Do you get a lot of outsiders?' and had her answer from another girl: 'They come to listen to your life.' Many youngsters apparently do not know that the public are not admitted to the juvenile court, and certainly in a busy central court, with twenty or more people present, all strangers to the defendant, there is nothing to suggest that this is so unless it is directly stated.

The arrangements to protect the child defendant from publicity are not adequate as seen from the defendants' point of view. Though the particulars given in the Press account effectively prevent the culprit being identified by the general public (most of whom have no interest in him whatever), a collection of such items as the home district, the age of the offender, the nature of the offence, and the address where it took place, may easily identify him for the neighbours who are then able to pin onto the correct person whatever details of previous appearances and domestic circumstances emerged in court and have been reported. Girls who have been before the court as being in need of care, or in moral danger, or out of control feel particularly strongly about this. As one girl said, 'Somebody came up to my mother and asked if it was her' (referring to the mother's comment in court). Others commented that everything their parents said about them was 'put in the papers'. To be rejected thus openly by one's parents is very painful indeed, whatever the justification. In some cases where local people are witnesses – e.g. shopkeepers or neighbours – and remain in court during the whole of the rest of the case after having given their evidence, they hear not only the previous record but also much private history as well. Some children report instances of being unable to go to certain parts of their own neighbourhood afterwards because of what the neighbours have repeated, not necessarily with strict accuracy. Whether this is a good thing or a bad thing is not the point at issue so much as the fact that the statutory prohibition upon the publication of identifying particulars in its present form is only partially effective in ensuring that all publicity is avoided.

Infringement of the spirit of the statutory provisions to ensure privacy for all concerned in juvenile court proceedings may take a more subtle form as, for instance, where the employer of a person concerned in care or protection proceedings obtains permission to attend as a visitor simply on the ground that he is interested in the case. If such a person is handed a copy of the probation officer's report, he may, without his employee being even consulted, learn a great deal of the latter's private life. The undesirable features of such situations are accentuated for quite other reasons if visitors, who have asked for permission to attend on the ground that they are personally interested in one of the parties, are also friends of the magistrates and are entertained in the magistrates' private room before the case. While this sort of thing may certainly conduce to a family – or even welfare committee – atmosphere in the court, it is not consistent with the ordinary requirements of a trial. With the best intentions, there are dangers of such happenings where the fundamental legal basis of the juvenile court as a court of law is not kept continually in mind.

In spite of laudable efforts to make the procedure in court more understandable to juveniles by means of modifying the wording, etc., it is likely that communication between the court and the defendant is in some instances still very imperfect indeed. The following is part of a description written by a fourteen-year-old boy (one of a class of eight contemporaries) at a remand home after his second appearance in court:

The Judge said to me i will send you to a remand home for a month and two years probatshin. I said the truth to the Judge. And I told im i was fonde of animals. He said do you want to have it put into custerddy and i said yes.

Another account contains the following:

He said you have 7 Fansis. I said yes He riad out to me.

The first writer had an estimated mental age of eleven and the second of under ten. The class of eight represented all the boys aged fourteen in the home at that time. It contained one boy of superior mental ability and one borderline normal; the performance of the remainder was on a level with the extracts quoted. It cannot, of course, be assumed from a boy's inability to express himself in speech or writing in an adequate manner that he has not at all understood what was taking place. Most of the children who have been in court seem to have understood in a very rough, vague, and approximate way, and from the context, the general drift of what was happening.

VERBAL USAGE IN DIFFERENT SOCIAL GROUPS

There are several aspects of this problem of communication in the court. In the first place, many children do not know the meaning of words such as 'charge', 'summons', 'prosecution', 'defence', which are the everyday language of a court of law, even after they have been to court more than once. A great deal can be done, and is done, by experienced magistrates and clerks to avoid the use of any technical language at all in the juvenile court. For instance, such a clerk, instead of saying, 'You are charged that between 3 p.m. and 5 p.m. on April the fifth you . . .' may say, 'They say that last Saturday afternoon . . .' Similarly, a child can be helped at certain stages to understand the procedure if the clerk makes prefacing remarks such as, for example, 'You've heard what the officer said, Barry, and you asked him some questions. Now, the magistrates want to hear what you've got to say about it yourself', before proceeding to invite the boy to give his evidence. The announcement 'You are to go to the remand home for full reports before we make an order' is probably almost meaningless to a child as far as the exact content is concerned (though it effectively confirms his general fear that he is to go somewhere else instead of going home), whereas some such statement as: 'We know very little about you, David. We think we ought to find out more before deciding what is best for you so we are going to send you to stay for three weeks at the boys' home. The people there will be able to tell us, when you come to court at the end of that time, more about what kind of a boy you are. Your mum and dad will be able to come and see you.' Similarly, the announcement 'We are going to adjourn this case' conveys very little indeed, whereas 'We are not going to decide about you today . . .' is understood. It is, however, possible to go too far in the avoidance of special terms and so create misunderstanding as, for instance, when a mother happily accepted the suggestion that the boy might go to 'boarding-school', but, on hearing the words 'approved school' in the committal order, created a very angry scene. She thought that the court had attempted to practise a mean deception on her. Her feeling seemed to be similar to what she might have felt had she herself accepted an invitation to spend a month or two in London with all expenses paid and then found that the invitation was a euphemism for a sentence to Holloway Gaol. It is of little use to attempt to persuade such a woman at such a moment that an approved school is not Dartmoor but a boarding-school recognized by the Ministry of Education, and, moreover, one at which many of the boys learn how to conduct their lives without getting into further serious trouble.

When a juvenile is put on probation the chairman or the clerk usually explains in simple terms what is meant by this. The explanation varies in different courts. One chairman may say: 'We are giving you someone to advise you and help you, someone who will be a real friend to you', or his explanation may run more along the lines of 'You are to be of good behaviour and do what the probation officer tells you', according to the particular chairman's general approach to such matters and his understanding of the realities of the work of the probation service. Whatever is said, the important point to remember is that the young offender also brings something to the situation. He brings the picture he has already formed before hearing any explanation at all. It is helpful, therefore, when a specialized term such as probation has to be used and explained, to find out first of all what impressions the offender has already. This may save time. It may also give useful guidance as to what points should be emphasized in the explanation about to be given, as when a fourteen-year-old boy was asked, 'Do you know what is meant by being placed on probation?' and replied, 'Yes, sir, it's a man what lays in wait to catch you out and bring you back to court!'

With the youngest defendants it is never possible to be sure what has been understood when any words not known to them in their daily life are used in court. During a recent case, a little boy had been called up to the magistrates' table by the clerk. As the child stood at a right-angle to the Bench and seemed to think he was to address his remarks to the clerk, the latter said helpfully, 'Just turn round and speak to the *magistrates*.' The defendant looked with alarm at the Bench, took a deep breath, and began nervously, 'Majesties!'

Most people who think about it at all grasp the fact that many of the words used daily in court are now so rarely used outside that they have come to be almost a specialized vocabulary, and that, while adult defendants may be vague about their exact meaning, children almost certainly do not understand them. It might come as a surprise, however, to many people to realize how very limited is the range of verbal comprehension of some of the children. A list of words in common use was drawn up by the writer and used by a youth leader for a quiz at a boys' club in a central urban district. There were twenty-one boys whose ages ranged from eleven to fifteen years. As far as was known, all were attending ordinary secondary modern schools. Among the words which none of the members understood were such common or garden examples as 'obliging', 'thorough', 'trustworthy', 'stubborn', 'protective', 'hasty', 'surly'. It is not unusual to find children aged eleven or twelve who have no idea what meaning to attach to the word 'credit' in the sense of 'to be a credit to', or to the word 'discipline' in any sense at all. To these children, a statement from the Bench such as 'We do hope that after a period of thorough discipline you will turn into a trustworthy person and be a credit to your family' loses much of its impact.

The range of verbal comprehension may, in general, be expected to increase with the age of the child. There are, however, subtler pitfalls in communication which are less easy to allow for. One of these is the fact that words seem to have different shades of meaning in different social and geographical groups. As an example, among the twenty-one club members previously referred to, the word 'ignorant' did not denote 'lacking in knowledge' so much as being 'unsophisticated' or 'half-soaked' – in fact, a 'dope'. The adjective 'rough' did not describe a way of handling a person or thing, but was reserved exclusively to describe people very low in the social scale and behaviour which indicated this – e.g. 'sleeping rough' meant sleeping in old bomb shelters, etc. 'Rudeness' was not verbal, but to be 'rude' meant actually to manhandle a person by shoving them about. 'Smart' was used entirely in reference to appearance and never in the sense of being clever or quick on the uptake. 'Spiteful' was used in appreciative and half-admiring reference to a friend who had been able to 'get one in', i.e. had successfully played a practical joke. It was not used for really vicious or malicious behaviour. Here again a comment from the Bench such as 'That was a mean and spiteful thing to do and not smart at all' loses half its force at the receiving end.

VERBAL COMPREHENSION AND INTELLIGENCE

The extent of a child's own vocabulary, his understanding of the meaning of words used by others, and the shades of meaning he himself attaches to particular words are all affected by such matters as his age and intelligence and social environment. Magistrates do not know by intuition, and simply because they have become magistrates, what level and range of verbal comprehension to expect in any given child. It is likely that among magistrates serving in juvenile courts there is a majority who were educated at least at grammar school level. Roughly speaking, this is probably also true for the rest of the court regulars – the clerks, solicitors, children's officers, probation officers, Press – in fact, probably everyone except just possibly the police officer on duty. The defendants and their parents, however, are preponderantly working class, and received their education in a less academic setting. This means that the two sets of people talking to each other in the juvenile court, as described by Dr Younghusband (see page 215), may not only be making quite different assumptions but also may be using a rather different vocabulary too. An intellectual understanding of the kinds of differences which may exist, and when these are to be expected, is not the same as operational knowledge. The normal range of vocabulary tends to spring irrepressibly to the lips and it is in practice most difficult to establish a sufficiently effective internal check to prevent the use of such sentences as 'You appear to have had no justification for doing this' in addressing a well-grown thirteen-year-old, who has already been stated in the school report to have a mental age of not more than ten.

A similar difficulty led to a twelve-year-old boy, whose mental age was that of a seven-and-a-half-year-old and whose ability to recognize words was stated to be that of a child of six, being told bracingly by the magistrate, 'You're not *unique* you know!' which the lad took as a fresh reproach of some kind. His sister with a mental age of eleven-and-a-half, though in years aged thirteen, had previously received with distinct caution the information that she had proved herself to be 'adaptable and accommodating' while at the remand home. Such instances are quoted in no spirit of derision since the writer is certainly as guilty as most, but by way of illustrating the fatal ease with which people who ought to know better may slip up in this way.

The headmaster of a well-known school for backward children recently told the writer, with some chagrin, of an analogous experience of his own. He was called out of class to an interview between one of his older boys and a police officer who was investigating a local incident. The officer had evidently no experience of backward children and with rising irritation the headmaster found himself obliged to act almost as interpreter not only of the words used but also in regard to the ponderous adult sentiments and exhortations which the conscientious officer felt it his duty to deliver. On returning to his class of very much younger children, however, the teacher himself found it almost impossible at once to adapt either his vocabulary or his concepts to their understanding. For some moments, even he had the greatest difficulty in translating words and content suitable for his fifteen- and sixteen-year-old pupils into meaningful statements for the eights and nines.

People whose work or leisure bring them into close and frequent contact with working-class children are often outstandingly good at making contact with such children in court. It is not enough to have a working-class background. It is necessary in addition to be, so to speak, 'child conscious'. The facility is easily lost without incessant practice. The best teachers and social workers have it and other people whose jobs or lives bring them into direct contact with people living in the social conditions and backgrounds from which most of the defendants come. It is always helpful to the magistrates if they can induce teachers and social workers who visit the court to discuss with them, from the point of view of its comprehensibility to children of different ages, the actual wording used by the Bench. If the visitors are people working with educationally backward children, their observations may be very helpful indeed, since many of these workers have made a close study of verbal ability and comprehension in children from poor backgrounds and can pick out immediately which words and phrases used by the Bench have probably been misunderstood by the defendants. The position of many juvenile defendants is made more difficult by the fact that the educationally sub-normal child from an adverse background is likely to display an even lower level of verbal comprehension than his low mental age would appear to justify.

A magistrate new to the juvenile court may well feel un-certain as to what he or she is to understand, from a state-ment in the educational psychologist's report, that a particular defendant has a mental age of such-and-such. The magistrate cannot usually hope to become an expert in the subject, and that is in any case not his function. But he may hope to gain an idea of the implications of such statements for some of the children in court, as far as their understand-ing of words is concerned. The educational psychologist will usually be found eager to help with a talk or demonstration if appealed to, and actual examples can do more than any-thing else to show the layman some of the practical realities of a mental disability.

As an example of the difficulties of mentally handi-capped children, the following account may be interesting. Nine boys were seen recently in a residential school for educationally subnormal children. Five were aged between thirteen and fourteen, while the other four were already fourteen and some months. Mental ages ranged three to four years behind chronological age. They were given a word and asked to find, out of several other words, the one which meant the same, e.g. '*timid* means (strict, shy, bold, tiny)'.[3] Four boys thought the word *timid* meant 'tiny', two plumped for 'strict', and one for 'bold'. When the word given was *wealth*, three of the boys thought it meant 'honesty' and two guessed 'poverty'. Similarly, *to escort* was thought by two boys to mean 'to cure', by one 'to watch', and by one 'to send'. Four of the boys were unable to say correctly which was the smallest of the numbers: 1486, 7301, 4000, 1852, 1849.

The writer once attended, with a party of other magi-strates serving in juvenile courts, a demonstration of intelligence testing by an educational psychologist. The party sat in a room of which one wall was transparent from their side but opaque from the other. A one-way microphone allowed the party to hear what was going on in the other room without themselves being either seen or heard. An anonymous child of low intelligence was being tested. The demonstration was extraordinarily convincing since the party soon found themselves participating in the search for the correct solution to each problem as it was placed before the boy by the psychologist. The time-lag between their own decision as to the correct answer and the boy's reply, often incorrect when it came, was very telling. The most dramatic moments, however, were those spent in waiting for the boy to attach a tail to the correct portion of a cardboard donkey. Even after the lessons learned by the party during the previous part of the test a slight gasp could be heard when, after minutes of thought, the boy pinned the tail carefully to the donkey's shoulder. The insight gained through such a participatory experience, if it, or something similar, can be arranged, is worth any number of academic lectures. What is needed by the magistrate is a true and sympathetic insight rather than book knowledge.

MAKING THE ORDER — THE RECEIVING END

After finding a charge proved, it is the custom in many juvenile courts for the Bench to talk confidentially with the child in an effort to find out more about his attitude to the offence. It is at this point, and also at the later stage when the court is pronouncing the order and perhaps accompanying the pronouncement with a homily, that the magistrates are most free to talk to the defendant in what appears to *them* to be ordinary language. Since the child gets least help from the context at this stage, much of the point of the communications may be lost if no effort is made to keep the vocabulary used within his probable range. This is doubly important since it is at these two points that many juvenile court magistrates hope to get into really fruitful contact with the offender and make some impact upon his character. A word of warning is necessary. S. and E. Glueck, in their valuable study of the characteristics of delinquent boys as compared with those of non-delinquents,[4] found that a high degree of suggestibility was enormously more frequent among the former than the latter. The suggestibility of many delinquent children is very noticeable in court, especially among those defendants who are described in the school report as backward. The children themselves take it for granted – for example, 'Colin said, "Let's go in there and get some stuff" ', is often the sort of explanation advanced in quite good faith as a complete explanation of the offence.

If the magistrates are not consciously aware of this characteristic of the delinquent child, misunderstanding can easily arise, since in an informal situation it is very easy for questions to be put, with the best of intentions, in a form which suggests a particular answer, e.g. 'You went into the shop to see what you could pick up, didn't you?' Many children can be guaranteed to nod emphatically in reply to such a question even though they have just said, 'I didn't mean to take anything, I just did it suddenly', in answer to 'Whatever made you do such a thing?', which may be described as an open-ended question. The child does not realize the possible effect of what he is saying upon the content of the order about to be made. The magistrate may not realize that the child is simply doing his best to cooperate by giving the answer which seems to be expected. It has sometimes seemed to social workers, who know particular defendants well enough to have a shrewd idea of the probabilities, that the same mechanism operates when a little gang is lined up in court and the charge is read over, to be followed by the question put to each in turn: 'XY, is this charge true or not true?' By the time the inquiry reaches number six, aged ten, he is falling over himself to oblige, and delivers himself of his squeaky 'Truessir!' with a more than military precision. Where a fairly detailed account of the events alleged is to be given later, there is a safeguard against unfortunate mistakes. Where the offences concerned are not the subject of charges but are said to have been admitted, and there is a request that they be taken into consideration, this is an additional reason for not being content with the formal inquiry 'Do you admit these charges?' It is better to spend some time making sure that everybody knows what is alleged against him personally and what he is 'admitting'.

This suggestibility may expose the defendant to special risks where the atmosphere of the court is very informal. It is most important that the magistrates should not, in their anxiety to find out exactly what the background situation is, slip into another form of questioning which sounds to the child like a statement – for example, 'Now I wouldn't mind betting this isn't the first nor the second time you've done this kind of thing. You've taken things before, haven't you, but you've been lucky and you didn't get caught?' If this kind of thing were to happen in an adult court, in between the police statement of the record and the pronouncement of the sentence, it would be recognized and objected to at once by the adult defendant or his legal representative as most unsuitable. An undefended and guilty juvenile, anxiously wondering what will be done to him, is unlikely to know what his legal rights in these matters are, or to assert them at such a moment if he does know. This is one of those points at which the juvenile defendant needs the safeguards of the law more, not less, than his adult counterpart, precisely because of his childish suggestibility. Much responsibility rests upon the clerk in the informally run juvenile court if it is to function as a court of justice at these moments, in fact as well as theory.

Other characteristics of the delinquent child's personality noticed by S. and E. Glueck[5] were that, as a group, such children were less critical of themselves, less able and less willing to size up their own faults and virtues. They were also more obviously self-centred. These characteristics may often be seen in the delinquent child in the court situation. At the time the order is made, a certain amount of admonition or encouragement may be offered from the Bench in the hope of helping the child. But in many instances it is difficult to avoid the impression that the defendant's awareness is so highly selective, so egocentrically focused around himself and his predicament and what is to happen to him in the immediate future, that he is actually incapable of grasping anything said to him by the Bench that does not appear to him to bear directly upon these points. Sometimes he does not seem to take in any words at all except those pronouncing the order. Afterwards he is again involved in his own relief or anxiety, related directly to the facts of the situation – he is not interested in advice or opinions from the Bench. Some years ago, having a suspicion that communication between Bench and child at this stage in the proceedings was considerably less effective than is sometimes assumed, the writer made a practice over a short period of calling at the remand home after an interval of two days or so from making an approved school order. In talking with these boys and others at the remand home it was a salutary experience to find that often they did not know that anything whatever (other than the order) had been said by the Bench. They were delighted to have a visitor, but usually did not know that they had ever seen the particular person before.

This situation is perhaps not surprising. It is probably similar in essentials to what might be expected from the reactions of a nervous adult placed in a similarly critical position. It has been noticed before by people working in other capacities with the same type of child. C. A. Joyce,[6] writing of the boys of his senior approved school, mentions that they 'do not, on the whole, remember very much of the Chairman of the court or of his homily'. Dr May Pearce, talking to the writer recently about a group of senior approved schoolgirls among whom she was doing psychiatric work, noted that they retained no impressions of any kind relating to the magistrates. An educational psychologist to three remand homes remarked briefly that the boys seemed only to have seen some vague shapes with no faces. They had no recollection of anything whatever being said by the shapes.

In view of all the circumstances it rather appears that, in spite of the relative informality of the juvenile court, the likelihood that the magistrates will be able to affect the child at all deeply by what they say from the Bench is somewhat smaller than might have been hoped. The court is not a suitable field for the deployment of Messianic ambitions or needs and feelings of an evangelistic kind on the part of members of the Bench.

There is, however, one thing which does seem to get across to the child in the Bench's remarks, and that is the tone of voice in which they are spoken and the attitude this seems to express. This again is not surprising. It is the kind of comprehension which even the youngest child or any little animal has, and it seems to be a surer way of communicating than the actual words used could be. An instance may illustrate this general point. Reports had been obtained on a difficult but intelligent boy who had been remanded in custody for the purpose. His record was not long but the contents of the reports were so serious and so much in agreement with each other that the magistrates thought an approved school committal order ought to be made. The youth had no reason to suppose that this was contemplated. The chairman was anxious that he should thoroughly understand how and why the magistrates had reached their decision. With this in view he took the boy through each of the reports with its highly unattractive picture of his attitude and behaviour. He was shown how particular incidents were the basis for various comments and how the total picture had been built up. It was pointed out how each of the reports was corroborated by what was said in the others. As the youth had been described as having a very hostile and difficult disposition, with a bad reaction to any kind of authority, particular care was taken to do all this in the tone of voice one might use in helping a traveller to read and use a map. In the end, and to no one's surprise, a committal order was made. On returning to the remand home the youth described what had happened at the court. He referred to his future hopefully and to the Bench as having been 'lenient with me'.

CHAPTER 10

DEALING WITH CRIMINALITY
BY COURT ORDER

IT appears very likely that most of the boys and girls who
come before a juvenile court charged with offences for the
first time do not appear again in that or any other criminal
court. A study of the relevant figures[1] shows that the
number of first offenders within a particular age group is
much larger than the number of recidivists in the suc-
ceeding age group. This confirms the impression that only a
fraction of those dealt with by the courts for the first time
reappear before them. Whether this is due to their having
been brought before the court and to any results which
follow from that, or simply to the ordinary progress of social
maturation, is not known. It seems unlikely that the court
has been able in so many cases, and by means of only one
appearance before it, to set in motion processes which can
be given the sole credit of being responsible for the reformation of a criminal character. It seems on the whole more
likely that the offence which led to the appearance in
court indicated in many, if not most, of these cases a
temporary degree of maladjustment to the demands of
living in society, which later, owing to changes in the
developing personality perhaps accompanied by a shifting
of the pressures upon it, disappeared.

The problem for society is not young people like these but
the very much smaller percentage who come back repeatedly, making their wretched way up the ascending
scale of punishment until, going forward to the sessions
under a recommendation for a borstal sentence, they bridge
the gap between the methods of sentencing open to the
juvenile courts and those others at the disposal of the
ordinary summary court, sessions, and assizes. For the
really persistent offender the dreary end of this road in

middle age or later is the sentence of preventive detention which, under the Criminal Justice Act, 1948, may amount to as long as fourteen years.

THE ROOTS OF CRIME

Norval Morris in his book *The Habitual Criminal*[2] provides an unforgettable picture of the recidivist – recently confirmed by W. H. Hammond and Edna Chayen in *Persistent Criminals*[3] – in the detailed analysis he has made of the characteristics – as shown by their records – of two groups of prisoners. He considers, firstly, thirty-two men who were, in October 1948, undergoing sentences of preventive detention under the 1908 Act, and, secondly, 270 other recidivists whose records would have much more than qualified them for sentencing under the Criminal Justice Act, 1948. The first group are a nuisance rather than a public danger. They are almost all unskilled, have practically never been employed, have very few personal relationships and owing to their mental and/or physical condition 'many are totally or partially incapable of facing the rigours of non-institutional life'. They return to prison in the minimum of time after release.

The larger group contains men with more serious offences. There are fewer men of poor mentality and more psychopaths and abnormal personalities. But there is the same, though much less pronounced, abnormal pattern of disturbed marital and other relationships, lack of skills, poor employment records, poor physical and mental condition. Of this larger group, forty per cent had been committed to prison before the age of twenty-one. Neither of the two groups represents a cross-section of the general population. Both are far below normal in the adequacy of their physical, mental, social, and psychiatric condition.

When a boy appears in court for the second, third, or fourth time, it is the deepening shadow of such a future as that depicted above which seems to be falling across him.

It is in these cases that the juvenile court feels its heaviest responsibility. There is the fear of doing something which may push the young offender farther along the wrong road, or at best of failing to do something which might put him in the way of being able to turn over a new leaf. There is the unspoken assumption that whatever is eventually done will have an important effect upon his future. The magistrates are anxious to make the order which will be in the best interests of the offender – but how are they to know which this might be?

We do not know what are the causes of crime. Margery Fry speaks[4] of the *climate* of crime, i.e. the social conditions which 'in greater or less degree go to the makeup of the "weather" in which offences multiply or dwindle', and of the *roots* or personal factors which make certain individuals more vulnerable than others to 'temptation weather'. For every delinquent child whose characteristics or circumstances or both appear to have been the factors predisposing him towards delinquency there are others with similar characteristics or in similar situations who have not become delinquent. Whatever may be the results of later researches, one conclusion unlikely to be upset is that there is no single cause of juvenile delinquency.

In the writer's experience, the offender is often the last person who has anything helpful to offer upon the subject of his delinquency. Many young offenders do not know why they committed the offence. Sometimes a boy with a considerable record, who knows very well that another appearance in court will inevitably lead to the long-dreaded removal from home, nevertheless, on little or no provocation and almost openly, commits some stupid trifling offence the immediate rewards of which are practically nil. In answer to the question, 'What did you think would happen to you if you broke the law again?', such a boy may say at once, 'Be sent away, sir.' But in answer to the further question, 'Then why did you do it?', he can only mutter, 'Don't know, sir', gazing helplessly back at his baffled questioner – or, as a sixteen-year-old girl in this situation said desperately, 'I don't want to sound like a clot, but if I knew why I do things I wouldn't do them. I don't *want* to go away from home!' – and burst into tears. It is not sufficient explanation to say that young delinquents steal because they want things. Everybody wants things and such desires are part of the normal healthy personality. But we are probably right in supposing that not everyone indulges in larceny and certainly that still fewer are invited to answer a charge in court.

It is much easier to show what are the concomitants of crime than what are the causes. Dr Cyril Burt's unequalled researches,[5] followed by those of a number of other workers, have convincingly demonstrated that certain situations are more likely than others to accompany the development of delinquent tendencies. The magistrates' interest in either the causes or the accompanying circumstances of crime is centred particularly upon any light which these may be able to throw upon the treatment advisable for each of the children with whom the court is concerned.

THE PREDICTION OF CRIMINAL BEHAVIOUR

Of more immediate practical relevance to the work of the courts than studies of the personal characteristics or circumstances which appear to have conduced to delinquency, are the investigations into the after-conduct of delinquents related to the different methods of treatment used by the courts. It would seem that a rational sentencing policy must be based upon knowledge not only of the characteristics of the offender but also of the effect of different methods of treatment upon different types of people. Such 'after-conduct' investigations have led to what are probably the most interesting contribution to penological studies in recent times, namely, those concerned with the statistical prediction of criminal behaviour. Leaders in this field have been S. and E. Glueck in the United States, with Hermann

Mannheim and Leslie Wilkins in this country. The work of these authorities suggests that it is possible to use past experience in a much more accurate way when assessing individual cases, with a view to forecasting probable success or failure, if this experience is presented in the statistical form of a properly validated prediction table.

Prediction tables have actually been used to forecast the proportions of successes and failures among groups of delinquents in different correctional-treatment situations. It is claimed that the prediction table technique can be used in relation to sentencing, to classifying in institutional treatment, and to problems of selection for conditional release 'on licence'. In sentencing, for example, a judge, or presumably also a lay magistrate, might consult separate prediction tables from which he could obtain information, in a properly organized form, as to past experience with regard to hundreds of people sentenced in particular ways. Such tables would be worked out for people resembling the particular offender in certain ways shown to be crucially important in this connexion, and would show the relative chances of success for offenders of this kind under alternative forms of treatment – for example, if conditionally discharged, placed on probation, sent to detention or to an approved school, and so on.

It is obvious that a prediction table of such a kind – or indeed of any kind likely to be produced in the near future – could not tell the judge whether the offender actually before him would make good on a particular sentence or not. There is no suggestion that a statistical calculation should, as it were, supersede the use of experience in judicial sentencing of offenders. On the contrary, it is an attempt to forecast the future on the basis of past experience. It is claimed that in this way the maximum use is made of past experience since the tables represent the total pooled experience of far more cases than could lie within the knowledge of an individual judge. It is suggested that, without the use of such a properly validated prognostic device, a judge who tries to act in the light of his own experience will in reality be acting in a way which, although based on fundamentally the same principle, is very fallible and open to all sorts of errors – of bias, selective memory, lack of knowledge of other cases, subjective assessments, etc. Although the tables cannot show whether a particular offender will commit further offences but only what the chances of others of his kind are if treated in particular ways, yet nevertheless it is claimed that the predictions made in the tables are more likely to afford accurate prognoses than the judge's 'hunch' or the guess from experience made in the ordinary way.

Clearly, this is not to say that all the judge would have to do in sentencing would be to look up and compare the chances in the book of tables, or to invite the appropriate expert to work them out and report to the court under Section 14 of the Magistrates' Courts Act, 1952! In the case of a first offender convicted of a minor offence, for example, it is unlikely that an English court would ever regard as relevant the information that his chances of success if given four years' corrective training are higher than his chances if fined or given a conditional discharge. But it might be very useful indeed in the case of an eighteen-year-old recidivist to know that records of past experience with other young offenders of his sort showed conclusively that, while success could not in any event be guaranteed, there was generally a greater chance of such people achieving it after a period of punitive detention than after borstal training. The chance of success would not be the only point to bear in mind but, in considering each case, the judge would be also able to review the results of wide experience accurately estimated and presented, instead of a limited experience dimly and incompletely recalled. He would also have to consider what evidence, if any, there was to suggest that the particular offender was likely to be one of those included in the percentage of successes in the group of similar offenders to which the prediction tables related, and also which penalties it would be appropriate on other grounds to consider in the particular case.

A number of questions leap to one's mind at once in considering the limitations of the assistance which courts might expect from the use of such prediction devices in sentencing. As already implied, the method which appeared to offer an offender the greatest chance of success might be one which is normally held to be appropriate only to confirmed recidivists, while the proved criminality of the offender in question might be very slight. Alternatively, exactly the opposite might, even if more rarely, occur. Furthermore what is to be done with those offenders whose chances under all forms of treatment appear to be poor? Ought an offender to be deprived of any opportunity of making good on probation, simply because his chances on punitive detention appear to be better? How far ought the probability of the offender's success under certain lenient treatment to weigh against the judge's estimate of the extent to which such a sentence is likely to fail to deter potential offenders?

These questions are, of course, not specifically related to the use of prediction tables and would doubtless occur at once to any experienced judge anxious to make the best use of his powers in sentencing. The use of tables would mean only that one of the points at issue in the mind of the sentencing judge was more accurately defined than would otherwise be possible. The questions themselves involve the functions of the court and the judge's duty in sentencing, the rights of the community over the individual, and questions of individual liberties.

THE EFFECTIVENESS OF SENTENCING

It must be admitted, however, that, in the present state of knowledge, the assistance which a judge may expect from prediction tables in choosing the appropriate sentence is, in one sense, very limited.

H. Mannheim and L. T. Wilkins[6] explored the relationship between background factors (such as previous treatment received, employment history, drunkenness, living with parents or not, type of home area, etc.), which were already in the records of boys when they entered borstal, and their subsequent success or failure after discharge. The boys were classified into five groups, A, B, X, C, and D. Group A had a success rate of seven out of eight, B had two out of three, X boys had an even chance, C had a success rate of only one out of three, and D, one out of eight. It should be noted that the classifications were made on the basis of *factors which already existed before the boys went into borstal at all* – in other words, the so-called treatment did not affect the percentage of success and failure to be expected from each group of boys.

When young prisoners were classified in the same way it was found that imprisonment gave results identical with borstal training for each group A, B, X, C, and D.[7] Moreover, it appeared that among 700 young ex-prisoners studied, some of whom had served four months and others fifteen months, the length of prison sentence had no effect on the outcome. The same result was obtained at Goudhurst senior detention centre where an average period of eleven weeks was served. For boys in each group it made no difference whether the sentence involved eleven weeks' detention, eighteen months' borstal, four or fifteen months' prison: the result would be the same.

In 1958 Wilkins[8] compared the outcome of treatment of offenders convicted in two different courts. One court used probation to the extent of treble the national average and ninety-seven probation cases from this court were matched (for offence, sex, age, record, etc.) with cases from another court which made only an average use of probation, using fines, discharges, prison, and borstal in its other cases. After a five-year follow-up there was no significant difference in the outcome of treatments in terms of further convictions. It suggests that probation could be used for a large proportion of the cases now sent to prison or borstal without any change in the reconviction rate as a whole.

Research done by the Metropolitan Police in 1937, on

the after-conduct of 20,000 first offenders during a five-year follow-up, showed that the reconviction rate varied with age but sentence seemed to have little or no effect. Fine, dismissal, imprisonment gave identical results. Sir George Benson of the Howard League, commenting in the House of Commons on these and other results of research, pointed out that it appeared that on a given type of individual all forms of penal treatment gave the same result. He also referred to a comparative study he had made between the results for different forms of sentence given in the Metropolitan area in 1932 – a period when we had nearly three million unemployed – with results from the same sentences on first offenders in Scotland in 1954 'when we had pretty well revolutionized our penal system and there was no unemployment'.[9] Here we have different places, times, and social conditions. Each age group had its own reconviction rate, but the rate for all forms of treatment was approximately the same.

Under the provisions of the Criminal Justice Act, 1948, it is possible for an offender to be required, as part of a probation order, with his own consent and on expert medical advice to the court, to receive mental treatment. In 1960 Max Grunhut[10] published a study of the results of such orders in terms of reconviction rates. For a variety of reasons, it is difficult to match and compare these 'Section 4 probationers' with other probationers who are not having mental treatment, and the similarity of results is therefore all the more interesting. Reconviction rates closely followed normal expectation. As with other probationers, they decreased for higher age groups and for women, and first offenders had a much better success rate. Moreover, the usual experience in regard to success rates by type of offence was repeated here, in that the highest rate of reconviction, nearly fifty per cent, was for offenders against property, while the reconviction rate for sexual offenders was low. Whether the medical prognosis at the end of treatment was good or bad, favourable or not, did not seem to be a determining factor in regard to subsequent criminality. There

seems little ground in this experience to justify courts in, for
instance, relying on mental treatment to cure criminal
behaviour in the mentally disturbed. Indeed, in our
experience of the results of sentencing to date, it seems that
there is little to justify courts in supposing that they can
reform or deter the offender before them through the sentence at all. We do not at present know how to affect
criminal behaviour by means of penal sanctions or other
orders made by the criminal court.

Certain aspects of the problem which have emerged from
recent studies such as those reported in *The Sentence of the
Court: A Handbook for Courts on the Treatment of Offenders*[11] –
are of especial interest to the juvenile court. Two of the
most important factors from the point of view of the
probability of reconviction are age and number of previous
convictions.

Thus, over fifty per cent of offenders aged under 14 at their first
offence were reconvicted within five years, compared with 30 per
cent of first offenders aged 21–29 and only 9 per cent of first
offenders aged 40 or over; similarly all offenders aged 8–11 who
had two previous offences were reconvicted, compared with only
just over 40 per cent of such offenders aged 30 and over. Secondly,
the more offences an offender has already committed, the more
likely he is to be reconvicted within a given period. The effect of
the number of previous convictions on the proportion reconvicted
differs somewhat according to the offender's age . . . , to his age at
the time he was first found guilty, and to the rate of committing
the intervening offences. For juveniles, one previous conviction
increases the five-year reconviction rate from about one out of
two to two out of three offenders. But adult offenders with one
previous conviction are about twice as likely to be reconvicted as
first offenders of comparable age.

Justices may obtain a free copy of this important publication through their own Magistrates' Courts Committees,
and, in view of the importance of the information it contains,
it ought to be possible to assume that every juvenile court
justice has made it his business to obtain a copy and to
become thoroughly familiar with its contents.

On the general topic of predictive tables it must be emphasized that the identifying of factors which appear to have predictive value in relation to future criminality, and the assessment of degrees of value, do not necessarily imply a causal relationship between these factors and the criminality. Nevertheless there is a strong suggestion that some kind of relationship exists between these factors and the causes, whatever they are, of the criminality. For practical purposes the important point is whether the predictive tables do predict. Professor and Mrs Glueck claim that this is a matter of demonstrable fact which is, in principle, no longer open to serious disputè. In their work with children the Gluecks[12] go so far as to suggest that it is possible to predict future criminality in children not yet delinquent at all by reference to the presence or absence of certain factors in the social background of the children. These social factors are respectively concerned with the discipline of the boy by the father, the supervision of the boy by the mother, the affection of the father for the boy, the affection of the mother for the boy, and the cohesiveness of the family.

The matter is of great relevance to the juvenile court and to the social services. Early prognosis of future criminality could lead to early action to prevent the development of the delinquent tendencies. In the case of children who have actually committed an offence, the prognosis of delinquent tendencies, on grounds independent of and additional to the offence, may alert the court to the fact that the offender is a much poorer risk for the future than the nature or seriousness of his offence might suggest. The prediction of future criminality in an unoffending subject raises different though related questions from the prediction of behaviour in the event of various alternative methods of treatment of a proved offender. The whole subject does, however, throw into the sharpest possible focus the question as to what should be the relation of the order to the offence and record. Are such prediction tables the final word in the argument as to how far the court, in making an order, is justified in ignoring the degree of proved criminality in the defendant, in the shape of the offence of which he has been convicted, and in dealing not with what he has done but with what he is or may become?

Thus prediction tables and other prognostic devices tend to highlight questions which are significant and important in a much wider context than that of the courts. It may or may not be right to argue that a child convicted of a minor offence in the juvenile court should, as a consequence, be dealt with by that court in relation to social factors in his background, the connexion of which with his delinquency appears to be one of statistical correlation rather than cause – to argue that the court is under no compulsion to maintain any relation between the offence and the order. But if it is right so to argue, then it is only one step farther to ask why a child who has not yet committed any offence at all should not be brought into court and dealt with, on the ground that his background suggests that he will very probably commit delinquent acts in the future.

It might perhaps be suggested that this is, in effect, what is already being done under care, protection, or control proceedings, since in very many cases it is not alleged that the child has yet committed any offence. But the main focus of care, protection, or control proceedings is not upon law-breaking at all, either present or future. Their scope is much wider than such a suggestion would imply and the proceedings are centred upon the presence or absence of proper care and guardianship. Allegations that the child who is the subject of the proceedings has committed offences may be made and proved as part of an attempt to show that he is out of control, but this by itself is not usually enough for the care, protection, or control proceedings to be successful. It is usually necessary, in addition, to show that he is not receiving proper care and guardianship, and the evidence on this point does not, in the majority of cases, rest upon whether the child commits or seems likely to commit criminal offences.

It is true that within its criminal jurisdiction also the court has power to take a child out of the control of his parents and commit him instead to the care of a fit person. But within its criminal, in contrast to its civil, jurisdiction the court has power to do this only after it has found the child guilty of a criminal offence, and, having done that, it does not require that anything further to the offence should be proved. In practice, 'fit person' orders are not usually made, in the case of first offenders at any rate, unless there appears to be a definite connexion between poor home conditions and some fairly serious delinquency. Although the home conditions may be unfavourable in the opinion of the social experts and of experienced members of the Bench, nevertheless, if the larceny of a bottle of milk is the total extent of the delinquency which has resulted, there would not appear to most people to be adequate grounds for a criminal court to remove a young offender from the control of his parents. One of the points to which an English judge or magistrate would be likely to give weight, when considering the order appropriate in such a case, would be that the offender must not be treated as guilty of further offences before he has committed them and they are proved against him.

This is not to deny that, where, on general grounds, a child appears to a criminal court to be a bad risk and likely to develop serious delinquent tendencies, this situation will, of course, weigh more heavily in the mind of the court as subsequent offences increasingly confirm the initial forecast. A court which is properly informed by the reports on the school and home background of an offender, and on the connexion which appears to exist between the conditions revealed and the child's delinquency, will usually, for example, place him on probation, when another child might have been given a conditional discharge or a fine. On committing further offences, such a child may very probably be sent to an approved school or taken into the care of the local authority rather earlier in the criminal career than might have happened to other offenders. But even here the court is relying upon the confirmation of delinquent tendencies offered by the further offences rather than simply on the suggested statistical relation between the poor home and delinquency.

The social backgrounds of the children identified as predelinquents by statistical methods such as the Gluecks' tables, though admittedly poor on the emotional side, would not necessarily provide adequate grounds for care, protection, or control proceedings as the law stands at present. Opinions differ as to whether this is a situation which calls for alterations in the law or whether the best approach is by some other method. At present, it is in these cases that the social worker may hear almost with relief that an offence has been committed and the child is to come before the juvenile court on a criminal charge, since this is likely to be the only way in which he can – by good fortune and a subsequent offence or two – be removed from home. In the meantime, there is also the hope that the home may be improved during the operation of a probation order.

Thus the civil court is not concerned with delinquency and its prevention as such, but with the welfare of children who come before it in every aspect which indicates the presence or absence of proper parental care. In its criminal jurisdiction, on the other hand, the court is concerned only with children who have, or are alleged to have, actually committed offences. Where the offence is trivial and the court leaves the child under the control of his parents, the social workers, teachers, and other people on the fringe of the case may be very irritated and annoyed indeed. But to make an order removing the child in such cases might well be to telescope the two different jurisdictions of the juvenile court, the criminal and the civil, and the two different procedures, that for the trial of offences and that for the hearing of applications in regard to children alleged to be in need of care, protection, or control. An order would have to be made which could not be said to be consequent upon the criminal proceedings but would in fact be based upon an implied finding that the child was not receiving proper care or guardianship – although this issue had not been before the court at all and the parents had not been given proper opportunities of refuting such an allegation.

Such a short-circuiting of the procedure proper to a care, protection, or control case may be very tempting, but, where the advisability of removal from home is not in any way suggested by the degree of criminality of an offender, the criminal court will need to consider very carefully any grounds upon which it is alleged that a 'fit person' order should be made. If the court normally receives reports in writing, the Bench will need to ask themselves whether they are being influenced by information given in those reports but not shown or read to child or parent, and which therefore the latter have had no opportunity of refuting. Sometimes, too, the reporting social worker or the magistrates themselves hold very strong personal views that certain circumstances (sexual irregularities on the part of the mother, for instance) *ought* to be regarded as adequate proof of a need for care or protection. This, however, is not how the law stands at present, and in the writer's view it would not be right for a magistrate to give such opinions the force of law by making a 'fit person' order upon these grounds alone. Efforts to stretch the provisions of the criminal law to meet needs for social action which ought to be faced and met by other means can only lead to confusion in the courts and to delay in taking more appropriate steps elsewhere.

In sentencing there are already, owing to such attempts, considerable differences in policy, as the following example will show. Under Section 54 of the Children and Young Persons Act, 1933, a juvenile offender may be committed to detention in a remand home for a period not exceeding one month if the court considers that none of the other methods in which the case can legally be dealt with is suitable. This restriction finds an echo in the prohibition under the Criminal Justice Act, 1948, Sections 17 and 18, on sentences of detention in a detention centre, or of imprisonment on persons under twenty-one, unless the court is of opinion that no other method of dealing with him is appropriate. Public opinion seems now to have moved very distinctly in the direction of general restrictions on imprisonment of people of any age if they are first offenders, and the First Offenders Act, 1958, extended this prohibition to first offenders aged twenty-one or more.

In a recent case a thirteen-year-old boy was found guilty of three offences of larceny and asked for thirteen others to be taken into consideration. The probation officer reported that neither boy nor parents took the matter at all seriously, and this was corroborated by the boy's attitude in court. It was the opinion of the magistrates that he needed a short, sharp lesson in the shape of detention, and that nothing else would be adequate to bring home to him or his parents the seriousness of his behaviour in the eyes of the law. The clerk, a man of great experience in the juvenile court, was horrified to hear this proposal, since the youth was technically a first offender and detention in remand home or detention centre is the juvenile court substitute for imprisonment. After considering this view of the legal aspect of the proposed 'sentence', and in the interests of justice, the court decided to impose fines instead.

Within a few days of this event the writer heard of a case decided in another court, in which a boy, also a first offender, had been committed to a month's detention as a consequence of a single offence of petty larceny. It was explained that this had been done on the suggestion of a social worker, as the boy's mother was not well and could thus obtain freedom from domestic responsibilities for a few weeks.

Two such widely divergent views as to the proper use of sentencing powers in the juvenile court cannot both be right. Certainly in the second case they seem to have been used simply to secure a convenient substitute for the 'short stay' provision not being made by the children's department of the local authority. In theory the possibility of an appeal acts as a check on the action of a summary court in sentencing. But as juveniles are seldom legally represented, appeals from the juvenile court are in practice very rare, and there is considerable freedom for the magistrates to exercise their sentencing powers in whatever way they think best.

It is probable that this rather flexible use of sentencing powers, coupled with a lack of scrutiny by the higher courts, and an extensive use of probation orders, with or without requirements, has helped the juvenile court to go some way in meeting changing views on the most effective approach to the treatment of delinquency in children and yet to remain ostensibly within the legal framework of the ordinary courts. This process has probably gone as far as it can go, and there are now signs of considerable dissatisfaction with the system, by which childish misdeeds may be made the subject of criminal charges.

THE PAUCITY OF REMEDIAL SERVICES AT THE DISPOSAL OF THE COURT

The first half of this century, and especially the period since the last war, has seen a great expansion of provision for the welfare, health, and education of the young, and these developments have left the special provisions made under the penal system far behind. Modern child-welfare services are related to need conceived in wide terms and indicated in a variety of ways of which delinquent behaviour is only one. Under these services the local authorities now have at their disposal, or have power to provide, every known treatment for the mental, physical, or emotional difficulties of children, including the power to act as a parent if necessary. In comparison, the treatment to which the juvenile court can commit direct, viz. punitive detention, attendance at a day centre run by the police, and a small range of segregated approved boarding-schools, is limited in the extreme.

Since, in dealing with offenders, the court can make the use of a recommended treatment a requirement in a probation order, it might be concluded that in this way the

juvenile court does, nevertheless, have the whole range of
preventive and remedial services at its disposal for the
treatment of children with behaviour difficulties. In practice, however, the court not only cannot provide the treatment itself but it also lacks power to compel the providing
bodies to act. For example, to touch upon a particularly
sore point, a requirement to reside at a school for maladjusted children would be impossible of fulfilment unless
the local education authority regarded such special educational provision as both appropriate and necessary in the
particular case and were prepared to pay for it. How and
where a child is to be educated is in modern times a decision
for the parents and the education authority, whether the
child is an offender or not. The court cannot take that
decision out of their hands except under the guise of a penal
measure, i.e. by committal to an approved school.

The court is in a similar position in regard to decisions
as to where, and by whom, a child shall be brought up. In
making a 'fit person' order, the court may have intended
that the child should leave his parents and be brought up
by foster-parents or in a children's home. But this is a
decision which is not theirs to make. The effect of a 'fit
person' order is simply to hand the responsibility for such
decisions to the children's officer instead of leaving it with
the parent. At no point does it belong to the court. The
children's officer may take the child placed in his care
straight out of court and back to its own home. If he does
so, he is acting well within his powers, functions, and responsibilities. The court has no power to interfere and it
has no supervisory function in the matter. The only way in
which a court can say directly where a child shall live is,
again, under the guise of a penal measure, namely, by
sending him to an approved school or detention centre.

INADEQUACY OF PROVISION BY THE HEALTH EDUCATION AND WELFARE AUTHORITIES

In modern times, then, the remedial treatment of children showing delinquent tendencies probably falls more appropriately within the sphere of the social services rather than of the penal system.

If this were fully recognized it would not, however, do away with some of the difficulties which exist under the present system but yet are in no way related to it – indeed are quite extraneous to it. From the point of view of the courts, the biggest gaps at present in the treatment of young offenders appear to be due to the failure of the local authorities to provide enough special educational treatment, especially for the educationally subnormal and the maladjusted, enough boarding-school education for children who could benefit from it, enough child-guidance services and, above all, enough (or any!) professionally trained social case-workers available to every social service which comes into contact with families in difficulties. It is very hard not to think that most of the children who come before the juvenile court for the first and only time in their lives could have been dealt with equally well outside the penal system, and would have been so dealt with if adequate facilities for early diagnosis and treatment had been available. The shortage of teachers and the resulting large classes mean that many children are not noticed to be in difficulty at all until the matter has become serious. Nor can the teachers give the time to parent contact which might be so fruitful. At the present time a remedial teacher with some knowledge of social work, or a trained social case-worker with some teaching experience, attached to every large school and available also for consultation and advice to the educational welfare officers, might help immensely towards the earlier observation of behaviour difficulties and the handling of these, within the school or home setting, with the help of the school health service.

In many areas at present there seems to be little hope of providing services adequate to deal with every child who could benefit. In the meantime, the policy has seemed to be to let things drift and sometimes to give priority on the waiting lists, not necessarily to those cases which are in most urgent need of treatment but to those which have registered themselves as a public nuisance by being the subject of criminal proceedings in a juvenile court. In view of the strong feelings expressed in some quarters about the iniquity of giving a child a criminal record, a system whereby a criminal conviction may be hoped for as the open sesame to the child-guidance clinic strikes oddly, to say the least. Yet many courts are faced with cases of truancy or pilfering of long standing, where children have not been seen at the clinics, or referred for ascertainment as needing special educational treatment. The court has no power to provide either of these facilities and there is no reason whatever for children to go through a court for the sole purpose of benefiting from them. The services have usually no powers after the court appearance that they did not have before. The court's time is wasted in this sense, and the child is left with a court case against him.

The offender's delinquency is very often only one aspect, and possibly quite a minor one, of the difficulties which beset the family of which he is a member. Being a problem family or a member of one is not in itself an offence. But the concern of the court is with the offender and his delinquency and if, for example, he completes his probation period satisfactorily, the advice, help, and friendship which the probation officer has been able to offer to him and the family will, thereupon, cease officially to be available. This will happen even though the family's difficulties and inadequacies, which helped previously to conduce towards the delinquency, may be showing themselves in forms such as eviction for non-payment of rent, truancy in another member of the family, or severe psychiatric illness in a third. Each of these difficulties as it develops fully may attract the attention of the relevant social agency or department, and as each is put right, even temporarily, the family will again be left to its own devices until further trouble appears in the same or some new direction.

It seems likely that much less attention would need to be given to the end products of social inadequacy – such as homelessness, delinquency, maladjustment, unemployability, etc. – if more attention could be concentrated on helping handicapped families to function better at an earlier stage, before the results of their inadequacy become too difficult or impossible to remedy. It would also lead to an economy of social effort in the long run, and probably in the short run too, if the difficulties which led to interference with the family by the authorities were regarded as indications of social problems with which the family needed help, and were not treated as ends in themselves.

A further attempt to meet this problem is the duty laid on every local authority, under Section 1 of the Children and Young Persons Act, 1963, 'to make available such advice, guidance and assistance as may promote the welfare of children by diminishing the need to receive children into or keep them in care ... or to bring children before a juvenile court', including 'provision for giving assistance in kind or, in exceptional circumstances, in cash'. This section opens the door to the social services to get in early at the slightest indication of even 'predelinquent' tendencies. However, the social services have no power to compel offenders as such to accept treatment, and it is, indeed, an open question whether the alternative of prosecution in the background would suffice to make treatment on a voluntary basis feasible in many cases.

In practice, the local authorities in many areas have proved quite unable to do more than make a feint at dealing with the ball now placed so squarely in their court. The task is enormous. To deal with it there is a shortage of most kinds of social and educational facility. This varies from one area to another, but tends to be disastrous in the more populated urban areas where the juvenile courts are kept busiest. There is heavy overcrowding in the schools, a long waiting-list in the child-guidance clinics (where these exist) and a desperate shortage of nurses in the children's hospitals. Above all, there is a shortage of trained and experienced probation officers, and of both residential and outdoor staff in the children's departments. Pressure points very obvious to people working in the juvenile court are the inadequate provision for boarding and for special education, especially of the maladjusted and the educationally subnormal, and the almost complete absence in some districts of trained and experienced child psychiatrists and psychiatric social workers. At the court end, the detention and approved school places which in theory are at the disposal of the court have, over the last few years, proved very inadequate indeed. In some areas, boys committed to approved schools, after having already spent six or seven weeks awaiting trial and a further three weeks in custody, on remand for full reports, have had to spend up to a further three months waiting in the remand home after committal, before there was even a vacancy in the classifying school to which they must go first for four to six weeks. These shortages exist in spite of determined, ingenious, and often quite desperate effort on the part of the departments concerned to make provision. They are the result of a persistently adverse public attitude to expenditure on provision for offenders. It cannot be too strongly emphasized that no change in the procedure for examining each offender's case and considering the results of the examination will of itself remedy these deficiencies.

CHAPTER 11

THE FUTURE: PROPOSALS FOR REFORM

THERE seem to be two major considerations involved in the problem of how to deal with child offenders. The first question is whether children who break the law are to be dealt with as children whose parents need assistance in bringing them up, or, primarily, as offenders against whose activities the community must protect itself. The second question relates to the procedure to be employed in implementing whichever of these two different approaches is preferred. It is clear that a court of justice might be used in either approach – exercising a civil jurisdiction in the first setting or a criminal one in the second. It is not so clear that a non-judicial administrative procedure – at least in Western democracies today – is an equally versatile device.

The juvenile court in the British Commonwealth countries is a well-known example of criminal jurisdiction, but ours is now practically the only European system which still brings schoolchildren before a criminal court. On the Continent, the civil or guardianship court is usual, while in Scandinavia the administrative welfare board is the rule. In California, in the U.S.A., the system is a mixed one of trial court and treatment tribunal. The differences between these alternatives are not nearly so clear in practice as their names might suggest, and in fact very few inferences indeed – for example, as to the pre-eminence of considerations of justice or, alternatively, of welfare – can safely be made merely from the descriptive title of a particular body. As has been clearly shown by Paul Tappan,[1] in policy, authority, and composition there are more points of similarity between some courts and the administrative committees or boards than there are between those courts and other courts. Nevertheless it might, prima facie, be expected that a criminal court would be, comparatively, the body most appropriate to the task of preventing crime, protecting society, and regulating the exaction of vengeance. Indeed, any judicial tribunal at all might be expected to be better adapted, both to the finding of facts and the apportionment of consequences, than a committee; but a committee might perhaps be thought to offer advantages in securing the rehabilitative treatment and reformation of offenders.

Thus the English juvenile court has been criticized on the ground that the criminal jurisdiction makes it difficult to deal with an offender's social needs. Guardianship courts have been criticized on the grounds that they are not suitable for dealing with minor and non-maladjusted offenders, that they lack adequate sanctions because of the necessity of preserving a welfare image, and that, in their paternalistic zeal, they are in danger of ignoring questions of individual freedom and civil liberties. The welfare boards have in recent years been under very heavy fire in their own countries on the same sort of grounds as the guardianship courts and, additionally, because in general no special procedure is laid down. Thus in Sweden, where the welfare boards have very wide compulsory powers, there is no legal duty on the board to find the facts before taking remedial steps, and they have been criticized for not taking enough care to satisfy themselves of the truth of allegations before deciding upon remedies. It is unusual for a board to see either parent or child, and, although the parent has a right to be heard, he has no right to cross-examine the complainant and, indeed, very few boards even inform the juvenile or his parents as to the material facts which have come to light during the investigation on which action is to be based. As non-judicial tribunals with very wide powers, the door is open to arbitrary decision and action, especially so in that in most of the welfare board systems appeal facilities do not include recourse to the courts. The Californian solution is criticized in that, with the best of intentions, it involves throwing over the protections afforded by the criminal jurisdiction at the very point where, it might be argued, the guilty defendant needs them most, i.e. at the sentencing stage. Thus the offender may be handed over to a treatment board under an indeterminate sentence of rehabilitation, its actual length depending on the decision of at least two of the six members of the youth authority, taken at their own time and neither in public nor published.

It must be pointed out, however, that both the characteristic advantages and disadvantages respectively of each of these systems are likely to present themselves in very different lights according to whether the particular examples under examination are good or bad of their type. Whether the type is to be rated as good or bad *per se* will, of course, depend on the personal view held by the particular observer. Thus there are juvenile courts purporting to exercise a criminal jurisdiction, but so informally run that they are hardly recognizable as criminal courts and appear to present many of the features popularly associated with the guardianship courts. On the other hand, there are civil or guardianship courts showing less regard for welfare than would be expected in a criminal court.

The more specific characteristics also are not always what might be expected. In England the procedure in criminal courts is by prosecution and is 'accusational' in character. It is not the court's responsibility to find out whether the accused did the act with which he is charged but for the prosecution to prove their accusation and for the court to decide finally whether they have done so or not. But in most Continental courts, whether civil or criminal, the procedure is as much one of inquiry as it is in the Scandinavian welfare boards and the court or board is in the position of actively investigating the allegations for itself.

In some of the systems the procedure in the courts is such that there are not two separate adjudications, i.e. the arrival at the verdict and then the decision on the sentence (with provision for remand for reports in between), but both decisions, on verdict and sentence, are taken as one and in the light of information already known to the Bench as to the record and character of the accused. This is also true of welfare boards. Again, it is not necessarily only the welfare boards which omit the requirement of formal proof: this may also be true of a court as, for example, under the New Zealand Child Welfare Act, 1925.

Even the qualifications and categories of personnel presiding are not characteristic specifically of courts or of welfare boards. Thus, while English summary courts use entirely lay persons on the Bench in contrast with the professional judiciary found elsewhere, some welfare boards require that a legally qualified person sits as one of the members, and a compromise is seen in some of the Continental courts where the system requires lay assessors to sit with the professional judge, as indeed is the case in England where the recorder hears an appeal from the juvenile court.

The most important question, therefore, is perhaps not whether to deal with young offenders in criminal or civil courts or through welfare boards as such, but how, under whatever system is in use, to ensure that the public is protected from crime, that liberty is preserved, and that the young offender gets the treatment he needs. The age of criminal responsibility is, of course, crucial, but it is important to clarify one point immediately. The age of criminal responsibility is not a statement about the psychosocial development of children but about the legal system. It embodies a social policy decision as to the age at which it is thought expedient to have penal sanctions available for use in suitable cases when dealing with offending juveniles. The decision is one of social expediency and is related to problems of keeping the peace, the solution of which, in regard to juveniles especially, has, as limiting factors, considerations of the rights and the welfare of the offender, as well as 'justice' and the basic need to substitute for private reprisals by regulating the exaction of vengeance.

Our own juvenile court is at present simply a summary court dealing with offenders aged ten to sixteen inclusive under ordinary summary procedure, only slightly modified as to procedure and constitution in ways which are intended

to assist the defendant, *in his capacity as a defendant,* by off-
setting as far as possible the handicap of his youth and immaturity. Thus we have no special sentencing structure
specifically related to the juvenile court, but young offenders
join in receiving the general benefits of our differentiated
sentencing structure – the differentiations relating mainly to
being over or under twenty-one years of age (e.g. in relation
to attendance centres, detention, borstal, etc.) and to the
seriousness of the record (e.g. restraints on the punishment of
first offenders, and on sentencing to preventive detention,
corrective training, etc.). The distinctive features of our
own juvenile court are simply the age of the defendant and,
most important, the statutory provision which, under
Section 35 of the main Act, compels the court to inform
itself as to the social background and surrounding circumstances of an offender before passing sentence. This
is a matter which is usually optional in dealing with
adult offenders. In law the welfare of the offender is
not the primary consideration even when dealing with
a juvenile, though in practice it may often turn out to
be so.

The ideas put forward in the White Paper on *The Child,
The Family and The Young Offender*[2] have been under discussion in one form or another since well before the setting
up of the Ingleby Committee. In fact, the juxtaposition of
the first and second parts in the terms of reference of that
Committee seemed almost to imply an assumption that
dealing with a child's social needs would often render it
unnecessary to deal with his offence *per se.* Ingleby saw the
difficulty of dealing primarily with social needs in a
criminal court as the 'dilemma' of the English juvenile
court. The solution was to push further the attempt to get
the best of both worlds within the present framework. The
juvenile court should be retained, but more of the younger
offenders should be dealt with by means of the civil procedure, by raising the age of criminal responsibility to
twelve, and later to thirteen or fourteen. It was to be made
easier to prove a civil case so that, on proof of the child's

alleged acts, it would no longer be necessary to prove lack of guardianship in addition. In criminal cases the court should 'move farther away from the conception of criminal jurisdiction' in deciding upon the order – and in all cases, both criminal and civil, the choice of order should be related simply to the treatment needed but not otherwise likely to be received.

These suggestions, even if adopted wholesale, would not have dealt with the 'problem' of the 'disproportionate' order. These were orders which appeared disproportionately heavy because they were made to meet grave social needs in cases where the actual offence proved was trivial. The real difficulty neither faced nor even mentioned was that, in such cases, the alleged needs were unproven. Not only are they cases in which criminal procedure excludes from the actual trial, as being irrelevant, the consideration of the needs of the offender, but often enough the evidence of need, had it been produced in a civil case, would not have sufficed to secure a finding. The so-called 'problem' is basic to the judicial procedure, whether civil or criminal. It is that specific allegations must be made and proved before a person can be subjected to compulsion on account of them, and that the weight of the order is traditionally likely to be apportioned by the court in relation to the gravity of the acts or situations established.

The subsequent Children and Young Persons Act, 1963, fell considerably short of the Ingleby proposals in their entirety, yet nevertheless brought changes which set the stage for what could have developed into a bloodless revolution in our method of dealing with juvenile offenders. In care, protection, or control cases it is no longer necessary to prove that guardianship is not being given but only to show that it is not, in fact, being received. The out-of-control procedure, formerly only available to the parent, is now available instead to the local authority, and in this procedure it is unnecessary to prove anything at all as to the quality of guardianship. But potentially the most important provision is that which, under Section 1, lays a duty on the local authority to do preventive work, thus 'diminishing the need . . . to bring children before a juvenile court'. Complementary to this important provision is the administrative arrangement made by the Home Office for police forces to consult the local children's department before bringing proceedings against children under the age of twelve.

The next step logically would appear to be to cover the whole range of juvenile offenders, thus enabling them to be dealt with entirely outside the courts wherever possible. Where powers of compulsion were required, these could be sought by bringing an out-of-control case under the civil procedure. That this is not happening may well be due to the need for punitive sanctions which are not at present available either to the court exercising a civil jurisdiction or to the children's departments outside the court altogether. It would also appear, however, to be due to the extreme inadequacy of the social treatment facilities in many fields. In the past the juvenile court has, in many instances, had to use the penal provisions to try to fill the gaps left by the social services. It has been the demands of the courts which have necessitated the continued existence and expansion of a system of boarding (approved) schools for offenders who need boarding-school education, and a probation service for those who need social case-work, and even in some areas special psychiatric and psychological services for assessment and treatment recommendations. A juvenile court which is of the opinion, on expert advice, that a young offender ought to go to boarding-school, or be supervised, or attend an attendance centre, or go to the remand home for reports, may simply make an order accordingly, i.e. on the basis of the treatment required for the particular child. The convenience or difficulties of the administrative authorities in making the required provision are not directly the court's problem. To that extent the court is in a very good position to draw public and official attention to the inadequacies of provision. It has been for the court to say what is required and for the administration to provide it.

This, then, is the system which, according to the radical proposals put forward by the 'Scottish Ingleby' (i.e. the Kilbrandon Committee's Report on Children and Young Persons, Scotland)[3] and the milder version in the White Paper on *The Child, The Family and The Young Offender*,[4] is to be superseded.

The proposals made by the Kilbrandon Committee bear considerable resemblance to certain aspects of Scandinavian practice. It should be borne in mind that the juvenile court idea has never really developed in the Scottish legal system, in contrast with that of England and Wales, and the position at present is that, in most areas of Scotland, charges against juveniles are still not heard before juvenile courts. The main proposal is that, in dealing with juvenile offenders, the juvenile courts should be done away with altogether. Offenders under sixteen years of age and admitting an offence should be dealt with by a lay panel of suitably knowledgeable people vested with powers of compulsory action and appointed by the sheriff on the nomination of the education authority in each education area. Behind the panel, and operating as its executive agency, would be a new social education department, responsible for the preparation of social background reports, treatment recommendations, and the subsequent application of treatment. Referrals to the panel would always be through a single independent official who would also present the case to the panel and act as legal adviser to it. He would be called the 'reporter' and be qualified in law and by experience in administration. Where the basic facts or the panel's decisions were disputed the disputed matter would go before the sheriff's court. Appeals against decisions of the panel would go to the sheriff sitting as a judicial officer. The measures available to the panel would include admonition of the child or caution of the parent, attendance centre, supervision, and reception into the care of the local authority (including power to send to a children's home or a residential school). It would be for the panel to decide which of these measures was appropriate in the particular instance. There would be no right of legal representation before the panel.

This Report was well received as a vigorous and forward-looking document, but recently a more critical view has been emerging. It seems not to have been realized at first that what was being proposed was that, on the admission of any offence, however trivial, by an offender of any age under sixteen, the local authority in the shape of the social education department would *ipso facto* acquire power to take over the parental rights, to board out, send to an institution, or deal with as seemed best according to its assessment of need from time to time, and that this power would remain in existence, unless successfully appealed against, until the child reached the age of sixteen and the ordinary protections of the law were restored to him. In the juvenile courts of England and Wales, in 1965, out of 120,698 offenders under seventeen only 1,370 were made the subject of 'fit person' orders. It is certainly a surprising suggestion that it is either necessary or advisable to give such very wide powers to a non-judicial body which will be dealing with many ill-educated and ignorant people who are to have no right to legal representation except on appeal. Not everyone thinks that the Scottish children's departments and probation services, which are already doing much of the kind of work involved, should be pushed aside. Objection has also been taken to the proposal that sixteen-year-olds should be exposed to the full rigours of the ordinary courts, a proposal made at a time, too, when there is so much talk in other circles of the need for special youth courts to be set up for the sixteen- or seventeen-year-old to twenty-one-year-old age group. The position of the reporter has also raised doubts and as F. V. Jarvis, for example, writing in *Probation* in June 1964 points out:

Not only would a child be 'prosecuted by the reporter', but that same official would give legal advice to the lay panel before whom he has brought the child and additionally act as the panel's secretary. It is necessary only to imagine the police in this county combining their prosecuting function with that of the clerk to the justices to see what distortion of the normal processes of justice would be involved.

In favour of the Report's proposals, it is pointed out that the new procedure would avoid the criminal stigma and bring the child directly into the hands of the treatment authorities, and that these would be dealing with him alongside other children in need of help and not as a member of a group regarded as morally reprehensible by legal definition. It is also pointed out that the extensive powers assumed would make possible a much more flexible plan of treatment as the situation changed from time to time, while the liberty of the individual would be safe-guarded by the sheriff's court determining all 'not guilty' pleas and by the possibility of resort to appeal against treatment recommendations at once or at annual intervals.

In a written Parliamentary answer on 23 June 1965,[5] the Secretary of State for Scotland stated:

> The Government propose to bring forward legislation in due course for the establishment of juvenile panels in Scotland on the lines recommended by the Committee. The effective establishment of a system of juvenile panels will require suitably organized support from the social work services, though not necessarily based, as the Kilbrandon Committee recommended, on the education authority. The Government are at present considering how best the social work services in Scotland may be reorganized in order to provide the comprehensive casework service recommended by the Kilbrandon Committee.

Proposals (*Social Work and the Community*, Cmnd 3065) for reorganizing local authority services in Scotland were published in October 1966.

The White Paper, put forward by the Government for the purpose of discussion before legislation is prepared, contains proposals which had been foreshadowed a year previously in the Report, *Crime – A Challenge to Us All*,[6] of a study group under the chairmanship of Lord Longford. As under the Kilbrandon scheme, the proposal is that (in

England and Wales) offenders under sixteen years of age should be dealt with quite outside the court and that the juvenile court should be done away with. The children should appear before 'family councils' including at least two people, one man and one woman, on any one occasion and 'consisting of social workers of the children's service and other persons selected for their understanding and experience of children and, in particular, for their awareness of the problems facing the children and adults likely to come before them.' The members of the family councils would be appointed by the local authority through its children's committee. Like the Kilbrandon panels, the councils would deal only with offenders who formally admitted guilt and/or agreed to treatment, but, unlike the panels, the councils would have no compulsory powers, applying remedial treatment only on the basis of agreement with the parents. The methods of treatment suggested are: agreed compensation for loss, supervision up to three years, short-term detention for training, and longer-term training which would include taking the child into care and using placement arrangements as at present, but giving the local authority the use of junior and intermediate approved schools which would become part of 'a wide range of residential establishments' at its service.

Cases would be brought to the notice of the family council by any of the persons who at present can bring a child before the juvenile court. The councils are expected to 'require more numerous and fuller social inquiries than many courts do now' and to spend more time in discussion 'in an unhurried manner' with the parents. Observation centres providing facilities for assessment of children, both resident and living at home, would house children on remand and also act as classifying centres before allocation to residential training establishments, thus replacing both remand homes and classifying schools. These will be important places since 'although the family council would not be a court of law, it would seem right that it should have power, *even in a case in which the parents disagree* [italics ours], to refer a child to an observation centre for a limited period for assessment and for a report of the type of treatment that is likely to prove beneficial in his case.'[7]

Where the facts of a case were in dispute, the case would be referred to a proposed 'family court' for judicial determination (of the facts), being referred back again to the family council for the discussion of treatment. The court would only find itself in the position of making an order in the case if no agreement on treatment was reached in discussion between the council and the family at this post-trial stage. In making an order 'it would be open to the family court to make any order which is now appropriate to a juvenile court' except that the approved school committal would be replaced by the 'fit person' order. 'It would, of course, remain open to the family court, in the case of any child coming before it, to impose such monetary penalty as it thought fit.'[8] Where it was thought desirable for any reason, a family council could refer any case at any stage to the family court. Homicide cases would continue to be dealt with at assizes, after committal from the family court.

Offenders over sixteen would be outside the ambit of the family councils. However, unlike Kilbrandon, the White Paper makes provision for a young offenders' court. This would be the family court exercising a criminal jurisdiction when trying offenders aged sixteen to twenty-one. Very serious cases would be heard by higher courts or, in some instances, by the young offenders' court presided over by a legally qualified chairman, as at the quarter-sessions now. The court would be public and open, and a range of measures comparable with those already in use for this age group would be available. As with the arrangements for dealing with children under sixteen, 'the determining factor in deciding what is to be done must be the welfare of the particular child or young person', yet at the same time 'what is needed is firm discipline', though this includes 'constructive treatment directed to the welfare or rehabilitation of the individual child or young person'.

These suggestions are put forward because 'children

should be spared the stigma of criminality' and they are said to offer the best means of directing social inquiries, deciding on the appropriate treatment, encouraging parental cooperation and responsibility, and ensuring a flexible treatment programme which can be adapted to the child's progress and changing needs.

If it is thought that the 'stigma' attaches to having been convicted in a criminal court it could, of course, be avoided by dealing with offenders by means of civil procedure, as can now be done with persistent offenders under 'out of control' proceedings. Since, however, the word describes not an objective fact but the way in which people generally (and perhaps the offender in particular) are thought to regard law-breakers – at any rate those who have been found out and brought to book by authority – it might attach to a finding in any court, and it would remain to be seen whether being dealt with by the family council acquired a stigma or not. It would be unfortunate if 'He's been seen by the council' came to carry whatever weight of disapprobation 'He's been up before the court' does now. This may well depend on how far the councils are dealing with non-offenders also, but the experience of the Scandinavian welfare boards suggests that the clientele will be overwhelmingly one of offenders, with all that this entails in public image.

It almost appears from the references in the White Paper that, except when it is sitting as a young offenders' court, the family court's jurisdiction will be civil, but, if that were what was intended, the suggestion[9] that 'It would, of course, remain open to the family court, in the case of any child coming before it, to impose such *monetary penalty* [author's italics] as it thought fit' would be likely to be unacceptable, since presumably this euphemism is intended as a statement to the effect that the court may impose a fine. In practice, a family court exercising a jurisdiction as described in the White Paper would usually be sitting as a criminal and not a civil court. On present showing, cases against young offenders (sixteen to twenty years old) are likely to amount to something near present juvenile court totals on the criminal side. These much outnumber the business of magistrates' courts in adoption cases (which applicants are tending increasingly to bring in the county court), consent to marry and affiliation order applications. In addition, there would be at least a trickle of cases remitted from the family councils and these, on present juvenile court showing and for other reasons, are likely to be criminal far more often than civil cases.

As persons over sixteen will not come before the family councils and the juvenile courts will no longer exist, it seems that the wayward sixteen-year-old, who commits no offence but is beyond the control of his parents and getting into bad associations or moral danger, is to be left to his or her own devices. Presumably something similar to the present arrangements, whereby a seventeen-year-old who is already the subject of a supervision order may be dealt with by the court for a breach of supervision until he or she is eighteen, will apply to those boys and girls who are the subjects of such orders at the time when they reach their sixteenth birthdays. However, the general position, under these proposals, of the sixteen-year-old prostitute, who is sometimes both mentally and morally immature and emotionally also quite at sea, certainly calls for very serious consideration.

Many people would find it difficult to accept, as proposed, the power of a family council to refer a child for assessment, even 'for a limited period', to a residential observation centre against the wishes of the parents and without the matter going before a court. The legal powers implied would presumably need to be such as to enable a family council compulsorily to remove from home an offender whose condition was not recognizably urgent or serious enough for him to be dealt with under powers at present existing for removing an endangered juvenile to a place of safety. However convenient such a procedure might be where a local authority wished to explore the ground and possibly to get the evidence needed before taking unwilling parents before the family court, the process might well involve physical force and, in any event, the situation presents itself somewhat in the light of an imprisonment by administrative instead of judicial procedure. Indeed, the end result might well be that judicial caution as to the reasonable use of such an enlargement of administrative power might render it ineffective in practice.

It seems a little naïve also to include attendance centres, at least as we know them at present and in view of the results to date, as a means of rehabilitating a young offender. They were intended to punish offenders by subjecting them to compulsory activities during their free time. Some centres now engage in reasonably constructive activities, others less so. The same sort of criticism can be made about the proposal for the councils to send young people to detention centres for 'short-term training'. These are to be provided and administered by the Home Office 'as now' – in other words, by the Prison Department. There is no evidence to date that either of these treatments has the slightest reformatory effect. They are reserved for youngsters who have committed prisonable offences, and are regarded by them and by the courts which impose them as what they are, i.e. a punishment.

It now appears that, when the junior and intermediate approved schools are taken over by the local authority, the department concerned is to be the children's department which will administer the schools and place and remove children as it thinks best. This would reverse an eighteen-year-old effort to ensure that children in local authority homes attend ordinary schools outside the homes. If a boarding-school education is what is required, the education authorities have power to provide it. It is not clear what elements are to be provided by the children's department in their own boarding-school; to these they will send children in their care who need 'long-term residential training' which would not be found in residential special educational treatment, e.g. in a school for the maladjusted under the aegis of the education authorities.

It is proposed that the family councils will obtain 'more numerous and fuller social inquiries' than the courts do now. This seems unlikely since social inquiries are to be carried out 'where necessary'. A great advantage of the present system is that inquiries are made as a matter of course (Section 35) in every case except the very trivial, and it is often only possible to assess the 'necessity' after the inquiry has revealed the facts of a situation. In some of the large urban centres it appears that, at present, a very sizeable proportion indeed of indictable offenders are remanded for further reports after the trial and on the basis of what the routine social inquiries revealed. Thus in very many cases the court finally has from four to six or more reports before it when deciding on the appropriate order.

Moreover, 'there would be sufficient councils to enable discussion with parents to be conducted in an unhurried manner' and 'meeting-places would be so arranged that parents and their children would not have far to travel'. In a well-run juvenile court today, the formal structure of the procedure enables the essentials of each case to be brought out, discussed, and assessed with the minimum of irrelevance and waste of time. Without formal procedure being laid down and followed it is almost certain that it will take considerably longer to elicit facts and feelings by means of 'unhurried discussion'. About 1,600 juvenile court magistrates are used to man the present juvenile courts on a part-time basis. It is questionable indeed whether it will be possible to obtain the services of a trained social worker at each family council meeting on this scale. If this is not possible, it becomes even more important to define clearly what the contribution – and therefore the relevant qualities – of family council members is intended to be.

Something similar to the proposed family councils already exists in the procedure by which, in some areas, persistent truants and their parents are interviewed by small subcommittees of the local education authority as the last stage before the authority reluctantly decides to prosecute. In these cases the 'council' may consist of either one or two members of the education committee, supported by the chief or a senior officer of the education welfare department. The 'council' receives the relevant information from the officer who has actually been concerned in trying to get the child to go regularly to school, and then sees the family and discusses the situation. The truancy must have been very persistent indeed for matters to have reached this stage. In theory all other relevant means have been tried and have failed. In practice, it has often not been possible to offer the necessary skilled social case-work to family or child, nor the individual attention in a small class – nor yet the exciting leisure time activities, attractive clothes, and regular pocket money which might have made tolerable some problem of daily life of which the truancy is only a by-product. Although the culprit has not been able to pull himself up by his own boot-straps he must be exhorted once more to do so, with the alternative of being brought to court, since the missing remedial services have not been brought into existence by his appearance before the sub-committee. If he finally is dealt with by the court, he may at long last be lucky enough to get skilled assessment of his situation and help from trained workers. This is perhaps rather an extreme picture to compare with the workings of the proposed new family councils, since, of all services, the education welfare service, while rich in human experience, is probably one of the poorest in knowledge of professional social work and in formal training. But unless there is a realistic appraisal of the present inadequacies of the social services, and a most energetic and determined effort to improve matters, there is no reason to suppose that the finished picture will differ greatly from that given above. Nor will the proposed power of the children's departments to punish by a period in a detention centre or attendance centre be a very fruitful substitute for a proper diagnosis and treatment of the root causes of trouble.

The treatment plan is to be arrived at by agreement at the family council, instead of by order in a juvenile court (though this surprisingly often includes agreement – for what it is worth). But it is not clear what the social worker brings to the informal 'family council' situation which he was unable to bring to the family in the even more informal social case-work situation. The council has no resources except those already at the disposal of the children's service. Still more obscure is the position of the other members. If the doctor or the teacher know the case, why has the social worker not consulted them before as a matter of course, and will the council be differently and appropriately constituted for each individual case? If they have relevant expertise but no knowledge of the particular case, why are their opinions to be preferred to those of their opposite numbers already involved with the family? If they have no expertise at all but simply an 'understanding and experience of children' and an awareness of the problems facing the families it is still open to doubt why their personal opinions are to weigh against those of professional personnel who have made a study of – and have by definition enormously more experience of – such families and their problems. Two alternatives appear to remain. One is that the members should be lay persons who would be intended to act 'judicially' – but, if so, between whom or what is a decision to be made, and on what grounds and with what effect, since the council is not a court and has no powers of compulsion? The second is that they should be lay persons representing the body which would, in the last resort, ask the court for power to compel the family to accept the treatment recommendations – in other words, members of the children's committee reviewing an intractable situation with the family concerned as the last stage before agreeing to the social worker's demand that compulsory powers should be sought. Here we have the pattern of the 'truancy sub-committee', in some local education areas called the 'appeal committee'.

Both Kilbrandon and the White Paper rest their proposals on the fact (which Ingleby glossed over) that most offenders plead guilty. Both wrongly assume that the criminal court has therefore no real function to perform in such cases.

But the criminal jurisdiction protects the liberties of the offender not only by requiring proof of offence before liability to compulsion but also by limiting the exercise of compulsory power over a convicted offender. In the juvenile court it is the child himself who is prosecuted and who receives these protections. But the position in the proposals for juvenile panels or family councils would appear to be that the child himself has no standing or rights as an individual. Once having admitted the commission of an offence it is only if *his parents* refuse to accept, carry out, or continue treatment that he would find himself before a court with the opportunity of being heard in his own behalf. This seems an extraordinary proposal for dealing with, for example, boys of fifteen, or even fourteen, faced with punitive sanctions such as 'short-term training' in a detention centre. To reply that nothing will be done by the councils except by agreement does not quite meet such objections. Neither set of proposals seems to have had in mind a type of parent commonly seen in the juvenile court, muddled, inadequate, beaten, pathetic, or truculent. Agreement, disagreement, and discussion are not very realistic terms to describe the part to be played by such families which appear before the family council, representing officialdom and authority, as failures by definition and unprotected by the provisions of any formally laid down procedure for observing, or even informing them, of their rights. There is no provision for legal aid.

The Ingleby Committee recommended that punitive sanctions except the fine should be available to the court in civil cases even where no offence was alleged, but this was not accepted by the legislature. It remains to be seen whether re-labelling the detention centre will alter this situation. Such considerations make it difficult to forecast the effect which the setting up of family councils might have on the present picture. The proportion of not guilty pleas might rise. The councils themselves might become simply a sieve, like the truancy subcommittees, the size of the holes which determine the volume of cases remitted to the court depending very greatly on the services available to deal with non-offenders by non-punitive means and, on the other hand, on how much public opinion will stand in regard to the escape from punishment of the trivial and the non-maladjusted offender.

There is to date no evidence to suggest that we know how to change criminal behaviour by any acceptable means. There is no reason to suppose that there will be fewer juvenile offenders committing offences if the White Paper proposals are accepted. There may well be a tendency towards an increase of private redress in the shape of physical vengeance by the victims of theft or damage, and a further leap forward in the development of informal police supervision schemes outside the purview of either courts or social services. The present gross scarcity of adequate remedial services, and the difficulty of applying punitive sanctions under the proposed arrangements, means that less rather than more might be done to deal with the offender in the immediate future.

In conclusion, it cannot be too strongly emphasized that what has been said does not add up to a case against the setting up of family councils *per se*. They are almost certainly inappropriate as a means of dealing with juvenile offences. But the fact that a child's social needs happen to have come to official notice only when he commits an offence is, of course, no reason whatever for not dealing with them by social means. Many child offenders are involved in a struggle against physical and emotional situations which might well prove too much for the stability of a mature adult. There is no excuse in an affluent society for not bringing help to such children. As far as the administrative structure is concerned the way is, as has been shown, already wide open for doing this, if the resources were available, and the efforts being made behind the scenes to increase training and recruitment of personnel are impressive. But the formidable lack of resources will not be affected by the setting up of family councils, though it may well appear to become even more acute as more needs – whose priority in social terms will not necessarily be related to the gravity of the offences committed – are revealed. However, the pros and cons of family councils should be seen as distinct from the attempt to deal with the offender or his criminality as such. It would be a great mistake and a pity if the work of family councils – should they be set up – were to be evaluated in terms of any expected effect upon criminal behaviour.

The White Paper appears to have been shelved for the moment and if offenders, even juvenile offenders, are to be dealt with by some body outside the family *for their offences*, that body should probably be a court. But, though the court has regard to the welfare of the offender in deciding upon the order to be made, it should not be expected to take on those responsibilities or functions which the social services of modern times have been set up to fulfil. The health, education, and welfare authorities should no longer be allowed to sit back in the comfortable hope that, in the last resort, the criminal court will do their job for them.

NOTES

CHAPTER 1
The Magistrates' Court: I

1. *Criminal Statistics, England and Wales*, H.M.S.O., 1965.
2. Methuen, 1952.
3. Longmans Green, 1951, page 368.
4. Report of the Royal Commission on Justices of the Peace, Cmnd 7463, H.M.S.O., 1948, paragraph 72.
5. March 1964, page 40.

CHAPTER 2
The Magistrates' Court: II

1. [1951] 2 K.B. 109.
2. Cmnd 1289, H.M.S.O., 1961.
3. Longmans Green, 1951, pages 341 and 368.
4. Gollancz, 1951, page 86.
5. *The Times*, 12 September 1956.
6. *The Magistrate*, December 1956, page 139.
7. Report of the (Streatfeild) Interdepartmental Committee on the Business of the Criminal Courts, Cmnd 1289, H.M.S.O., 1961, paragraphs 343–6.
8. Ibid., paragraph 345.
9. Ibid., paragraph 346.
10. Report of the (Wolfenden) Departmental Committee on Homosexual Offences and Prostitution, Cmnd 247, H.M.S.O., 1957 (reprinted 1962), paragraph 179.
11. Stevens and Sons, 1955, page 36.
12. [1963] *Criminal Law Review*, 207.

CHAPTER 3
Juvenile Court Procedure

1. Report of the Departmental Committee on the Treatment of Young Offenders, Cmnd 2831, H.M.S.O., 1927, pages 17–21.
2. Report of the (Ingleby) Committee on Children and Young Persons, Cmnd 1191, H.M.S.O., 1960, paragraph 66.

3. Report of the Departmental Committee on the Treatment of Young Offenders, Cmnd 2831, H.M.S.O., 1927, page 37.
4. Ibid., pages 35 and 36.
5. Ibid., page 25, Part 4, 'The Juvenile Court'.
6. Ibid., pages 26–8.
7. 179/1949, 27 August.
8. 191/1952, 1 September.
9. Report of the Royal Commission on Justices of the Peace, Cmnd 7463, H.M.S.O., 1948, paragraph 185.
10. Report of the (Wolfenden) Departmental Committee on the Treatment of Young Offenders, Cmnd 2831, H.M.S.O., 1927, pages 34–5.
11. Ibid., page 21.
12. Ibid., pages 38–9.

CHAPTER 4

The Powers of the Juvenile Court

1. 3 All E.R. 673.
2. The Report of the Departmental Committee on the Treatment of Young Offenders, Cmnd 2831, H.M.S.O., 1927, page 57.
3. *Criminal Statistics*, H.M.S.O., 1965, pages xxiii, xxiv, xxix and xxxi.
4. Report of the Departmental Committee on Social Services in Courts of Summary Jurisdiction, Cmnd 5122, H.M.S.O., 1936, pages 40–5.
5. Annual *Criminal Statistics*, H.M.S.O.
6. *Supplementary Statistics*, H.M.S.O.
7. Report of the Departmental Committee on Social Services in Courts of Summary Jurisdiction, Cmnd 5122, H.M.S.O., 1936, page 73.
8. [1919] 2 K.B. 278.
9. Cf. *The Sentence of the Court; A Handbook for Courts on the Treatment of Offenders*, H.M.S.O., 1964.
10. Cf. ibid.
11. Report of the Departmental Committee on the Treatment of Young Offenders, Cmnd 2831, H.M.S.O., 1927, page 69.
12. *Detention in Remand Homes*, ed. Radzinowicz and J. W. C. Turner, Cambridge Studies in Criminology, Macmillan, 1952, page 77.
13. *Seventh Report on the Work of the Children's Department*, H.M.S.O., 1955, page 34.

14. Cf. *The Sentence of the Court; A Handbook for Courts on the Treatment of Offenders*, H.M.S.O., 1964, page 52.

15. *Report on the Work of the Prison Department*, Cmnd 2708, H.M.S.O., 1964, page 42.

16. Memorandum of Evidence submitted by the Magistrates' Association to the Royal Commission on the Penal System, 1965.

17. Cf. *The Sentence of the Court: A Handbook for Courts on the Treatment of Offenders*, H.M.S.O., 1964.

CHAPTER 5

Approved Schools, Borstals, Attendance Centres, and 'Fit Person' Orders

1. *Criminal Statistics*, H.M.S.O., 1965, page 206.

2. Report of the Departmental Committee on the Treatment of Young Offenders, Cmnd 2831, H.M.S.O., 1927, page 70.

3. Ibid., pages 73 ff.

4. Ibid., pages 75 ff.

5. Annual *Criminal Statistics*, H.M.S.O., 1959, 1964.

6. Report of the (Ingleby) Committee on Children and Young Persons, Cmnd 1191, H.M.S.O., 1960, paragraphs 488–9.

7. Report of the Advisory Council on the Treatment of Offenders, The Organization of After-Care, H.M.S.O., 1963, page 66 (reprinted 1964).

8. H.M.S.O., 1964.

9. *Criminal Statistics*, H.M.S.O., 1965, Table VI.

10. Report of the Departmental Committee on the Treatment of Young Offenders, Cmnd 2831, H.M.S.O., 1927, pages 63 ff.

CHAPTER 6

The Juvenile Court at Work

1. July–August, 1953.

2. Cf. J. Piaget, *The Moral Judgement of the Child*, Kegan Paul, 1932.

3. The Rt Hon. Sir Hartley Shawcross, Q.C., J.P., M.P., as reported in *The Magistrate*, December 1957, page 146.

4. Report of the (Ingleby) Committee on Children and Young Persons, Cmnd 1191, H.M.S.O., 1960, paragraph 197.

5. Judges' Rules, H.M.S.O., 1964, page 8.

CHAPTER 7

Avoiding the Stigma of a Criminal Conviction

1. Kee in the *Sunday Times*, 29 September 1957; Gale in the *Observer*, 31 March 1957.
2. The Chief Constable of Liverpool, *The Police and Children*, Liverpool Police Force, 1956.
3. Report of the (Streatfeild) Interdepartmental Committee on the Business of the Criminal Courts, Cmnd 1289, H.M.S.O., 1961.
4. Cf. J. A. F. Watson, *The Child and the Magistrate*, rev. edn, Jonathan Cape, 1965, pages 49–51.
5. J. A. F. Watson, *The Child and the Magistrate*, rev. edn, Jonathan Cape, 1965.
6. Report of the (Ingleby) Committee on Children and Young Persons, Cmnd 1191, H.M.S.O., 1960, paragraphs 233–6.
7. Home Office Circular Number 20, H.M.S.O., 1964.
8. Cmnd 2742, H.M.S.O., 1965.

CHAPTER 8

The Finding and the Order

1. [1956] 1 Q.B. 439, and [1956] 1 All E.R. 450.
2. Memorandum of Evidence submitted by the Magistrates' Association to the (Ingleby) Committee on Children and Young Persons in 1958, paragraphs 73–4.
3. Report of the (Ingleby) Committee on Children and Young Persons, Cmnd 1191, H.M.S.O., 1960, Appendix IV B, page 172.
4. Cassell, 1952, page 9.
5. *Proceedings of the Fifth International Congress on Social Defence*, Stockholm, 1958, pages 456–7.
6. Report of the (Ingleby) Committee on Children and Young Persons, Cmnd 1191, H.M.S.O., 1960, paragraph 216.
7. Ibid., paragraph 217.
8. N. O. G. Wooler in *Probation*, March 1957, page 74.
9. F. G. Hait in *Probation*, June 1957, page 92.
10. Cf. E. Glover, 'Prognosis or Prediction', *British Journal of Delinquency*, Volume VI, Number 2, page 17.
11. Cf. *The Sentence of the Court: A Handbook for Courts on the Treatment of Offenders*, H.M.S.O., 1964.
12. *The Times* Law Reports, 10 March 1956.

CHAPTER 9

The Child and the Court

1. Cf. Lord Hewart, c.j., in *R.* v. *Sussex J. J.* [1924] 1 K.B. 256.
2. 'The Juvenile Court and the Child', *British Journal of Delinquency*, January 1957, pages 187–95.
3. These words and numbers taken from F. J. Schonell and R. H. Adams, *The Essential Intelligence Tests* series, Oliver and Boyd, 1948.
4. *Delinquents in the Making*, New York: Harper and Row, 1952, page 15.
5. Ibid., page 134.
6. *By Courtesy of the Criminal*, Harrap, 1955, page 28.

CHAPTER 10

Dealing with Criminality by Court Order

1. *Supplementary Statistics*, H.M.S.O.
2. Longmans Green, 1951.
3. Home Office Research Unit Report, H.M.S.O., 1963, pages 183 ff.
4. 'The Roots of Crime', the *Sunday Times*, 13 April 1952.
5. *The Young Delinquent*, London University Press, 1925.
6. *Prediction Methods in Relation to Borstal Training*, H.M.S.O., 1955.
7. Sir George Benson, *British Journal of Delinquency*, Volume IX, Number 3, January 1959.
8. *British Journal of Delinquency*, Volume VIII, Number 3, January 1958.
9. Hansard, Volume 630, 1960–1, 17 November.
10. *Probation and Mental Treatment*, International Library of Criminology, Tavistock Publications, 1963.
11. *The Sentence of the Court: A Handbook for Courts on the Treatment of Offenders*, H.M.S.O., 1964, page 42.
12. *Unraveling Juvenile Delinquency*, Harvard University Press, 1950.

CHAPTER 11

The Future: Proposals for Reform

1. 'The Competent Authorities', *Proceedings of the Fifth International Congress on Social Defence*, Stockholm, 1958.

2. Cmnd 2742, H.M.S.O., 1965.

3. Cmnd 2306, H.M.S.O., 1964.

4. Cmnd 2742, H.M.S.O., 1965.

5. Hansard.

6. Labour Party Study Group, 1964.

7. White Paper: *The Child, the Family and the Young Offender,* Cmnd 2742, H.M.S.O., 1965, paragraph 16.

8. Ibid., paragraph 18.

9. Ibid., paragraph 18.

GLOSSARY

Adjournment: a putting off to another time or place, without a day fixed, or generally

Attendance centres: centres provided by the Home Office for the occupation and instruction of boys and men aged at least ten but under twenty-one years of age who are ordered by the court to attend as a punishment

Approved school: a school approved by the Home Secretary and intended for the education and training of juveniles committed by the court

Borstal: establishment administered by the Prison Department of the Home Office for the training of offenders aged at least fifteen but under twenty-one committed by the court. The first such establishment was at Borstal near Rochester

Corrective training: a sentence of not less than two nor more than four years as determined by the court, which may be passed on conviction by indictment of a person not less than twenty-one years of age whose offence and previous record are of a specified seriousness

Detention centres: places administered by the Prison Department of the Home Office to which persons aged not less than fourteen but under twenty-one may be sent by the court as a punishment and kept for short periods, usually three months, under suitable discipline

Fit Person: a person capable of undertaking the rights and duties of a parent, to whose care a juvenile is committed by order of the court. In practice the fit person is usually the children's officer of the local authority

Indictment: a written accusation that one or more persons have committed a felony or misdemeanour. Cases heard on indictment are heard before the higher courts

Jurisdiction: the extent of power of a court. Limits of jurisdiction may be as to the character of the question to be determined or geographical

Larceny: the unlawful taking and carrying away of things personal with intent to deprive the rightful owner of the same

Plea: used colloquially to mean a plea of guilty. It has other meanings also, e.g. the defendant's answer of fact to the plaintiff's declaration

Preventive detention: a sentence of not less than five or more than fourteen years as determined by the court, which may be passed on conviction by indictment of a person not less than thirty years of age whose offence and previous record are of a specified length and seriousness

Probation: where a person is convicted of an offence the court may make a probation order placing him under the supervision of a probation officer for a period of not less than one or more than three years. If he fails to observe the conditions of the order or commits another offence he may be brought up and sentenced for the original offence and also dealt with for the breach of the probation order

Remand home: a place established or used by the county council of a county or county borough for the temporary accommodation under court order of juvenile offenders or those in need of care, protection, or control, or awaiting a court appearance

Remand centres: places for the detention of persons not less than fourteen and under twenty-one years of age who are remanded or committed in custody for trial or sentence

Summary court: a court of summary jurisdiction; any justice or justices of the peace or other magistrate authorized by statute to act; magistrates' courts

Summary jurisdiction: the power of a court to give judgment or make an order forthwith; the power of magistrates to hear or dispose of a criminal case without sending it for trial at sessions or assizes

SUGGESTIONS FOR FURTHER READING

FOR readers who may wish to go further into the general problem of offenders and their treatment H. Mannheim's *Comparative Criminology* (Routledge & Kegan Paul, 1965) is an impressive guide. Nigel Walker in *Crime and Punishment in Britain* (Edinburgh University Press, 1965) provides a study of the penal system as, on a smaller scale, does Howard Jones in *Crime and the Penal System* (3rd edn, University Tutorial Press, 1965). Two valuable White Papers dealing in a general way with crime and punishment are *Penal Practice in a Changing Society* (Cmnd 645, H.M.S.O., 1959) and *The War Against Crime in England and Wales 1959–1964* (Cmnd 2296, H.M.S.O., 1964).

In the juvenile court many disciplines meet. Books listed in relation to the content of particular chapters contain references which could lead a reader into almost every field of the social sciences. They are only a selection.

CHAPTER I

A standard comprehensive account and discussion of the system of law courts and the administration of justice is R. M. Jackson's *The Machinery of Justice in England* (4th edn, Cambridge University Press, 1964). A short, lively account of the magistrates' courts is *The Magistrates' Courts* by F. T. Giles (Stevens & Sons, 1963). Detailed and practical discussion by the Streatfeild Committee of the work of the criminal courts, mainly the higher courts, is contained in Part A of the Report of the Interdepartmental Committee on the Business of the Criminal Courts (Cmnd 1289, H.M.S.O., 1961).

A stimulating discussion of the facts of crime and other manifestations of 'social pathology' is provided by Barbara Wootton in the first two chapters of her book, *Social Science and Social Pathology* (Allen & Unwin, 1959), while the Home Office annual publication *Criminal Statistics* gives statistics relating to crime and criminal proceedings in England and Wales each year (H.M.S.O.).

The Report of the Royal Commission on Justices of the Peace 1946–48 (Cmnd 7463, H.M.S.O., reprinted 1959), makes interesting and still relevant reading. A White Paper, *The Training of Justices of the Peace in England and Wales* (Cmnd 2856, H.M.S.O., 1965), outlines new arrangements for obligatory training of lay magistrates.

The Magistrate, the monthly journal of the Magistrates' Association, which also publishes a useful little book: *Notes for New Magistrates* (revised and reprinted 1966), contains short articles and reports on matters of current interest to magistrates. The weekly *Justice of the Peace and Local Government Review* is essential reading on matters of current discussion and practice in the courts.

CHAPTER 2

Part B of the Report of the Interdepartmental Committee on the Business of the Criminal Courts contains discussion of 'the arrangements for providing the courts with the information necessary to enable them to select the most appropriate treatment for offenders'. The Home Office Research Unit Report on *Persistent Criminals* by W. H. Hammond and Edna Chayen (H.M.S.O., 1963) provides detailed examination of the sentencing of a group of persistent offenders and of the characteristics of the offenders and their behaviour. A smaller study, *The Habitual Prisoner* by D. J. West (Macmillan, 1963) is especially interesting in its emphasis on psychiatric aspects.

A useful little book on general aspects is C. H. Rolph's *Common Sense about Crime and Punishment* (Gollancz, 1961), while some general problems of the administration of justice are dealt with in an inspiring manner by Lord Denning in *The Road to Justice* (Stevens, 1955). A brisk and stimulating introduction to the whole subject of crime and criminals is provided by Barbara Wootton in her lectures for the Hamlyn Trust and published under the title *Crime and the Criminal Law* (Stevens, 1963).

CHAPTER 3

The juvenile courts have not apparently in the past aroused any great interest in legal writers. An exception, however, is provided by a standard work, *Clarke Hall and Morrison on Children* (Butterworths, 6th edn, 1960, and supplement, 1964) and *Notes on Juvenile Court Law* by A. C. L. Morrison, ed. Banwell (5th edn, Justice of the Peace and Local Government Review, 1964) is a useful little book. A new edition of *A Guide to Juvenile Court Law* by G. H. F. Mumford (Jordan & Sons, 1961) is in preparation.

The reports of the Departmental Committee on the Treatment of Young Offenders (Cmnd 2831, H.M.S.O., 1927) and of the Committee on Children and Young Persons (Cmnd 1191, H.M.S.O., 1960) contain much interesting and still highly relevant discussion. They are best read in conjunction with the Children and Young Persons Act, 1963, as is also the January 1957 special number on juvenile courts published by the *British Journal of Delinquency* (now the *British Journal of Criminology*).

CHAPTER 4

The *Eighth Report on the Work of the Children's Department* (H.M.S.O. 1961) contains much relevant information which may be supplemented by the *Report on the Work of the Children's Department, 1961–3* (H.C. 155, H.M.S.O., 1964). Max Grunhut's *Juvenile Offenders before the Courts* (Oxford: Clarendon Press, 1956), reports a study of variation in both incidence and treatment of juvenile delinquents. *The Probation Service*, 2nd edn, by Joan King (Butterworths, 1964), provides an all-round description of the modern probation service. Useful critical accounts of detention centres for juveniles are two articles by M. Grunhut in the *British Journal of Delinquency* (now *British Journal of Criminology*) – Number 5, 1955, and Number 3, 1960, respectively.

CHAPTER 5

A report on *Attendance Centres* by F. H. McClintock, for the Cambridge Institute of Criminology (Macmillan, 1961), is useful reading containing a number of case studies. *Borstal Re-assessed* by Roger Hood (Heinemann, 1965) is a comprehensive, critical account of development and use of the borstal system past and present. John Gittens's *Approved School Boys* (H.M.S.O., 1952) contains a detailed account of the observation, classification, and treatment of boys coming to a classifying school.

CHAPTER 6

John Watson's book *The Child and the Magistrate* (revised and largely rewritten edn, Jonathan Cape, 1965) contains vivid and detailed descriptions of court proceedings and their background, relevant particularly to this and the preceding chapter.

CHAPTER 7

A different view of police Juvenile Liaison Officer Schemes may be found in an article by J. Mack in *British Journal of Criminology* (April, 1963) and in the pamphlets entitled *The Police and Children* issued from time to time by the Liverpool Police Force. See also the Kilbrandon Report on Children and Young Persons, Scotland (Cmnd 2306, H.M.S.O., 1964), the White Paper *The Child, The Family and the Young Offender* (Cmnd 2742, H.M.S.O., 1965), and the Report of the Ingleby Committee previously mentioned for proposals to avoid the stigma of criminal conviction.

CHAPTERS 8 AND 9

Here again, see the Report of the Ingleby Committee for a discussion of the 'dilemma' of the juvenile court and a critical view of this discussion in W. E. Cavenagh's 'A Comment on The Ingleby Report' (*British Journal of Criminology*, July 1961).

Studies on the concomitants of delinquency throw light on the background of the children who come before the courts, their behaviour in court, and the matters likely to be in the minds of social and other experts reporting to the court. Recommended books are: Harriett Wilson's *Delinquency and Child Neglect* (Allen & Unwin, 1962), T. Ferguson's *The Young Delinquent in his Social Setting* (Oxford University Press, 1952,) K. Friedlander's *The Psycho-Analytical Approach to Juvenile Delinquency* (Routledge & Kegan Paul, 1949), H. J. Eysenck's *Crime and Personality* (Routledge & Kegan Paul, 1964), M. Woodward's *Low Intelligence and Delinquency* (rev. edn, Institute for the Study and Treatment of Delinquency, 1963), J. Bowlby's *Child Care and the Growth of Love* (the second edition (Penguin Books, 1965), contains two additional chapters with reference to the continuing debate on the effects of maternal deprivation), T. Morris's *The Criminal Area* (Routledge & Kegan Paul, 1958), and J. D. W. Pearce's *Juvenile Delinquency* (Cassell, 1952).

A survey of the state of opinion at the time is Lord Pakenham's *Causes of Crime* (Weidenfeld and Nicholson, 1958), while an impressive attack on most of the current criminological hypotheses is to be found in Barbara Wootton's *Social Sciences and Social Pathology* (Allen & Unwin, 1959).

CHAPTER 10

The Home Office Research Unit Number 7 reports in *Probation Research, A Preliminary Report* (H.M.S.O., 1966) the first stages of an investigation aimed eventually at discovering whether matching individual offenders and probation officers would increase the success rates of probation.

The Roots of Crime by Edward Glover (Imago, 1960) starts with a valuable review of the recent history of investigation and treatment of delinquency in Great Britain and goes on to deal authoritatively with the deep-seated causes of delinquent behaviour as they appear to a leading psychoanalyst. Basic reading on maladjustment with a special chapter on the maladjusted child in relation to the juvenile courts is the (Underwood) Report of the Committee on Maladjusted Children (H.M.S.O., 1955). Reports of the annual Child-Guidance Inter-Clinic Conferences, published by the National Association for Mental Health, show the striking failure in provision to meet the requirements forecast by the Underwood Committee. Reports by the Chief Medical Officer of the Department of Education and Science, *The Health of the School Child*, give a vivid picture of health problems among schoolchildren.

CHAPTER 11

The April 1966 issue of the *British Journal of Criminology* is a special number on the White Paper, *The Child, The Family and the Young Offender*. The last chapter of this book is included as an article (see acknowledgement in the preface). Other articles by P. D. Scott, Lord Kilbrandon, L. Neville Brown, and B. J. Kahan, are relevant.

The pre-White Paper position as to the law and the social services was analysed in articles in *The Times* ('New Ways with Delinquents', 23 August 1965) and *New Society* ('Out of Court?', 15 July 1965) by Winifred E. Cavenagh and Richard F. Sparks. *Crime – a Challenge to Us All* (1964, published by the Labour Party's Study Group) has provided the basis for much subsequent thinking on society's handling of young offenders.

AMERICAN LITERATURE

A great deal of American work has been done in this field, though not all of it is necessarily applicable to situations in this country. A well-known work on the causes of juvenile delinquency is S. and

E. Glueck's *Unraveling Juvenile Delinquency* (New York: Harvard University Press, The Commonwealth Fund, 1950), while *The Sociology of Crime and Delinquency* compiled by M. E. Wolfgang, L. Savitz, and N. Johnston (John Wiley & Sons, 1962) provides an introduction to many leading writers and numerous references.

Well-known works on the court are *Family Cases in Court* by Maxine B. Virtue (Duke University Press, 1956) and *A Court for Children* by Alfred J. Kahn (Columbia University Press, 1953). A recent publication *A View from the Bench – The Juvenile Court* by Justine Wise Polier (New York: National Council on Crime and Delinquency, 1964) is particularly topical in pointing out the gross deficiencies in the social services to meet the needs of the court. The last word to date is contained in *Standards for Juvenile and Family Courts* (Children's Bureau Publicity No. 437 – 1966, U.S. Dept. of Health, Education and Welfare), prepared in co-operation with the National Council on Crime and Delinquency and The National Council of Juvenile Court Judges. This reflects advances in American social and legal thinking during the last decade including the increased interest in the establishment of family courts.

TABLE OF STATUTES

INDEX

MORE ABOUT PENGUINS
AND PELICANS

If you have enjoyed reading this book you may wish to know that *Penguin Book News* appears every month. It is an attractively illustrated magazine containing a complete list of books published by Penguins and still in print, together with details of the month's new books. A specimen copy will be sent free on request.

Penguin Book News is obtainable from most book-shops; but you may prefer to become a regular sub-scriber at 3s. for twelve issues. Just write to Dept EP, Penguin Books Ltd, Harmondsworth, Middle-sex, enclosing a cheque or postal order, and you will be put on the mailing list.

Some other books published by Penguins are described on the following pages.

Note: *Penguin Book News* is not available in the U.S.A., Canada or Australia

THE INSECURE OFFENDERS

REBELLIOUS YOUTH IN THE WELFARE STATE

by T. R. Fyvel

The term 'juvenile delinquency' scarcely describes the worldwide malaise of youth which beset the 1950s and which – although Teddy Boys are now almost period pieces – continues into this decade. What causes this rebellion of youth in a Welfare State?

T. R. Fyvel's survey is in the tradition of George Orwell. He conjures up for us a world of sharp clothes, gang life, coffee-bars, motor-bikes, juke-boxes, pin-tables, cafés, and cinemas, and adroitly relates the toe-tapping young non-conformers of today to the conditions of an affluent society which for them is little better than a dead end. This is incomparably the best study of a grave post-war phenomenon in Britain.

'An admirable book – balanced, humane, perceptive and thorough' – New Statesman

'As an account of all that it means to be out of step in contemporary society his book deserves to be widely read for its detachment and humanity' – Economist

NOT FOR SALE IN THE U.S.A.

THE UNATTACHED

Mary Morse

Resentment, apathy, mistrust – the dead-end job, the Beat sound, and a rejection of the values of adult society. These are the kind of words with which journalists have tried to catch and understand the unattached – the teenagers who don't belong to anyone or anything. What kind of people are they? What are their attitudes, needs, aims, or resentments? How can they be approached or understood?

In 1960 the National Association of Youth Clubs set up a pioneer experiment to discover the answers to these questions and possible solutions to the problem of the unattached. Three young social workers were sent, each to a different town, under concealed identities, to find and to scrape an acquaintance with these particular teenagers. Over three years, the three, one of whom was a young woman, eventually became the trusted friends and confidants of the bored, the apathetic, the rebellious, and the defiant. This account of the workers' experiences offers an utterly authentic insight into the world of the unattached. But the book is more than this: it is also a fascinating description of difficulties, loneliness, fears, and setbacks of three social workers, working out on a limb in isolation and under assumed identities. It is a fascinating account of a remarkable experiment.